SYNOD '67

SYNOD '67

A NEW SOUND IN ROME

FRANCIS X. MURPHY, C.SS.R.

GARY MACEOIN

THE BRUCE PUBLISHING COMPANY/MILWAUKEE

NIHIL OBSTAT:

JOHN A. SCHULIEN, S.T.D.
Censor librorum

IMPRIMATUR:

✠ WILLIAM E. COUSINS
Archbishop of Milwaukee
January 22, 1968

Library of Congress Catalog Card Number: 68–22590

Foreword

To write contemporary history is a risky business, but the information needs of our age of instantaneous electronic communications demand that someone take the risk. The need for a history of the Synod of Bishops is doubly urgent, because the secrecy which enveloped the proceedings prevented meaningful day-to-day coverage in the newspapers and periodical press. Our purpose is to fill this need by delineating briefly and clearly the genesis and origin of the Synod, offering the reader the reflections of theologians and journalists to whom it proved an extremely significant development in the life of the postconciliar Church.

We have tried to provide a balanced expression of the many currents of thought and ideology present at the Synod, an account as accurate as possible under the conditions of time and circumstances in which the meeting was held, and in which the book was composed. If at times the narrative seems to favor one viewpoint more than another, this may well be an authentic sign of our effort to combine veracity with accuracy. The theologian or historian, to say nothing of the journalist, who professes disincarnate objectivity automatically exposes his prejudice. As theologians and journalists, we are well aware of a common bias. All we can say is that we have tried consciously and conscientiously to curb individual and mutually shared prejudices.

As our work progressed, it became gradually clear to us that two widely divergent evaluations of the facts are possible. One is from the viewpoint of the institutional Church. The other is from that of contemporary mankind, of those people of all races and colors, of all shades of belief and unbelief, whose joys and hopes, whose griefs and anxieties the Catholic Church proclaimed to be also hers in the opening words of Vatican Council II's Constitution on the Church in the Modern World. Since that time, the world has been insistently asking what is this something of value which the Catholic Church professes to want to contribute to mankind's struggle toward those goals to which we all feel irresistibly drawn. It asks the question respectfully and with an intense desire for a meaningful answer. But it also asks it with intense honesty. It requires and deserves a nakedly honest answer.

The two evaluations have been made in the Prelude and in the Postscript respectively. While we are in substantial agreement on the content of both sections, the internal logic of our individual viewpoints and the dialectic of the situation decided us to attribute exclusive responsibility for the one to the priest and for the other to the layman. For all that lies in between, we are jointly accountable.

In our efforts to obtain accurate information, trace down the origins of movements, eliminate unfounded rumor and pernicious as well as bland gossip, taking into account the reactions of non-synodal prelates, observant theologians and involved journalists, as well as reporting the interventions and observations of the bishops who constituted the Synod and the pope who summoned it, we hope we have acquitted ourselves according to the best traditions of the common disciplines to which we are committed. In the interests of truth and theology, we have tried in the text to let the facts speak for themselves.

FRANCIS X. MURPHY, C.SS.R.
GARY MACEOIN

Contents

SYNOD '67

Prelude

Priding itself as an institution whose perspective was focused on eternity, the Catholic Church entered the 20th century with a smug belligerence *vis-à-vis* the outside world. In 1896, for example, it had declared that the ordination of ministers in the Anglican church was not valid as far as the Catholic Church was concerned, and therefore, presumably, but an empty form in the sight of God. Five years earlier, Pope Leo XIII issued his encyclical *Rerum Novarum,* in which the Church turned its attention at long last to the plight of the working classes, and to the demands for justice in the economic and social ordering of nations and societies. It was taken for granted by many in the Vatican that this document would pacify agitators within the Church's ranks who incredibly sought to engage its pastors and teachers in an activist approach to worldly problems.

On the other hand, the Church was suffering persecution in various degrees in different parts of the world. In the Latin countries of both Europe and South America, masonic and anti-clerical groups within the governments and universities were hostile to the Church and its teachings. They were particularly inimical to Catholic schools and educative interests as retrograde in their objectives, and closed within an ideological framework harmful to the development of contemporary man.

Within the body of Catholic thinkers, likewise, stirrings of doctrinal aberrations were faintly audible, particularly on the part of intellectual adventurers who were so frequently tempted to cross the eternal wisdom of the Church with the passing fancies of contemporary philosophy, only to find themselves invariably betrayed by the temporary allure of worldly wisdom. Persecution and heresy were perennial problems, and the Church had a way of both living with the former, and of suddenly divesting itself of the latter by swift and sweeping condemnation of foolhardy intellectuals and disloyal clerics.

Thus the reaction against Modernism was building up at the turn of the 20th century, stimulated by an intricate network of clerical spies in various lands who regularly delated churchmen of all ranks to agents of the Holy Office in Rome on suspicion of heretical thinking, writing, and speaking. The trap was sprung in 1907 with the publication of St. Pius X's decree, *Lamentabili* and the encyclical *Pascendi.*

Further provisions for the running of a tight ship in the turbulent waters of the twentieth century were projected in a codification of the Church's laws. As conceived by its authors, all jurists to their fingertips under the guidance of Cardinal Pietro Gasparri, a Neapolitan greatly impressed by the positivist legal philosophy of the nineteenth century, their primary task was to wrap up in one comprehensive code of laws the whole of the Church's authority with the core of its doctrinal and moral teaching, thus giving absolute security to the Catholic way of life. It is true also that such a codification would bring order into the confused mass of Church laws by clarifying lines of jurisdiction. When this document of 2414 canons was promulgated in 1917, its authors were convinced that they had created a *monumentum aere perennius* — a monument that would last forever.

The counterpart of the Code, in the mind of the Vatican thinkers and of most Catholic bishops and teachers, was the revival of the *Perennial Philosophy,* the scholastic accomplishment of the thirteenth century, that would serve as an impeccable structure for the service of the Church's doctrinal and moral directives. This development had been consolidated in the Thomistic approach to theology. Through the perennial philosophy, there was no realm of worthwhile human knowledge that could not be judged and dealt with, and either absorbed or rejected as befitted the needs of a Church whose head was infallible.

Despite doubts and difficulties on the part of its restless thinkers and activists disaffected by two world wars within a period of forty years, responsible churchmen at the top persisted in this overall view of the church in the 20th century. So it had been from the beginning, they were convinced; such it was now, subject to persecution and agitation; and such it would be to the end of time. But the Holy Spirit had guaranteed its integrity; and the Vatican daily *L'Osservatore Romano* proudly proclaimed on its masthead each day: *Non prevalebunt* — its enemies would not prevail.

This state of affairs was rudely shattered by a simple announcement made three months after his election by the late Pope John XXIII, a pontiff of peasant origins then 77 years old. Troubled by the Church's apparent inadequacy in facing up to the problems of contemporary man, John called for a local Roman synod to update pastoral practice in his own diocese of Rome; a basic revision of the code of canon law, a short forty years after its promulgation; and the convocation of an ecumenical or general Council.

The first of these measures was run through in short order in 1960. Its immediate results in Rome were negligible. But it served two good purposes. It indicated that the problem of updating the Church could not be accomplished by the formulation of laws and regulations, but would require a great debate, eventually drawing into consideration all the Christian forces operating in the present world. It likewise experimented with a new kind of law — canons that were exhortative rather than menacing; regulations aimed at spiritual realization in the manner of the Gospel, rather than at obediential conformity after the fashion of civil law.

The four years of debate and resolution that characterized Vatican Council II provoked worldwide interest, as believer and unbeliever were treated to the spectacle of an institution as intransigent as the Catholic Church suddenly unbending and asking itself fundamental and far-reaching questions about its being and nature, its purpose, functions, and accomplishments. The Church as a spectacle before men and angels, in the concept of St. Paul, proved itself troubled but confident in its inner self-possession; and while buffeted by new movements and currents of thought, it showed itself capable of slowly and painfully regearing its thinking and activities to the requirements of the 21st century.

A minor but not insignificant development in the direction of this eventual realignment of the Church's interior organization was the Synod of Catholic Bishops which met in Rome from September 29 to October 29, 1967, at Pope Paul's invitation. It was at once a new venture in Roman ecclesiastical governance and a return to a time-honored procedure, and under both aspects it was fully in keeping with the style of a Church whose devotion to tradition is a cornerstone of its stability. While it tends, between times, to get stuck in a groove and to present the monolithic appearance of a perpetual resister to change and progress, the Catholic Church has in fact frequently been a catalyst of reactions that have led a world to new discoveries and mutational advances. This is not mere boasting. In the fifth and sixth centuries, it was the Church, particularly through its monastic organizations, that set about civilizing the barbarian nations. The Gregorian Reform of the late eleventh century prepared the way for the renaissance in learning that characterized the twelfth century and paved the way for both the Renaissance and the Reformation in the sixteenth. No one can prophesy the ultimate effects of Vatican Council II; but its immediate impact, again as a catalyzer of religious movements in the twentieth century, has been phenomenal.

The Synod of Bishops is an outgrowth of the Council. The idea of bringing a representative group of the world's bishops periodically to Rome as a continuing organ of Church government was read into the record during that assembly's second session; the Pope officially approved before the Council ended. Thus, in keeping with Roman tradition, and in the interests of continuity, an ancient practice was revived and given new significance. The antiquity of the practice is attested to by the fact that at the beginning of the fifth century, when the Roman See came to be acknowledged as predominant in the West, and was deferred to occasionally by the Eastern Churches, the synodal principle was a feature of Roman rule. The clearest evidence comes from the reign of Pope Leo I (440–461 A.D.). He frequently called the bishops not only of the dioceses close to Rome but of the entire Patriarchate of the West, from Northern Italy to Sicily, into consultation.

In the sixth century, synodal rule became a characteristic of the Eastern Churches, including those presided over by the previously powerful Patriarchs of Alexandria, Antioch, and Constantinople. The Byzantine Emperor frequently claimed ultimate authority over the Churches within his political jurisdiction. It was at such times in particular that deference to the primacy of Rome on the part of the other autonomous Churches by appeal for support or final judgment became apparent. Down through the centuries, rule through Synods has been the normal practice of the Oriental Churches both Orthdox and Catholic.

In both the ancient practice and the contemporary revival an Episcopal Synod is a gathering of bishops as the successors of the apostles. By means of discussions to establish a consensus and an exercise of their authority as successors to the college of apostles, the bishops settle issues of policy or doctrine, usually for a particular portion of the Church. In the present instance, the Synod of Bishops called to Rome represented the residential bishops of the whole Catholic Church organized into conference by regions, or (in the Eastern Catholic Churches) by patriarchates and major archbishoprics. While the governing structures of the Catholic Church vary greatly from place to place as a result of the conditions in which they were created and the historic evolution they have experienced, the pope presides as Supreme Pastor over all of them. His authority in settling problems of faith and morals is absolute. However, it is not arbitrary. Although in terms of governmental power his jurisdiction is universal and final, in fact his exercise of that power is conditioned by religious considerations that distinguish it from political and civil domination.

Attempts to understand or explain the Catholic Church in purely political terms are bound to prove inadequate, even though the Church as an organization tends to mirror or parallel the type of civil government predominant in each age. During the later Roman Empire, it took on imperialistic contours, expressing its laws and regulations in the form of decrees and canons. In the post-Carolingian age, it gradually became a feudal lordship, with certain popes claiming a universal suzerainty over the kingdoms and emperors of Christendom. In the age of the divine right of kings, it assumed the aspect of absolute monarchy that continued down to the abolition of the Papal States in 1871.

Today, Vatican City is a minimal sovereignty, with the bishop of Rome as its ruler, and the universal Church is vertically aligned with the pope as its supreme pastor. Without encroaching on his authority as such, however, there are movements within the Church seeking to give it a more representative flavor. And the Synod of Bishops is both a symbol and a fact in this line of development. It was a sounding board of international proportions. Involved in an exercise of quasi-parliamentary dialogue with the Church, its members constituted a pilot project in collegial governance of the people of God.

Called together by Pope Paul VI were some 138 bishops elected by 37 conferences of bishops. They sat down with the patriarchs and major archbishops of the Catholic Oriental Churches, six heads of religious orders of men elected by the Conference of Superiors General of Religious Orders and Congregations in Rome, the heads of Roman Curial congregations, and some 20 prelates selected by the Pope, making a gathering of nearly 200 members. They had come to give their views and recommendations on a series of problems concerning the Church's administration and way of life on which the Pope had requested advice.

There were no observers from other Christian Churches, not even from the Orthodox Churches which have a long tradition of synodal government. The reason given for their absence was that this Roman Synod of Bishops was experimental. In addition, Pope Paul added at the first working session on September 30, that the Synod was not a Council directly involving the whole Church. It was a meeting "which in both method and purpose is directed to internal questions of the Catholic Church." And while the exclusion of observers was criticized, the other Churches took it with good grace. The Orthodox Patriarch Athenagoras found no difficulty in accepting the invitation to visit the Pope during the last week of the Synod, a time chosen to stress that there was here at least a symbolic link between the Churches he represented and the internal affairs of the Catholic Church. Pope Paul emphasized the point in his September 30 speech to the Synod Fathers. Your presence, he said, "gives testimony that in the life of the Catholic Church there is active the time-honored synodal institution, which has been so well utilized in the Eastern tradition, and which will strengthen — in a new way adapted to our time — the bonds that exist between the Church of Rome, 'which holds the primacy of charity' (St. Ignatius of Antioch), and the various local Churches." At the formal prayer meeting of the Pope and the Patriarch in St. Peter's Basilica on October 26, the Synod Fathers were present, "forming a crown," as Pope Paul had earlier expressed it. They exchanged the kiss of peace with the Orthodox prelates in the Patriarch's entourage.

Earlier in 1967, a series of meetings had been held in Rome in preparation for the Synod under the sponsorship of IDOC, a non-official center for research and information concerning the impact on the Catholic Church and on the world of the continuing implementation of the decrees and spirit of Vatican Council II. Theologians and historians including bishops, priests, and laymen, had examined the *Motu Proprio* which established the Synod, as well as the constitution or *regolamento* under whose auspices it would be conducted.* Many of the observations were critical of the material to be handled, the limitations on the choice of topics, and the denial of legislative authority foreseen in these documents. Some speakers suggested that the principal aim of the Synod should be to encourage both the Pope and the entire Church to accelerate the *aggiornamento* decreed by Vatican Council II. In particular, they wanted the Vatican to adopt a tone of confidence when evaluating the Church's problems, and to restrict itself to the formulation of broad directives for guiding the great theological discussions and speculative advances now in progress. The secrecy decreed for the Synod was severely criticized. The dominant tone of the conferences was, nevertheless, one of encouraging promise.

On the double ground that the consultation would deal only with domestic matters and that it was experimental, the *regolamento* decreed total secrecy. It was a decision made by the Pope on the advice of his immediate aides, and they justified it with the argument that bishops might be reluctant to speak their minds freely, if their views would be reported in the press. Many bishops showed they did not agree. The Canadian Bishops' Conference made an official protest, asserting that the Synod needed the feedback of public opinion to perform its task properly. Conflict raged behind the scenes in Rome and contradictory statements were made to the press. Only after newsmen reached Rome to cover the Synod was the final word handed down. They would not even receive the facilities they had been accorded at the first session of Vatican Council II, facilities which it had subsequently been agreed were inadequate to permit them to do their work properly.**

The issue is deeper than that of the pope's prerogative to

* The texts of these documents will be found on pp. 189 and 193, below.
** For details, see p. 24 f., below.

consult his advisors in private, a right nobody challenged. What is questioned is the judgment of the circle of the Holy Father's immediate aides who were responsible for the decision. Even accepting the merit of their argument that bishops would speak more freely behind closed doors, one must ask — on a purely pragmatic level — if secrecy is in fact possible. Vatican Council II's first session showed how hard it is to maintain. It also showed how rumor and distortion flourish when facts reach the press via the back door. Had they been sensitive to the further changes in the Church in the direction of greater openness as a result of the Council, these advisers might reasonably have concluded that secrecy could not be maintained and therefore should not have been imposed.

On another level, if they were attuned to current reality, they might also have judged that the negative impact of secrecy on the Church's public image would outweigh the benefits they sought. The Council created a continuing sympathetic awareness of Church affairs among vast numbers of outsiders. It also made Catholics conscious of the right to complete and authentic information on everything affecting the life of the Church, a right based on the theological principle that the Church has an obligation to care for the whole people of God. Catholics are no longer willing to be treated as minors. They want to judge responsibly, and to have access to the information required for responsible judgments. Churchmen who fear that what they have to say would be dangerous for the laity to know, or that they will be misquoted or misinterpreted, should question their own competence for exercising their office. The Church is a public institution meant for the inclusion of all men. Its prelates are public officeholders, responsible to God but responsible before the people of God.

The public image of the Church has thus properly become of world concern. The Holy Father's advisers must take this fact into account when they make plans for a Synod. There is no longer place for half-news, just as half-truths are recognized as worse than lies. When the Synod is described as an approach to collegiality, the universal responsibility implicit in that term must be kept in mind. The official secrecy was consequently a blemish on the Synod. But, thanks no doubt in part to its ineffectiveness, it did not prevent the Synod from being a success. For, in final analysis, the Synod was truly a contribution to the Church's *aggiornamento* that would have rejoiced the man most responsible for the current dynamic progress of that venerable institution, the window-opening Pope John XXIII.

Evaluated against this total background, the Synod's inadequacies and possible failures are to be regretted but must not be regarded with alarm. In preparing an instrument as important as the government of the Christian Church in the 21st century, one of the things to be established by trial and error in the preliminary stages is the extent to which the proposed structures are inadequate or irrelevant. If the Synod had been merely a "dry run" to determine the suitability of the machinery for the intended tasks, that alone would have fully justified it. But in actual fact, it accomplished far more. It laid the foundation for a continuing debate within the governing body of the Church regarding essential problems affecting its well-being and the spiritual, moral, and material salvation of mankind that is the Church's main business.

Both the problems discussed and the ecumenical representation at the Synod will doubtlessly grow in ever widening circles. In a Church whose actual history embraces 1900 years of continuous being, and whose perspectives reach from creation to the final end of time, the Synod of Bishops was apparently only a minor event. But not unlike the mustard seed of the Gospel parable, it could grow and become a great tree whose branches might eventually encompass the whole of the universe.

FRANCIS X. MURPHY, C.SS.R.

CHAPTER 1

The Synod Opens

Saint Peter's, the great baroque basilica in Rome which in the eyes of the world is the center of Roman Catholic Christianity, witnessed a modest but religiously proper event on September 29, 1967. Punctually at 10 A.M., Pope Paul VI made his entry for Mass. The fourteen concelebrants who preceded him were bishops from fourteen different nations. In contrast to the pomp and fanfare of the opening of the Second Vatican Council five years earlier, the Pope came on foot, dressed like his fellow bishops in white chasuble and miter.

Such was the start of the first Synod of Bishops. Symbolism is one of Rome's deepest traditions, and here was a symbolic expression understandable to all who witnessed it of the detriumphalization which Vatican Council II had urged as part of the renewal of the Church.

The liturgy was celebrated in Latin, the official language of the Church of Rome. The choice was logical, not only because of the place, but also because the 182 Synod Fathers present represented at least a hundred countries, and spoke more languages than the frustrated builders of the Tower of Babel. The Gospel was read in Greek and Latin; the prayer of the faithful, in English, French, Spanish, Italian, German, and Portuguese. The form of the celebration not only reflected the liturgical advances introduced since the Vatican Council, but went beyond them by including the still-experimental three Scripture readings in the Liturgy of the Word. The first was the dream of Jacob, from Genesis 28; next the account of Saint Michael as head of the angels, from the Book of Revelation; and finally the meeting of Jesus with Nathaniel, from the first chapter of Saint John's Gospel. The concelebrated Mass was itself yet another significant symbol of the conciliar Church. It was an affirmation of the Gospel-oriented Eucharist as the source of the renewal.

Welcoming the bishops, the Pope stressed the point. "Together we have celebrated the eucharistic sacrifice, which has been called with particular appropriateness 'the mystery of faith and the mystery of love.' There is no other way to describe this sacramental mystery which brings to us, pilgrims in time, the real presence of Christ. . . . Two years after the Council, and in fulfillment of our undertaking, we find ourselves united again in this blessed place . . . to intensify our love in preparation for the happy celebration of the first meeting of the Synod of Bishops."

By late September the oppressive heat of the high summer is gone, but Rome is still a city of warmth and sunshine. It is a favorite time for tourists and pilgrims, and the Synod opening had increased their numbers and added substantial contingents of theologians and representatives of the press and the electronic media. They had converged on St. Peter's not only to witness the historic spectacle of the first Synod of Bishops in the modern history of the Church of the West, but also to catch a glimpse of the Pope still convalescent from his recent illness. The latest reports on the Pontiff's health were reassuring, yet everyone wondered how he would stand up to the strain of at least a month of intense involvement with his advisers.

Those who managed to squeeze into the basilica, and the many additional millions who watched the simultaneous teletransmission on Eurovision were cheered to find that, though Pope Paul walked rather slowly as he entered, there was no trace of fatigue; and his step was firm. He climbed the seven steep altar steps effortlessly, at the Offertory of the Mass. At the Consecration, he raised the host and chalice high and turned around each time for all to see and worship.

It was, nevertheless, not difficult to surmise that behind the carefully controlled features, features perhaps a little more fleshless after his illness than their normal ascetic appearance, grave matters were troubling Paul's keen mind. Some of these he expressed in his talk that day, and in another at the start of the Synod's first working session, the next morning, As on several occasions in recent months, he dwelt on many and serious dangers to the faith. "There is great peril because of the irreligious tendencies of the modern mentality," he said. "Even inside the Church, insidious menaces exist and are spread about by some teachers and writers. They want to express Catholic teaching in a new form, but often they seem more anxious to adjust the dogmas of the faith to profane thought and language than to accept the magisterium of the Church as their guide."

He was concerned, too, that some members of the Synod were absent because of improper political interference with their liberty of movement. "Especially to Cardinal Wyszynski, Archbishop of Warsaw, and with him to Cardinal Wojtyla, Archbishop of Cracow, and to the Polish bishops who in solidarity did not want to come to Rome without their Primate, we send cordial and special greetings. This we do, not without expressing our strong sense of regret because of the obstacle put in the way of such a harmless voyage, and because of the unjust conditions imposed on the Church in various countries, where legitimate freedom is still denied her, where the Church is the object of unjustified suspicions, of moral and legal pressures and an even fierce antireligious opposition. You know, venerable brothers, how much Catholic life in some nations is restricted in its vital needs, both organizational and functional, and deliberately reduced to hardship and the danger of gradual extinction."

But the Pope's concerns were not confined to the Church's internal issues, doctrinal and operational. He also needed the help of the bishops, he told them, for an issue that was not on the agenda but which Paul has missed no opportunity of promoting: peace in the world. "A subject of such great and all-embracing importance as world peace cannot escape the attention, the interests, and the prayers of this gathering. . . . We cannot forget, not even in the calm of our Synodal sessions how this peace is being seriously violated and dangerously undermined. Without interruption, a bloody war is being waged in South-East Asia; another in the Middle East is being barely held in check by a fragile truce; we see conflicts out of control and guerilla operations in various parts of the world. Despite many resolute and praiseworthy efforts, a state of general insecurity seems to be abroad in the world that inevitably foreshadows other misfortunes."

Pope Paul is known for his gift of balancing the pros and the cons, the positives and the negatives of a situation, and his opening talks to the Synod were no exception. The gloomy observations just quoted were nuanced by other elements to give a total perspective that many judged more positive and self-assured than the generality of his previous analyses.

He stressed, for example, the importance he gave to the Synod itself as a new structure full of promise for the Church. Vatican Council II, he said, had highlighted "the collegial characteristics inherent in the constitutional structure of the Church," and though the Synod is not a Council, it has some of its elements. "It reflects its spirit and method, and — please God — will obtain the Council's own charisms of wisdom and charity."

By these and similar words, the Pope proclaimed his confidence that the Church's new vision of herself as a communion in which the pope is surrounded by his brothers was a guarantee of their ability in union to face and overcome the difficulties he had mentioned earlier. He had entered St. Peter's without his Noble Guards, his Knights of Cape and Sword. His reliance was not on them but on his fellow bishops, and on the people who thronged the basilica and joined vocally in the liturgy. Pope Paul would follow up this symbolic gesture in the following days by frequently visiting the Synod Fathers while they dealt with their agenda, and by joining them in their mid-morning coffee break, making every effort to talk to each in turn and give each a chance to speak his mind. Here was another positive indication that the Pope realized the need to break out of the isolation into which popes were forced in an era of formalism, to engage in dialogue in the literal sense of the expression.

Not less important was his insistence that his criticism of "some teachers and writers" was not intended to, and should not be used as an excuse to stifle legitimate theological discussion. What he sought, he insisted, was to strengthen in particular the faith "of those who devote themselves to the study of theology and of religion, so that, with a renewed and alert understanding of the established and unchanging teachings of the Church, they will cooperate wisely to promote the sacred sciences."

The similarities and differences of his charge to the Synod Fathers and that of Pope John to the Fathers assembled for the first session of Vatican Council II are significant. Pope Paul recalled in his opening address part of what Pope John had said on the earlier occasion, that part concretely in which he had told the Council Fathers it was their duty to transmit in its integrity, without omission or alteration, the teaching of the Church. Unlike John, however, he did not remind the Synod Fathers that the teaching should be reformulated in terms of the research and presentation of today's world, nor did he draw John's distinction between the substance of the teaching and the form of its expression.

Some commentators seized on that detail to contrast the two men. Perhaps it is more pertinent to contrast the two situations. At the start of the Council, John XXIII recognized the urgency and the difficulty of shaking the Church out of its fortress mentality, forcing Catholics to think again for themselves after several centuries of following quasi-military orders. Two years after the Council, people were asking if some had not learned the lesson too well, opening a breach within the Church between those who were moving ahead quickly in implementing the decrees and spirit of the Council and those being left behind either because they were temperamentally incapable of change or — much more frequently — because the need to change and the elements requiring change had not been properly explained to them.

Whatever else Pope Paul is, he is certainly a pope of unity. "The first purpose in establishing this new instrument of the Church's pastoral government is unity and solidarity in the Catholic hierarchy." At the very moment he is following so energetically the lead of his predecessor toward unity with his fellow Christians, this man who has given the Orthodox Patriarch Athenagoras the kiss of peace, in Jerusalem, Constantinople, and Rome, and has cancelled the excommunications fulminated centuries ago against the Orthodox Churches, this man who stresses incessantly the many bonds by which we are united "spiritually and substantially" with other Christian Churches and communities, is determined not to go down in history as a pope who caused or permitted a schism in his own Church. One might argue that this determination sometimes becomes so obsessive as to cloud his mind to the side effects of the decisions it dictates. But the Pope's intention and its basic correctness can hardly be called in question.

How would the Synod help the Pope to advance these causes so dear to his heart? Nobody was too clear, perhaps least of all the bishops themselves assembled for the event, and probably not even Pope Paul. There was a vagueness about the situation which disturbed many observers. As the days passed, however, the conviction grew that Pope Paul had wished this vagueness for much the same reasons as Pope John had launched the ecumenical council in a welter of confusing directives and conflict of jurisdictions. Rather than impose a ready-made constitution in Rome's traditional manner, both popes seem to have sought a fluidity in which the true lines of power would gradually reveal themselves, in which the underlying forces would gravitate around their appropriate poles.

Cardinal Bernard Jan Alfrink, of Utrecht, Holland, had called in November, 1961, for "an ecumenical council in miniature" as a continuing organ of Church government. The proposal was motivated by the experience of bishops from around the world working together on the central preparatory commission for Vatican II. In 1962, Pope John indicated that he liked the idea. Pope Paul expressed agreement specifically in an address to the Curia in September, 1963. "If the Ecumenical Council wishes to see some representatives of the episcopacy, particularly bishops heading dioceses, associated . . . with (the Pope) in the study and responsibility of ecclesiastical government, it will not be the Roman Curia that will oppose it." He repeated the thought in his first address to the Council Fathers at the inauguration of the second Council session September 29. Their response was quick and enthusiastic. On October 1, Archbishop Maxim Hermaniuk, Exarch for the Ukrainians in Canada, said on the Council floor: "This government could take the form of a large college, a kind of episcopal council beside the Pope, which would include the patriarchs, the cardinals who are residential bishops or archbishops, and delegates from episcopal conferences or missionary areas." Maximos IV Saigh, Melchite Patriarch of Antioch, repeated substantially the same formula the following month, adding that "there should be constantly in Rome, in addition, what the Eastern Church calls the *Synodos endemousa,* that is to say, some members of the Sacred Apostolic College taking their place in turn beside the Pope . . . the supreme executive and decision-making council of the universal Church, to which all Roman offices would be subject." He was supported by Cardinals Giacomo Lercaro of Bologna, Laurean Rugambwa, of Bukoba, Tanzania, and Ermenegildo Florit, of Florence. A written request to the Pope, signed by 500 Fathers, followed.

In early 1965, Pope Paul announced that he was expanding the college of cardinals to increase the representation of the non-Italian world. Earlier, at the close of the third Council session in November, 1964, he had indicated his intention to accede to the many requests from the Fathers to establish the collegial body they favored. The expansion of the college of cardinals was widely understood to be his way of fulfilling his promise, and many were gravely disappointed. An expanded college of cardinals would still be handpicked by the pope. Because cardinals are named for life, it would be dominated by men in their seventies and eighties. In addition, it would be an organ of the pope as bishop of Rome rather than as pastor of the universal Church.

It would be in keeping with Pope Paul's techniques of government to have let the matter rest there, had the reaction been favorable. In fact, he took an early opportunity to announce that a new body would be created alongside the expanded college of cardinals. To give effect to their wishes, he told the Council Fathers at the inauguration of the fourth and final session in September, 1965, it would be "composed of bishops to be chosen for the greater part by episcopal conferences."

The following day, with a speed unusual in Rome, the constitution of the new body was issued as a *Motu proprio*. It was an extremely vague document, a deliberately vague document. The Pope wanted to start with experimental forms and let them be clarified gradually in the light of experience. The very nature of the Synod was left in doubt. Professor Edward Schillebeeckx, O.P., insisted in a talk in Rome early in 1967 that it fulfills all the requirements for a "truly collegial act" as specified in the Constitution on the Church. "Counsels given by the Synod and adopted by the Pope (or deliberative decisions ratified by the Pope) are non-conciliar but nonetheless strictly collegial acts of the world episcopate in union with the pope." Another leading theologian, Professor Giuseppe Alberigo, a layman and professor of the History of Christianity at the University of Bologna, in the same series of conferences sponsored by IDOC, insisted on the contrary that the Synod as established is not strictly a manifestation of collegiality, both because its function is normally consultative (advisory), and because its potential deliberative (decision-making) function does not derive from God through the episcopal consecration of its members, but from the pope. He agreed with Cardinal Paolo Marella in describing it as a symbol or token of collegiality, but not an express statement of collegiality in effect or doctrinally.

Pope Paul himself left the issue open when he spoke to the Synod Fathers on September 30, although the previous day he promised that this talk would touch on some points regarding the Synod's canonical status. "There are not a few scholars and publicists eager to analyse the juridical aspects of this institution," he said, "and to determine — as far as they can — its form and function according to certain new concepts of the Church's constitutional law. But it is enough for us to reflect how this new organ, at the very heart of the Church, is in harmony with that spirit of union and collaboration between the Apostolic See, the Catholic episcopacy and the major superiors of religious families, which the Council experienced and fostered, and to observe that it is the intention of this Synod to further the exchange of experience and information concerning the life of the Church."

The Synod is by its constitution a permanent institution, and its specific function is to advise the pope on matters on which he asks its advice. Synods can be of three kinds, general, extraordinary, and special. A general Synod is a formal assembly to discuss grave matters of interest to the Church as a whole. An extraordinary Synod is one summoned rapidly to deal with one issue of general concern that calls for a quick decision. A special Synod is called to deal with issues concerning only one region or a few regions. Although the Synod is of its nature permanent, the membership is chosen for each session, the procedure varying to meet the conditions of the general, the extraordinary, and the special synod. The members go out of office immediately on conclusion of the session. While this may seem an unusual provision, it reduces the danger that the same individuals will automatically be renamed time after time and thus raise the average age of members unduly. The danger is further lessened by a provision that members should be chosen each time who have expert knowledge of the issues on the agenda.

For a general Synod, such as that inaugurated on September 29, 1967, about two-thirds of the membership of approximately 200 are elected by national and regional conferences of bishops around the world. Conferences with 25 or fewer members elect one representative. Conferences with 26 to 50 members elect two; those with 51 to 100, three; and those with more than 100, four. Members by virtue of their office are the patriarchs, major archbishops, and most metropolitans (not controlled by patriarchates) of the Eastern rites. The Roman Union of Superiors General of religious institutes elects ten members to represent the religious orders and congregations of men. The pope, for his part, may name additional bishops, members of religious orders and members of the clergy who are experts, their number not to exceed 15 percent of the total.

The constituent document adds that "in a general session of the Synod of Bishops, there are also present the cardinals who head departments (*dicasteria*) in the Roman Curia." Some commentators pointed out before the Synod that the words did not make it clear that such cardinals would be full members with the right to speak and, as appropriate, to vote. Father René Laurentin, for example, said they seemed from the phrasing not to form part of the Synod but to be mere observers. Dr. Peter Huizing, S.J., professor at the universities of Louvain and Nijmegen, on the other hand, said that the word "also" in the paragraph favored including them as belonging to the Synod in the same way as the others.

The issue became somewhat more important when, in addition to the heads of the thirteen *dicasteria,* three other curial cardinals were introduced to the Synod meetings, Cardinal Eugene Tisserant, the 83-year-old dean of the College of Cardinals, Cardinal Dino Staffa, 61 years old, recently transferred from the post of secretary of the Congregation of Seminaries and Universities (now Congregation of Christian Education) to the less sensitive proprefecture of the tribunal known as the Signatura Apostolica, and Cardinal Antonio Ferretto, 68 years old, the Supreme Penitentiary. The explanation of the Vatican spokesman was that Cardinal Tisserant as dean had been omitted previously through an oversight, and the other two had the right to participate as heads of two important tribunals. Actually, Cardinal Francesco Roberti is head of the Signatura Apostolica, but as he was ill, Cardinal Staffa took his place. The constituent document of the Synod gives no support for this explanation. Other observers saw it as a maneuver to increase curial influence in a body in the evolution of which the Curia has an understandable interest. During the session, the curial cardinals intervened in the discussions, took part in the election of Synod commissions, and were otherwise given equal status with the other participants. The ambiguity seems accordingly to have been resolved in their favor.

Vatican II was always bogged down by the vagueness of the lines of authority among the directing bodies, the 4 moderators, 12 presidents, 6 members of a coordinating commission, and a secretary general. None of the presidents or moderators were elected by the Council. In addition, Cardinal Ottaviani insisted that the theological commission which he headed was the "competent authority," a claim stoutly resisted by Cardinal Döpfner and never definitely resolved. The result was that the directive bodies were unable to resolve major conflicts by themselves. As René Laurentin put it, "these bodies are more sluggish than the will of the immense majority of the assembly."

In the Synod, all officials are similarly appointed by the pope, but the structure is simpler and it functioned to the general satisfaction when put to the test. The final authority is a president or group of presidents. Three were actually named, Cardinal Jean Villot of the Roman Curia (until early 1967, Archbishop of Lyons, France), Cardinal Pericle Felici of the Curia, and Cardinal William Conway of Armagh, Ireland. All were extremely young, as cardinals go, 54, 56 and 54 years respectively. Cardinal Villot, named as undersecretary of Vatican Council II by Pope John in October, 1962, is known for his liberal tendencies. Cardinal Felici had proved himself efficient and charming, and also extraordinarily skilled in keeping his personal views to himself, as general secretary of Vatican II. Cardinal Conway has the reputation of being rather conservative, more concerned with pastoral than with speculative issues.

The secretary general is the key man. He prepares the agenda and controls the material arrangements. In addition, he is the one permanent element in the Synod. All other members and officials function simply for the session in which they participate, but he continues in office as long as the pope wishes, thereby ensuring continuity. Named to this post was a "dark horse," Bishop Ladislas Rubin, a man who combines to an extraordinary degree the qualities needed for his delicate tasks. Affable, self-possessed, and determined, he enjoys the reputation of being nobody's man. It is a reputation that fits with his record. Born in Galicia, Poland, in 1917, he knew life in prison camps in Siberia when Stalin joined Hitler in gobbling up Poland, next fought in the Polish Liberation Army of General Anders, made his way to Lebanon, completed his studies and was ordained a priest in 1946. Since

1949, he has lived in exile in Rome as chaplain of émigrés and rector of the Polish College. He speaks the major European languages, Slav, Germanic, Anglo-Saxon, and Romance, as well as Arabic. He has a reputation for administrative and diplomatic ability. Though long in Rome, he has remained on the margin of the Curia. Or, as the phrase goes, "he is not one of the family."

Ten other officials were also named, a rapporteur and a special secretary for each item on the agenda. The primary function of the rapporteur is to set the scene by an opening statement on each item of the agenda. Both he and his special secretary answer queries from the Fathers regarding the document distributed to the Fathers in advance, in which the meaning and purpose of the agenda item are developed.

Cardinal Felici, who was primarily responsible for the document on reform of canon law, was rapporteur for that item. His special secretary was Father Raimondo Bidagor, S.J. Cardinal Browne and Father Edward Dhanis, S.J., a Belgian, were rapporteur and special secretary respectively on the item on doctrinal issues. Henri Fesquet of *Le Monde* of Paris has described them as "two men with the reputation of being passably hostile to theological renewal." Cardinal Garrone and Msgr. Flaminio Cerutti followed for seminaries; Cardinal Marella and Msgr. Joseph Tomko, for mixed marriages; and Cardinal Lercaro and Father Annibale Bugnini, C.M., for the liturgy. Father Bugnini, to quote Fesquet again, is "gravely suspect by the integralists." All in all, the ten men between them reflect well the broad range of opinions in today's Church.

The synod in its present tentative and experimental form falls far short of what the institution of the same name means in the life of the Orthodox Churches. Juridically, it has no authority. The pope summons it, if and when he chooses. He ratifies the delegates elected by the episcopal conferences. He fixes the agenda. He accepts or rejects the advice it gives him. It is restricted to "informing and advising" unless he authorizes it to make binding (deliberative) decisions and ratifies such decisions after they have been made.

Unlike the Orthodox, who regard synodal life as a fact lived continuously at the core of the Church, the Western Church sees it as simply one method or manifestation of unity, exercised for the well-being of the Church. That is how the differing viewpoints were recently defined by Father Emmanuel Lanne, O.S.B., rector of the Greek College in Rome. The Orthodox Synod is deliberative by nature, and the laity play an active part. "The Orthodox conscience," to quote Father Lanne, "considers participation of the Christian people in the synodal life of the Church as advisable, and non-participation as anomalous." The Orthodox synodal system is consequently quite different from anything the Western Church has known or knows today, basically because of the different ecclesiological perspectives.

In spite of the differences, Pope Paul was quite right in stressing the ecumenical significance of the initiative. As Melchite Archbishop Edelby, of Edessa, expressed it, "we have here a beginning. It is still only five percent of what the Eastern Churches understand by a synod, but the next time it will be more, and the following time still more.* Ecumenical Patriarch Athenagoras' reception at the Vatican, returning Pope Paul's visit to him at Istanbul, while the Synod was meeting, had also a significance. Though the Pope did not receive his guest in a session of his Synod, at least the Holy Father was surrounded by the Synod members when he welcomed the Patriarch and prayed with him in St. Peter's.

Secrecy is not mentioned in the constituent document, but the operational directives dated December 8, 1966, and issued over the signature of Cardinal Amleto Giovanni Cicognani, the 84-year-old Secretary of State, dealt with the point. "All who have a part in the Synod are bound to

---

* That was Archbishop Edelby's summation in early October. By mid-month, he had raised his assessment to 15 percent; by the end, "perhaps even 65 percent."

secrecy regarding both the preparatory acts and the work of the assembly itself, particularly on matters concerning the decisions and conclusions of the members."

Secrecy is one of the most elusive of Roman concepts. Its purpose is often not to hide information but to arrange for its release in a form and at a time calculated to promote the interests of those in the know, interests which may be institutional, ideological, or personal. A different interpretation is worked out on a pragmatic basis in each instance, as the circumstances indicate.

The first tests gave promise of a liberal interpretation. Episcopal conferences had to choose their delegates on the basis not only of their general knowledge and prudence, but of their "theoretical and practical knowledge of the issues with which the Synod will deal." This meant that almost 2,500 prelates and several thousand advisers had to know the agenda months ahead of the meeting. The United States bishops in fact received the agenda before their meeting in Chicago in April, 1967, and the press immediately published what the bishops quickly confirmed as an accurate copy.

The Canadian bishops also held a plenary meeting in April, and there they discussed the secrecy issue and put themselves on public record in a strongly worded resolution. Since the action of newsmen during Vatican II, they said, "furnished an important dynamism for the life of the Council, we feel it our duty to urge that all facilities be given by the Vatican to the great media of information, so that they can provide the people of God with the services they expect from the press . . . complete and accurate information on all subjects discussed, and also a feed-back to the Synod itself of the views formed and discussions provoked by this information among the people of God."

Subsequently, in the United States and many other countries, the names of the bishops elected by the episcopal conferences as their representatives were leaked to the press without waiting for the papal approval of the choices, as specified in the rules. And at a press conference in Rome, on April 19, 1967, Bishop Ladislas Rubin, Secretary General of the Synod, assured his audience that the rule would be interpreted as liberally as it was during the Council.

The press had every reason to believe Bishop Rubin's sincerity, and to think in addition that he could make his words stick. He had, nevertheless, been over-optimistic. During the summer, rumors of an unresolved conflict on the secrecy issue flourished. Msgr. Fausto Vallainc, Vatican press officer, made no attempt to hide his personal desire for procedures in keeping with Bishop Rubin's promise. But right up to the eve of the Synod opening, he was unable to get any official instructions. He went ahead, nevertheless, with preparations to provide the facilities offered the press at the second and subsequent sessions of the Council. This included engaging the services of Father Edward Heston, C.S.C., who had attended the Council meetings and immediately afterwards each day had given an English-language briefing, to the general satisfaction of the press. Similar stand-by arrangements were made for the other major languages. As the Synod date approached, the Vatican officials in touch with the press were increasingly optimistic.

The disillusionment of the journalists, who had come in great numbers as representatives of all the media from every part of the world, was consequently great when, on the very eve of the session, the word was handed down that secrecy would be as strict as at the first session of the Council. In fact, as they learned after the first working session on September 30, it was even stricter. Only Msgr. Vallainc was allowed to attend the session. He made notes as it progressed and, about an hour after its end, produced a statement in Italian containing summaries of the speeches.* However, he had been

* The physical strain on Msgr. Vallainc was such that after about a week, he was allowed to bring Father Heston along as his assistant. French newsmen protested that this gave their English-language colleagues an unfair advantage. From Oct. 17 onwards, Msgr. Dominick Pichon, head of the Public Opinion Secretariat of the French Bishops, also attended

forbidden to give the names of the 12 cardinals and 7 archbishops and bishops who had spoken that day. In addition, as he notified the press, he had been instructed to "scramble" the summaries of what had been said in such a way as to complicate the task of identifying the speakers. Without such identification, the information was almost valueless to the newsman. He could not say who was speaking on behalf of a bishop's conference with 200 or more members, and who spoke only for himself. He could give his reader no indication of the dynamic interplay of the participants, or the added importance of a given viewpoint in the light of the previous positions adopted by the person who expressed it. Words without context, and particularly without the vital context of the speaker's known attitudes and assumptions, mean little.

Two Italian newsmen had earlier addressed a letter to the Secretary General of the Synod, in which they had touched on the "delicate problem" which the upcoming Synod offered to specialists in religious information to give their readers "an exhaustive and timely account," and expressed the hope that they would not "be forced by their professional sense of duty to violate the obligation of secrecy, to have recourse to speculative suppositions or to humiliating expedients in order to acquire information."

The reaction of most Italian newsmen to the service offered by the Synod authorities was to ignore the event altogether. Not a line about it appeared in the Rome dailies the day after the first working session. Other newsmen, including representatives of major news agencies and newspapers of the world, as well as the editors of many United States and other Catholic newspapers, decided it was their professional duty to cooperate in breaking secrecy by utilizing the "underground" service of the Center for Coordination of Communi-

---

the Synod meetings and reported on them to French-speaking journalists. The official explanation for his presence inside the Synod was that he had been designated by the French episcopate "to make profound studies on mixed marriages and on the liturgy," the agenda subjects then being discussed.

cations for the Synod (CCCS). A similar operation, the CCCC, had been developed as an independent source of information and backgrounding for newsmen during the Council. When the Council ended, it was fused with a parallel service for theologians into the permanent center for information and research on the implementation of the Council, IDOC. While maintaining the service for theologians, IDOC suspended that for newsmen on the ground that it was needed only for special occasions. However, it revived it as the CCCS for the Synod, and the CCCS was able each afternoon to give the press a list of the morning's speakers, with a summary of what each had said, as well as additional background material designed to help the newsmen give their readers some perspective on what was happening. The CCCS center was in fact *underground,* in a basement under a bookstore on Via della Conciliazione, the great boulevard opened by Mussolini to provide a vista from the Tiber to St. Peter's. Here each afternoon, a panel of theologians met the press and answered their questions about the meaning of the information they had just been given, a service performed during the Council by the U. S. Bishops' Panel.*

As the days went by, various newsmen made additional contacts with what the French Catholic news magazine, *Informations Catholiques Internationales,* delicately referred to as "episcopal sources." The situation lent itself to legitimate mistakes and malicious rumors. The Rome rightwing daily *Il Tempo,* famed for its distortions of Vatican news and often the mouthpiece of the hardline curialists, charged Cardinal

---

* Gary MacEoin developed the CCCS program for the Synod while on assignment in Rome from March to June, 1967, as a management consultant to IDOC. John Horgan, an Irish journalist specializing in religious information, headed the operation during the Synod. Regular panel members were Abbé René Laurentin, Fr. John Long, S.J., Fr. Jorge Mejía, Fr. Francis X. Murphy, C.SS.R., Fr. Thomas Stransky, C.S.P., and Fr. Peter Hebblethwaite, S.J. Occasional visitors included Fr. Enda McDonagh, the Maynooth (Ireland) moral theologian, Fr. Robert Rouquette, S.J., of *Etudes* (France), and U. S. canonist Fr. Edmond D. Walsh, S.J., of Chestnut Hill, Newton, Mass.

Veuillot of Paris with having made an "antiroman, anticurial and antipapal" speech. The speech had in fact been made by Cardinal Léger of Montreal, and it contained nothing to justify the charges. But, in broad terms, though the journalists had to do a lot more legwork, they got the news with laudable accuracy and speed. To sum up in the words of *Informations Catholiques Internationales:* "The effort to wrap questions which interest the whole people of God in an artificial mystery . . . was once again shown up as unavailing. It testifies, nevertheless, to the survival of a disincarnated concept of the Church, and some lack of understanding of the rights and the elementary needs of religious information."

To describe the Synod as of interest to the whole people of God, far from being an exaggeration, is an understatement. As quickly emerged from the news coverage, people of all cultures and social conditions, of all religions and of none, wanted desperately to know just how serious was the Roman Catholic Church about the updating, the commitment to the concerns of mankind, to which Vatican II had pledged it. One of the great astonishments of the early days of that Council was the realization that the world was watching with intense sympathy the struggles of the biggest and most venerable Christian institution to unshackle itself from the rusty chains which bound it to cultural forms long meaningless to the world and rapidly becoming distasteful to its own members. Many prophesied that the end of the Council would see the end of the interest. On the contrary, it has grown and become more sophisticated during the subsequent years, as valiant efforts to start the process of reform revealed ideological and practical differences far deeper than had been at first suspected. To add to the general interest, it became steadily clearer that many of the problems brought into the open in the Catholic Church by the Council were problems shared in significant part by other Christian bodies and perhaps by all religions, particularly the challenge of atheism as formulated in contemporary society.

Thus, for example, the Roman Catholic and other Churches are hemorrhaging, losing especially the young who shun the traditional church services and proclaim a growing suspicion of structures and leadership. Vocations to the priesthood and to the monastic and convent life decline, at a time when the generosity of youth and its desire to serve others is more visible than at any other moment in history. Many clergy and nuns, not a few among them being the most highly motivated and best formed, return to civilian life in the hope of finding there more opportunity to express their dedication.

Observers describe this and like phenomena by drawing a distinction between religious reform and ecclesiastical reform. What happened during the two years between the close of the Council and the opening of the Synod would in this interpretation be a widening of the gap between these two reforms. Religious reform, a change in the norms and values of individuals, followed by a change in their behavior, can occur very rapidly today under the influence of the mass media operating in a social climate conducive to change. Ecclesiastical or institutional reform is more complicated and can with difficulty keep up. The problem is not simply to create new committees and organizations, to formulate new codes and policies, to shift personnel, though these are all complicated enough. There is the added problem that the heads of the institution, the bureaucrats, must look in both directions simultaneously. It is the nature of the bureaucrat to do this instinctively, but it is also in the nature of his situation. Leaving aside entirely his vested interests, he is committed to the immovable no less than to those in motion, to those floundering along in the rear as well as those adventuring ahead of the front lines.

Yet the obligation to keep a brake on reform in order not to shake the machine apart creates what is one of the toughest of the current dilemmas of the Church. It poses the question to which everyone hoped the Synod would give, if not a definitive reply and solution, at least an indication that a solution is possible. The Catholic Church was once the leader of the advance of mankind, the home of culture, the inspirer of art, the encourager of the genius which started Western civilization in the direction of its subsequent accomplishments. For several centuries, leadership has passed to other hands. The Church long resisted, attempting by all means in its power to retain or regain controls which it had forgotten how to use constructively. Finally, it has recognized its mistake. It has offered a new alliance to mankind, one in which it proposes for itself a much more modest role than previously. It no longer seeks to lead, except in a clearly defined and limited way. It seeks to serve. But it has made this offer at the precise moment when the world has entered on a phase of accelerated and accelerating progress. The last few centuries of the estrangement have witnessed greater change than all the previous history of man. The next fifty years promise to carry the human race further both in control of the environment and in development of man's own faculties than the previous fifty million. Can the Church, starting with a timelag of several centuries, hope to catch up with this superman? Or is it destined to see itself for the indefinite future in the position of one running at a rate of five miles an hour after a vehicle which is continuing forward at a rate of six miles an hour?

Catholics are giving three answers to this question. Some say we should stop running right away, because we shouldn't have begun to run in the first place. They form the conservative group who fought so hard at the Council but were proved to constitute a relatively small segment of Catholic opinion as reflected and expressed by the Council Fathers. There are those who say we can and must run faster, and that if we do, we will undoubtedly catch up. The Council established that the vast majority of thinking Catholics belonged at that time to this group. But there is a third and growing group separating itself from the second and simply dropping out of the race. It's no use, they say. The dead weight around our necks is too much. We can never make it with this institution, so let's forget about institutional forms and go on our own, each one writing his own rules. This is the famous "third man" about whom so much is being written these days.

It was only in October, 1966, that the expression was first used, by Father François Roustang, S.J., writing in the French magazine *Christus,* and the speed with which it has traveled is evidence of the extent of the phenomenon it describes. The reference is to an early Christian text, the *Letter to Diognetes,* in which the Christian is called a third race, a third people, a third man. The *Letter* is contrasting Christians with Jews and pagans, following an allusion of Saint Paul in *1 Corinthians.* The current meaning of the expression is, however, totally different. It is, as explained above, the man who is personally committed to moral values and faith in Christ, but who is detached from or unconcerned with institutional structures, as contrasted with the conservative who wants to defend existing Church structures, and with the progressive who wants to change them.

To add infinitely to the complication of the situation, these three groups between them form only a minority, possibly no more than a tenth of Catholics. As in all societies, so in the Church there is a relatively small proportion of opinion-makers. With the modern expansion of mass literacy and of higher education, the opinion-making segment of society has increased significantly in relation to the whole. But the vast majority of people still depend more on others than on themselves to make their decisions for them.

In former times, it was usually easy for an individual or group in this category to pick a man of integrity and intelligence, and follow his lead. The electronic age of instant communications is changing that situation radically. Everyone is now exposed to all the opinions, and often in a form so oversimplified as to be distorted. This is hopefully a transitional phenomenon, to be overcome with the wider utilization of the opportunities for education already at hand. But transitional or not, it is a basic datum of our current condition. This great group, alerted and disturbed, looks for quick and easy answers, just as the same group on the level of society demands simple answers to the great issues of war and peace, of wealth and poverty.

Such people are building up pressures on the leaders of the Church, just as they — as citizens — demand from their political leaders more than these can deliver today, although in both cases the demands are in themselves reasonable. For the Pope and the Synod Fathers, they constitute what is perhaps their most anguishing problem. Two years after the Council, the Church is still inevitably in total transition. All kinds of reforms have begun but few if any have been completed. The Church has launched out into the deep of the ocean, and it is still not even possible to say when a new port will be reached. But those on board the ship must be reassured that the captain and officers know where they are headed, and that the supplies on board are adequate for a voyage of indefinite duration. It is in this perspective that one must approach the study of the first Synod of Bishops. It will help to explain why the issues on the agenda, if far from the most basic with which the Church must deal urgently, need to be resolved before the others can be tackled realistically. To continue the metaphor of a ship at sea, it is a clearing of the decks to prepare for storm or battle.

CHAPTER 2

Five-Pointed Agenda

"The substance of the ancient doctrine of the Deposit of Faith is one thing, and the way in which it is presented is another." This distinction between the reality of the truths revealed by God and constantly taught by the Church, and the way those truths are expressed in each age and for each culture, was made by Pope John in his opening address to Vatican Council II on October 11, 1962. Many of the older-minded theologians and Roman-trained churchmen who had hitherto managed to keep such an idea out of the textbooks and the official theology of the Church did not like it. They held that the way a truth was worded was almost an essential part of the fact it represented, and many of them came close to defining the Christian religion as a series of propositions to be believed and memorized.

In contrast to this attitude, Vatican Council II reaffirmed the fact that Christianity is essentially a relationship between God and man, wherein man's maker has not only spoken to his creatures, but demonstrated a personal love for man that is incredibly exercized in the incarnation of Jesus Christ the Son of God and capped with the redemptive action of Christ's death and resurrection. These mysteries, though inexplicable, have a direct bearing on man's immediate interests and activities as well as on his destiny. To be a Christian means that one believes in Christ as God and strives to conduct one's life in accordance with that belief. Christ is portrayed in the Gospels as having founded a church, and in the twentieth century, an institution calling itself the Catholic Church claims to be the same church established by Christ. It has been through innumerable vicissitudes in the 19 centuries of its history; it has been split into fractions, many of the members of which among the Orthodox and other Christian Churches claim to present authentic lineaments of the original institution. Vatican Council II provided a key to an acknowledgment, and possibly to the solution, of the problem raised by disunity among Christians. It likewise gave directives for an updating of the Church designed to bring it abreast of the religious and personality interests of contemporary man.

Pope Paul convoked the Synod of Bishops as a step in the implementation of this Council program. He saw it as an experiment, an attempt to lay down lines for a gradual involvement of the world's Catholic bishops in the government of the universal Church. Many outside observers as well as activists within the Church hoped that the Synod would take on immediately the proportions and functions of a Council in miniature. The existence of such sympathetic concern is one of the favorable signs of the times. The pressures it produces can, nevertheless, be embarrassing, especially when journalists and other publicists give free rein to their imagination in their effort to satisfy the legitimate and growing religious interests of their readers.

In this perspective, the agenda for the Synod proved somewhat disappointing to many of the Church's well-wishers and critics, and even to not a few of the bishops involved in its deliberations.

The Pope was from the outset faced with a dilemma. He did not want to submit an over-involved or excessively profound problem to the bishops. Since they are for the most part residential prelates, to keep them out of their dioceses for any great length of time would be an injustice to their people. In addition, part of his purpose was to enlist their aid in the major reform of the Curia in which he is engaged. Largely through default on the part of the world's bishops, policy-making has become concentrated in recent centuries in the hands of the Pope's administrative aides. He wanted the bishops to help in his program of restoring a more normal arrangement in which bishops, clergy, religious orders, and the laity will all play their appropriate part in the decision-making process.

The five topics finally selected for discussion proved to be of substantial value for this purpose. They were also generally indicative of the grave problems facing the Church today. As a matter of tactics, the most crucial issue — the advancing wave of atheism — was dealt with as a sort of appendix to the document on the essentials of the faith or doctrine. And as events may prove, this was probably a prudent thing to have done. The Synod's prime business was with matters more or less immediately important to the Church's inner well-being. While atheism is a grave peril, it is an outside problem.

One of the most difficult considerations facing the Church today is the place and purpose of law in a religious society. It is true that one of the Church's primary tasks through the centuries has been the safeguarding and interpretation of the Ten Commandments. It is likewise true that it has made major contributions to order in the medieval and modern world through the canon or church law. But many outside observers and many critics within the Church itself have long been asking if it has not allowed its concern for law to degenerate into legalism. In a simple analysis, these people say that instead of leading its members to holiness through direct participation in God's love and grace, the Church in recent times has concentrated its emphasis on having people keep its laws. The accusation raises a series of curious questions. Christ said explicitly that he had not come into the world to abolish the law and the prophets, but to fulfill them. At the same time, however, he eliminated the legal prescriptions of the old Jewish religion, as is clearly established by the teachings of St. Paul and the practice of the primitive Church. The problem bothered the apostles. It caused a dispute between Peter and Paul and was finally settled at a Synod in Jerusalem about 51 A.D. There it was decided — "It seemed good to the Holy Spirit and to us," is the way St. Peter announced the Synod's conclusion — that converts from paganism would not be held to the ritual or procedures of the Jewish Law. They would be asked merely to renounce the turpitudes of their pagan background — homicide, adultery, and idolatry — and introduced into the Holiness Code of the older Hebrew Prophets. This continuity between the Old and the New Testaments was emphasized; and Christ's fulfillment of the law and the prophets was accepted in a totally spiritual perspective.

The ancient Jewish concept of the Law seems, at least to the outsider, to have been ambiguous. It was first of all a philosophy of life. By contemplation of and meditation on the Torah or law, the devout Jew became a participator in the wisdom of God, so that it became his delight to observe and cultivate God's ordinances. But in addition, the term also described the almost innumerable laws dealing with the Jewish cult and hygienic regulations. By a strange paradox, while the early Christians seem to have had little difficulty in grasping the distinction, rejecting the idea that holiness was related to the observance of an externalized set of regulations, in later times Christians frequently succumbed to the temptation of regarding the Church's laws as in themselves a way to holiness. Part of the reason for this reversal was the return to a wider and deeper study of the Old Testament. The presence of God emerges so vividly from its pages that many persuaded themselves that particular regulations laid down in the Torah partook of the nature of divine laws and could consequently not have been abrogated by Christ. This is observable in the sermons of the sixth century, whose writers were influenced by the diffusion of the translation of the Bible made by St. Jerome toward the end of the fourth century. It was also characteristic of many of the Protestant Churches in the sixteenth century, similarly influenced by translations of the Bible into the vernacular after it had been available for many centuries almost exclusively in Latin.

Contemplation of the Torah put the devout Jew in contact with the *Shekinah,* that is to say, a divine insight that in turn led him to identify the way of wisdom (*hokmah*) with the right conduct of life. The Rabbis developed this idea, in a moral and spiritual sense, into a doctrine that described the *Shekinah,* or divine presence, as inhabiting the hearts of the humble and giving them wisdom. Contemplation of the Torah thus overcame evil inclinations, rendering the wise man gentle, kind, and pious.

Taken over by the early Christians, this concept is at the heart of the Christian teaching on grace, prayer, and contemplation as bringing man into an intimate relationship with God, a concept of a personal association that runs parallel to the sacramental system and the juridical bonds which bind the believer to God within the body of Christ that is the Church. It is at the core of the Christian practice of asceticism and mysticism.

On the practical plane, however, as the Church developed and had to deal with vast aggregations of people organized in parishes and dioceses, the necessity of specific laws and regulations made itself felt. Thus the early synods and councils passed a series of ordinances dealing with membership in the Church and the types of activity that would be improper in a Christian. Called canons, these regulations were modeled on the Roman legal concepts current in the world in which Christians then lived. Eventually, after the conversion of Constantine and the gradual christianization of the Roman Empire, those canons were included in the later codes of Roman Law. In the Middle Ages, when the Church itself became a secular power, canon and civil law developed side by side, with the jurisprudence of the Church always tending to consider its laws as reflecting directly the will of God. Thus the impression was given, particularly during the period following the Reformation of the 16th century and the Counter-Reform within the Catholic Church, that obedience to the Church's laws was a guarantee of striving for sanctity. With the codification of the Canon Law in 1917, a reign of juridicism was confirmed within the Church. On top of the harshness of the old Justinian sixth-century code, with its concept of debits and penalties, the positivistic spirit of 18th- and 19th-century law had also crept into the code. Attempts to introduce this type of law with its neat precisionings had always been warded off by the Eastern Churches, and efforts during the 1920's and subsequently to codify the canons of the Eastern Catholic rites caused no end of objections on the part of many bishops of the Byzantine, Melchite, Maronite, and similar Churches.

Vatican Council II brought this problem to a head. Even before convoking the Council, Pope John had announced that it was his intention to revise the Code. He had likewise experimented with a different type of Church law in the Roman diocesan Synod of 1960. While short shrift had been given to the code of some 754 articles that resulted from this assembly of the parish priests and prelates of the diocese of Rome, and vigorous objections were raised by the professors of canon law to the type of law thus attempted, John insisted that the Church's legal system should be exhortatory and stimulating rather than menacing and penalizing. When an angry Spanish ecclesiastic who had taught canon law for decades in Rome protested that "the synodal canons are not law," John replied: "They may not be law in your sense, but they are in mine. And I happen to be the pope."

John did not pursue the matter immediately, preferring to concentrate his full attention on the Council. Several of the Fathers returned to it during the first session of the Council in 1962, and shortly before his death Pope John, on March

28, 1963, named a commission for the reform of canon law. It was loaded with cardinals and Roman-trained canon law professors, and it got nowhere because they refused to consider the fundamental issue raised in the Council, namely, the nature of the Church's law. Should it reflect the spirit and procedures of civil law, or should it concentrate more on the Law of Christ with charity and holiness as its prime considerations? When Cardinal Pericle Felici succeeded Ciriaci on the latter's death, the new president of the commission at least seemed to recognize the problem. While he set its members to work revising particular canons, in his approach to the Synod of Bishops, he introduced the fundamental problem: revision of the code, or a new start from a totally different concept of law? And if the latter, should it begin with the notion of the law or Torah in the Jewish sense, and with the Holiness Code regarded by the early Christians as fundamental to their way of life? Merely to ask the question provided an interesting example of an important trend in the Church today, a sense of need to return to our sources, what the French call *ressourcement*. In the existential atmosphere of the twentieth century, it is being discovered, reform and emancipation can be achieved only by a return to primitive concepts and considerations. The Church was born in an atmosphere of much more existentialistic thinking than that in which it subsequently developed.

The second topic proposed for Synodal consideration had to do with the Church's doctrine. Again John's opening talk at the Council had a fundamental bearing. He had deliberately eliminated theological arguments at the Council in the sense of disputes regarding individual matters of faith. He had forbidden the Council to follow the long-standing conciliar practice of condemning doctrinal positions or individuals suspected of heresy. Vatican Council II could, nevertheless, not avoid doctrinal discussions. The Church's life is constituted by its beliefs. But the energies of the Council Fathers were concentrated on a pastoral consideration of the immediate consequences of its belief in a Trinity, in Christ as the Son of God, in his institution of a Church guided by the Holy Spirit, and in the Church's specific function as an enlightening and sanctifying institution leading men to the knowledge of and union with God.

As a result of the great changes of perspective in considering Catholic doctrinal truths, however, a path was opened for discussion and for a reconsideration of many of its pastoral teachings, from its views on freedom of conscience and the nature of membership in the Church, to the meaning of matrimony and the legitimacy of birth control. With the transformation of the Holy Office, likewise, into a curial congregation charged with promoting doctrinal development rather than suppressing dangerous opinions or speculations among theologians and philosophers, a generation of writers, propagandists, and popularizers, as well as a number of professional theologians, quickly felt the need to challenge the conventional ways of thinking about and expressing doctrinal and moral concepts. Some went so far as to take it upon themselves to ventilate extreme notions and ideas regarding even fundamental tenets of the faith. In Holland, in particular, the desire to exercise the new freedom produced attacks on very many of the basic procedures and conclusions of the older theology.

Actually the Council had accomplished a fundamental change in this area by downgrading the near-monopoly previously accorded to the theological methods and teachings of the 13th century Dominican mastermind, St. Thomas Aquinas. His systematic coverage of Catholic truth called the *Summa* had become the basis for most theological treatises and manuals in the post-Tridentine Church. And though somewhat different systems were cultivated by the Scotists and other independent-minded thinkers in the Church, Thomism had acquired the stamp of official approval of the Roman universities and through them of almost all the seminaries throughout the world. There is, of course, nothing wrong with Thomism as an expression of Catholic teaching, except that it is quite unsuited to modern ways of thinking. It concentrates heavily on the essences of things, while contemporary man feels totally uncomfortable with the idea that you can get closer to reality than an appreciation of the phenomena presented by the outward appearance and behavior of things spiritual or material. The beauty of Thomism was that it provided a simple yardstick for separating heresy from orthodox expressions of the faith. Unfortunately, despite an attempt to revitalize its procedures and update its doctrinal precisionings at the turn of the twentieth century, the yardstick's markings had become obliterated with the years. This left the Church with a problem. In order to exist, a society must have a way to determine who belongs to it and who does not. For the Church concretely, heresy has always been the basic point of division. Accordingly, the old Holy Office decided as a stopgap measure, at the end of Vatican Council II, to send a letter to the bishops and the superiors of religious orders of the Church asking ten specific questions about the presence of heresy in their areas of jurisdiction. The tenor of the replies was that many of the indicated heresies did in fact exist in various parts of the world, but that they were not anywhere a major threat to the Church. In spite of this assurance, the Congregation for the Doctrine of the Faith decided to utilize the same approach for the Synod and to reformulate the questions about current heresies under the general heading of "Dangers to the Faith."

After an introduction which speaks of a crisis of civilization reaching far beyond the field of religion, the position paper organizes the issues in eight chapters. The first presents what it calls "the foundations" of the faith, biblical revelation and the knowledge and objective expression of truth. Next comes Christology, including such issues as the historicity of Jesus, the reality of his miracles and his rising from the dead, his divinity and virgin birth. Ecclesiology follows, with comments on the relationship of the institution and charisms, and the nature and function of the magisterium. Chapter 4, entitled

"Anthropology," deals with the contemporary as contrasted with the traditional concepts of human nature. It leads into two chapters discussing "basic morality" and "special morality" respectively. The former touches on objective and subjective morality, the sense of sin, and the meaning of original sin. The latter evaluates the arguments in favor of an individualistic approach to salvation as contrasted with the need for commitment to others, then turns specifically to sexual morality. Next come some observations on the sacraments, especially the Eucharist and Penance. The final chapter is eschatological, relating the present to the future life.

The position paper closes with an appendix on atheism. Contemporary atheism is the Church's chief rival in today's world for the simple reason that it attempts to offer an honest and coherent way of life. Gone now are the vile misrepresentations of Catholic teaching and the calumnies of the 18th- and 19th-century anticlerical societies which offered a diabolical substitute for Christianity in the form of so-called "Black Masses" and demonic incantations. The effective atheist today is a humanist who regards the Church as well-meaning in its attempt to explain man in terms of a supernatural destiny, while judging that its claims are incompatible with the evidence now placed at men's disposal by modern science. What is more, the atheist maintains that an outdated institution such as the Catholic Church exercises a harmful influence by holding millions of intelligent people back from the progress they can and should be making by a leap forward in material well-being. He does not quarrel with most of Christianity's moral teachings. He will tolerate many of its doctrines as harmless myths. But he believes that the Church is no longer necessary. The God it preaches is dead, because the character and function the Church assigns to him lack meaning for modern man. Paschal once said that it is better to believe there is a God and serve him than not to believe, since if there is no God, it makes no difference, whereas if there is a God, it makes a great difference. This logical dilemma does not bother the contemporary atheist. With considerable sophistication he observes that if there is a God the atheist will be given credit for good faith in his honest disbelief. Following his conscience, he cannot be condemned.

These or similar considerations were in the minds of the drafters of the statement. Atheism had originally been listed first among the errors today threatening the Church, a decision which had its logic in view of the fact that atheism was never so widespread and so respectable in the eyes of civilized man. Father Dhanis, the special secretary for this agenda item, told the Synod that Pope Paul himself decided to downgrade it to its modest position as an appendix. That decision also has its logic. It may have been motivated in part, as in the case of Vatican Council II's avoidance of new condemnations of Communism, by the tentative efforts of the Roman Catholic Church to find practical accommodations with Communist governments. But a deeper reason exists. Catholic theology is still groping with the complicated and positive phenomenon of contemporary atheism. Much work remains to be done before definitive answers can be expected.

Concretely, a highly specialized body, the Secretariat for Non-Believers, has been in existence since 1965, headed by Cardinal Francis König of Vienna. Several international meetings have been held between Christians and atheists under its auspices. Although the results are highly tentative, they have created a climate of mutual respect, as well as agreement on the desirability of widened cooperation on purely worldly issues, such as the promotion of the material and intellectual betterment of mankind. The Synod Fathers took the observations of the appendix and the work already performed by the Secretariat for Non-Believers into account in their final expression of their views. While agreeing with the reality of the threat of atheism, they felt it should be handled at different levels and in diverse ways. As for themselves, they agreed with the Vatican Council that the less they said, the better. New condemnations would be not only ineffectual but harmful.

In broad terms, what the Church is today attempting is a new meditation, leading to a new formulation of such fundamental truths as the nature of God, the explanation of the humanity of Christ, the whole order of spirituality as it is represented in the Mass and the sacramental system. While Catholics adhere to these basic teachings, many feel that they need a new orientation because of the discoveries in the realm of science and in humanistic studies that are having a fundamental influence on man's thinking and on human psychology today. The possibility of such a re-evaluation is evident from the fact that the primitive Church accomplished a similar cultural mutation. It took the Gospel message that Christ had preached in a Hebraic atmosphere and Jewish culture and adapted it totally and substantially to the Greco-Roman civilization of the third and fourth centuries. It ran risks in so doing. The history of the first councils and the fundamental heresies condemned in the early Church are a witness to the struggle involved. But the effort was successful, and today's conditions call for a repetition. What informed Church leaders seek, however, is to avoid the condemnations and recriminations of the past by learning from history — another of Pope John's favorite expressions. This is all the easier nowadays because the Catholic Church enjoys the goodwill of the other Christian Churches, all of which feel that contemporary atheistic and materialistic tendencies increase the urgent need for Christian unity.

While recognizing the urgency, most of the Synod Fathers insisted that the task must be approached with calm and confidence. They disliked the tone of pessimism, the suggestion of "alarming news, . . . strange and audacious opinions . . . deeply troubling the spirit of a great number of the faithful," which carried over into the position paper from the earlier letter to the bishops and religious superiors signed by Cardinal Ottaviani. However, they seemed to a considerable extent to share the lack of awareness in the drafters of the document of a growing resentment among Catholic intellectuals, both lay and clerical, at the slowness of implementation of the decisions of Vatican Council II. It is a resentment that in some areas, not excluding the United States and England, could easily build up to an explosive level. The failure to take note of this phenomenon is perhaps the biggest defect in the document on "Dangers to the Faith."

The third item on the agenda was seminary reform. Since at least the start of Vatican Council II, seminary life and training have come in for violent criticism, particularly in the United States, Holland, Spain, and several South American countries. The system introduced after the Council of Trent of gathering young men into special colleges, cutting them off entirely from the world about them, imposing a monastic discipline on them, and imbuing them with a narrow theological outlook, had served the Church well for almost three hundred years. The reluctance of bishops and Roman officials to see its values questioned is understandable. In recent years however, both the strict discipline and the educational procedures have been progressively challenged, and a gradual relaxation of restrictions has been introduced. Until Vatican II such incredible rules were enforced as a total ban on secular papers and magazines, a strict censorship over books, a rigorous daily schedule of class, study, and prayer hours. Considerable control was exercised over leisure time and off-campus jaunts and visiting. While attempts had been made in more progressive countries to widen the focus of studies with courses in sociology, pedagogy, catechetics, and psychology, little attempt was made to break out of the structured metaphysics and the theological system that had its roots in 13th-century Thomism, and that was based on the so-called *philosophia perennis,* an integrated view of man and the world that left open few loopholes and barred the way to the research and questioning that are the very essence of philosophy.

In gauging the fitness of candidates for the priesthood, attention to psychological traits had in recent decades gradually invaded the more advanced seminaries. But the controlling bodies in Rome, the Congregation of Seminaries for diocesan seminarians and the Congregation of Religious for those belonging to a religious order, frowned upon psychiatric procedures or analysis. These Roman offices tried, in addition, to enforce a discipline which prescribed that Latin was the only language to be employed in class lectures and study. The curriculum set down in the document *Deus Scientiarum Dominus* (issued by Pope Pius XI in 1931) paid almost no attention to the cultural and educational requirements of local lands or situations. In countries like France and Germany, where seminary training had to be coordinated with a government-controlled educational system, most bishops and religious superiors ignored the regulations. Elsewhere, they were a constant source of irritation. When Pope John in March, 1960, was practically tricked into signing a document prepared by the Congregation of Studies reinsisting upon the use of Latin in seminaries, the dam burst. The Secretary of the Roman bureau had overplayed his hand, and a general if quiet revolution occurred in the seminaries.

These circumstances undergirded the criticisms levelled at seminary training in the second session of Vatican Council II. A new document *On the Pastoral Training of Priests,* for all its apparent deference to past procedures, radically changed the theological content and the routine of seminary life. It began by stressing that since priests were being trained to deal with people and their problems, they had to be exposed to both in the course of their preparation. Likewise, it said, the monastic routine is useless in everyday parochial life. What is needed is a sense of responsibility whereby the student becomes accustomed to rise, eat, study, attend class and retire, as well as say his prayers, on his own — all of which he has to do once he is liberated from the seminary and takes up his chores in a parish, a school, or other ecclesiastical occupation.

With these changes came a sudden wave of challenges regarding the question of celibacy, with a small but notable number of defections among newly ordained and older priests in the ministry. Reaction in the seminaries was considerable. Among the young men themselves questions arose as to the propriety of the Church forcing them to accept celibacy as a condition for admission to the priesthood. The two are not necessarily yoked together. The Eastern Churches, both Catholic and Orthodox, have married priests. Seminary directors, likewise, began to give considerably more attention to methods and techniques for judging the aptness of candidates. With the announcement of the Synod, seminary training thus became a crucial issue. Its importance was further highlighted by a dropping off of vocations in many parts of the world at the very moment when the need for priests was almost everywhere accelerating.

Mixed marriages, the fourth item on the Synod agenda, create problems which had been discussed at some length at Vatican Council II. Because the difficulties vary so much from country to country, nobody was able to come up with a broadly acceptable solution. Nevertheless constant pressure was being exercised on the Holy See for some sort of ruling that would prove universal in principle if diverse in application. In particular the canonical form of marriage as defined in the Code and applied more recently (1949) to the Oriental Churches was under attack. In marriages where one partner was non-Catholic, a dispensation had to be requested of the bishop or the Holy See to allow the Catholic to marry "outside the faith" and both parties had to give promises (*cautiones*) that the only ceremony would be the Catholic one, and that all the children of the marriage would be brought up in the Catholic religion. This rigid discipline had prevailed in lands where the Church was stabilized, such as Great Britain and the United States. Even in such countries, however, with the advent of Catholic participation in the ecumenical movement, more thought was given to the rights of the non-Catholic and to the possibility that he could have conscientious objections to the promises. One further result of the law had a sort of sinister twist. Catholics who had complied with the form and had consummated their marriage were bound "until death did them part." The Catholic, however, who defied the law of the Church and got married by a minister or civil official, could apply to the Church for an annulment, if the marriage did not work out. These and similar considerations caused much unhappiness in parts of the world where mixed marriages were prevalent. In the post-conciliar period the Pope decided to ask the Synodal bishops their opinions. In a world in which the forms and structures of marriage are breaking down rapidly, Rome needs a wide variety of information and guidance in this field. Bishops are faced with every possible complication from civil and cultural to legal and religious difficulties. They are consequently equipped to give evidence of a wide divergence of thought and practice. Again the pluralism of the Church's approach to the modern world was demonstrated as an absolute necessity.

The final item of the agenda dealt with the part of Vatican Council II's work which has been most fully implemented, though without yet reaching a new and generally acceptable equilibrium. In terms of pastoral needs, the liturgy occupies a more basic position than most Catholics, lay and clerical alike, yet understand. What was called for by the Council was a total inner reform of Christian religious practice, so that belief in Christ's divinity and his redemptive activity being still carried on in the Church would enter more vividly into the mind of the Christian. Emphasis on active participation in the ceremonies of the Mass, the translation of that act of worship into the vernacular, and a possible simplification of the rites, thus all become mere means to a total realization of faith in action. Resistance to liturgical change, whether expressed in a refusal to introduce a table-altar, or to involve the people by having the priest face them, or to resist lay participation in the ceremonies, results from a total misunderstanding of what the liturgy is all about. Fears that people will be scandalized by change is a venerable Roman habit, a bad habit conveniently adopted by older minded pastors and religious superiors grown set in their ways and convinced that theirs is the only acceptable expression of piety.

To complicate the issue further, a wide variety of experiment with the Mass and liturgical forms has occurred in different parts of the world, some with and some without the required authorizations. Plentiful publicity has been given in the daily and weekly press to so-called Beatnik Masses, mixed confessional agapes, and wild-cat experiments among young priests. An "instruction," issued unexpectedly by the Congregation of Seminaries in January, 1966, directing the retention of Latin as the primary liturgical language in seminaries, provoked a minor rebellion of seminarians in various places. And at the other extreme, the Catholic Traditionalist Movement served notice on the Holy Father in September, 1967, that he had 30 days in which to authorize it to establish in the United States a separate "traditionalist Latin rite" with its own bishop. Father Gommar De Pauw, its founder, said that if the Pope failed to comply, he and 156 other priests would go it alone, opening store-front churches. Father De Pauw also urged the Pope to annul the decisions of Vatican Council II and in particular to disavow the doctrine of episcopal collegiality. "Stop wearing that bishop's miter and place the papal tiara back on your anointed head," he ordered Pope Paul. In Italy itself, personal attacks on Cardinal Lercaro, head of the post-conciliar liturgical *Consilium,* were encouraged by at least one curial cardinal* and a number of well-to-do Italian families who regard the Latin liturgy as one of their last links to aristocracy. Hence the Liturgical Commission welcomed the opportunity to submit a series of questions concerning their present program to the Synodal bishops.

The one post-conciliar bureau that felt no such need was Cardinal Bea's Secretariat for Christian unity. Its incredible accomplishments in breaching the barrier between the Churches would be highlighted in the last week of the Synod by the meeting between Pope Paul and the Orthodox Patri-

* See p. 144, below.

arch Athenagoras in St. Peter's. With an astuteness that could not be better employed, members of the Secretariat played watchdog over the formulation of the five documents submitted to the bishops. And while they could not control Cardinal Browne's position paper and *relatio,* they saw to it that nothing truly disruptive to ecumenical relations was allowed to stand. During the Synod, members of the secretariat played proper court to the bishops whose support they required; and while the Synod as such was not of their immediate interest, they managed to make it conscious of the fact that the Secretariat is one Roman organization that does its job efficiently.

CHAPTER 3

Reform of Canon Law

Cardinal Pericle Felici has had a spectacular career as a curial official. Efficient, able, and charming, he emerged as one of the dominant figures of Vatican Council II. As general secretary, he was responsible for documentation, information, communication between the steering committee and the assembly, the collection and transmission of written and oral suggestions of the Fathers, and the drawing up of texts edited by the committees. He also saw the Pope several times a week, an opportunity most narrowly limited and giving those who enjoy it incalculable influence. Although identified with the conservative minority, he was adept at keeping on excellent terms with all elements, with one exception. His polish and finesse did not extend to the press. In November, 1964, he gave the *Osservatore Romano* an interview in which he described the newsmen covering the Council as "parasites and fungus growths . . . promoting confusion, insubordination and error."

That totally atypical outburst of temper in no way affected his progress. After the Council he became general secretary of the Central Commission which supervised five subordinate commissions in their work of drafting instructions to implement major Council decrees.

He seemed a logical choice for the post of secretary general of the Synod. Instead he was named pro-president of the Commission for the reform of canon law on the death of Cardinal Ciriaci in December, 1966. The decision was influenced by the fact that he was due to get the red hat of the cardinal, an honor which the secretary general of the Synod does not rank. So Bishop Ladislas Rubin was given the Synod post and Felici was made cardinal and president of the Commission for Reform of Canon Law in June, 1967.

In this capacity, Cardinal Felici presented to the Synod Fathers on September 30 the first agenda item. It was a document prepared by the Canon Law Commission he heads and clearly reflecting his own fine hand and lucid mind. It is a good document, an excellent one, yet inevitably limited by the preconceptions and assumptions of its drafters.

On the need for reform of canon law, there has long been total agreement. Canon lawyers had made collections of the laws of the Church at various times, the most famous being the 16th century *Corpus Iuris Canonici,* but the only attempt at scientific codification in the Church's long history was the Code of Canon Law ordered by Pope Pius X in 1904 and promulgated by Pope Benedict XV in May, 1917, to become effective a year later. It was drafted by a small group of canonists working in a strictly legalistic atmosphere and seeking to realize the ideal of 19th-century jurisprudence, the formulation — in an apparently complete and perfect system — of interlocking, abstract rules, so that the judge would simply have to pick the right one to resolve whatever problem might be presented to him. Their principal concern, accordingly, was to assemble and correlate for easy reference the rules and regulations which had been promulgated piecemeal during the previous centuries, particularly in the centralizing and autocratic atmosphere of the Counter-Reformation. The signs of the times had little meaning for them. They failed to recognize adequately that the Church was no longer European but worldwide, that the world was no longer rural and static but increasingly urban, industrialized, and mobile, that laity and unlettered were not only no longer interchangeable terms and concepts, but that many of the laity were in various respects more cultured than the clergy who served them.

The unsuitability of the Code for the twentieth century was bad, but its spirit encouraged and promoted something worse. That was the tendency to subordinate theology and even the Scriptures to law. The Code tended in practice to be regarded as the primary rule of the Faith, followed at an extremely respectable distance by speculative theology, with pastoral theology reduced to the status of an Amy Vanderbilt collection of practices and prescriptions, and the Scripture held in reserve as a source from whence to draw arguments to confute all who dared challenge any aspect of the bizarre system.

Pope John's announcement in January, 1959, of his intention to reform the Code was contained in the same speech in which he revealed that he was going to call an ecumenical council to renew the entire Church, and he linked the two points. The Council would have to come first, so that the Code reform would take into account the Council's decisions. It was only in March, 1963, that he named a commission of cardinals to assume responsibility for the work. Pope Paul twice expanded the commission in 1964, adding eleven cardinals in January and 70 consultors in June. For a long time, nevertheless, it did little more than receive and accumulate everything relating to canon law reform coming from commissions of the Council. The Council was not supposed to involve itself directly in the details of the reform. It simply proposed principles on the basis of which the Commission would act.

Just as the Vatican Council was ending, Pope Paul told the Commission in November, 1965, that the time to get to work had come, and he set out a number of specific guidelines. Law, he stressed, should be linked closely to theology. It should seek evolutionary forms in keeping with the acceleration of modern life. It should follow the broad lines sketched for it by the Council. In addition, it should study the desirability of one Code for the whole Church instead of separate codes for the Western and Eastern Churches. This last was a complicated and contentious issue. A papal commission had already been set up in 1935 by Pope Pius XI to prepare a code of canon law for the "Eastern Church." Over the years, to the satisfaction of nobody, it had completed some parts of its assignment. Catholics of Eastern rites in union with Rome had been offended by its interference with their age-long traditions, the constant pressures to "westernize," the assumption that the Latin Church was normal and all others unfortunate deviations. The Orthodox had been similarly offended, not only because the gap in liturgical forms and other customs between them and their brothers was being widened, but also because they considered the work of the Commission an unacceptable interference by the Patriarch of the West in the internal affairs of Constantinople and the other Patriarchates. Some Maronite bishops had suggested at the Vatican Council, as a possible way to de-escalate these tensions, that "a common and fundamental code containing the constitutional law of the Church" be drawn up. It would restrict itself to broad principles and provide a basis for separate implementing codes for the Eastern Church and the Western. This was the issue which Pope Paul asked the new Commission to study as part of its task.

The urgency of the Pope's charge was not reflected in any burst of activity from the Commission. Cardinal Ciriaci was 82 years old and in poor health. The secretary, Father Raimondo Bidagor, S.J., a 72-year-old Spaniard, was also a judge of the Holy Office, a consultor of the Congregation of the Sacraments, an official of the special commission dealing with requests for dispensations from marriages ratified but not consummated, a consultor of the Congregation of the Council, of the Congregation of Religious, of the Ceremonial

Congregation and of the Congregation of Seminaries and Universities, a judge of the appeals court in marriage cases, an official of several other curial bodies, and a professor at the Gregorian University in Rome. Whether in spite of or because of all these activities, Father Bidagor was no self-starter. In addition, he shared the "Roman" belief that change in the code should be kept to a minimum, that as it stood it constituted a monument to reason and justice to be venerated and observed as a perfect expression of the will of God; and that if it occasionally created an apparent problem, the solution could always be found by the application of "Roman finesse."

In an effort to break the impasse, a more dynamic man, Msgr. William Onclin, of Liège, Belgium, professor of canon law at the University of Louvain, was brought in as co-secretary. Father Bidagor, however, resented his appointment, and the new man was too far down the line of command to get action on his own initiative. It was only when Archbishop Felici took over in February, 1967, that things really came to life. In his address to the cardinals on Christmas Eve, 1966, the Pope had returned to the subject he had treated a year earlier, summing up his charge to the Commission in three criteria. The reform, he said, should take account of experience, of needs, and of the Council's directives. The new Commission head had studied and understood that speech. He went immediately to work and put others to work with the same efficiency and singleness of purpose which had characterized him at the Council. A central committee coordinated the work of groups belonging to more than twenty countries to produce in a few months a revision of several hundred of the 2,414 canons contained in the 1917 Code.

By this time, however, it had become apparent that the matter was more complex than had been assumed. All three criteria presented by Pope Paul — experience, needs, and Council directives — made it obligatory in one way or another to question the very bases on which the present Code rests. As they stripped away the plaster and ripped up floorboards to modernize the building, they were finding rotted beams and slipped foundations. Could they restore, or would they have to tear down and start afresh?

It was somewhat in this frame of mind that the document presented to the Synod by Cardinal Felici was prepared. It did not concern itself with the details of the canons already rewritten. Instead it quite properly formulated some basic prior issues which must be resolved before it is possible even to begin an organic revision. However, it ignored the issue that should be tackled before any other, namely, whether or not the Church needs a code, a rather curious oversight in view of the fact that it got along without one for all its millennial existence other than the last 50 years, 50 years which would not be universally regarded as the most successful in its performance of its mission. But accepting, as the document does, the need for a code, it asks the proper questions that follow. Should the code be in strictly legal form, prescribing acts which a Christian must perform, acts which he may perform, acts which he may not perform, in accordance with his function and service in the Church? Or should it, on the contrary, confine itself to presenting a rule of faith and morals, somewhat in the manner of the documents of Vatican II?

This is substantially the same question raised in the last chapter,* regarding the function of law in a religious society. Interestingly enough, a comment in Pope Paul's speech opening the Synod on September 29 can be read as a direct reference to it, with the Pope on the side of the spiritualists. Charity, he said, "is a vital and constitutive principle of holy Church, which is held together interiorly not by bonds of blood, of territory or culture, not by political ties or by interests, but by love."

The document had been prepared without the benefit of this observation, and it answers the question in a quite different framework. Without developing arguments as though the matter were too obvious to merit further serious discussion, it

* See p. 36, above.

plumps squarely for a retention of the legal structure of the present Code. "It is proper," it says, "that the new code should by all means retain a juridic character."

Most of the Synod Fathers who referred to this point agreed that the new code should be expressed in legal language. But the consensus was clearly opposed to Father William Bertrams, S.J., a member of the commission which had drafted the document, when he sought to defend this position by presenting law in the Old Testament concept as a sacramental instrument of salvation, something sacred and sanctifying in itself. Among those who challenged such a "sacramental" notion of law was another Jesuit, Bishop Hans Martensen of Copenhagen. The law is not identified with the Gospel, he said, because the law does not procure salvation. Neither was the Gospel made for codification, and it should not be suggested that the law is in any sense a sacrament. St. Paul said that the law could be the occasion of sin, whereas sacraments are the occasion of absolution. To suggest that the law is some kind of sacrament would introduce a new ecumenical problem, and even Catholics should be protected from the danger of imagining that the Christian life requires external compliance with the law. What Bishop Martensen was here emphasizing was that for the Christian, law was no more than a pragmatic set of rules for smoothing human relationships and in the final analysis for determining whether or not one was a member of this society or community of Christians, a sort of common law approach to human coexistence. The Christian establishes his relations with God through Jesus Christ in other ways. Specifically, he makes Christ present and unites himself to him in the Spirit by listening to the word of God and celebrating the eucharistic mysteries.

Cardinal Suenens of Belgium was in full agreement. The point of departure for the code of canon law, he said, should not be that the Church is a society for the sake of the hierarchy, but that the hierarchy exists because the Church is a society needing its service. The notion of law as a sacramental instrument of salvation is a Jewish concept and should be eliminated. Other points he made were that the excessively monkish description of the religious life in the current Code should be omitted, giving more weight to the needs of the apostolate, that laymen know more than clerics about matters concerning the world and should consequently be brought in to help in the revision of the law, and that marriage cases should be handled faster and more humanly.

The various Suenens comments just given refer to three basic principles enunciated in the document. They are that the canon law should be revised to give full weight to the principle of subsidiarity, thereby assuring to the bishops the powers they need to deal with the problems of the local Churches; that a pastoral spirit should replace the legalistic approach of the present code, reducing the severity of penalties and showing more concern for the rights of freedom and equality; and that personal rights should always be respected.

The extent to which the report dwells on the need for a pastoral spirit and on the rights of the individual is a measure of the gulf between the present Code and contemporary concepts of justice. In the law of the Church, it says, "there should shine through a spirit of charity, of restraint, of humanity and of moderation, all of which are supernatural virtues and as such distinguish our law from every human and civil law." Henceforth, the rule of law is to apply in the Church. "Because of the basic equality which should prevail among all Christ's followers, because of the dignity of the human person, and because of the reception of baptism [which makes the recipient a full member of the people of God], a legal status common to all should be drafted before the rights and services related to the various Church functions are listed." Further, the powers entrusted to the pope and the bishops must not be used arbitrarily. That "is forbidden by natural law, positive divine law and the law of the Church."

In addition, "rights in the strict sense are to be recognized as inherent in each person, so that the principle of the protection of the law is to be applied with equal measure to superiors and subjects, and appropriate means must be available for everyone to assert his rights and get justice when they are violated." While claiming that legal procedures of recourse for an injured party contained in the present Code are adequate, the report admits that canon lawyers as a group consider that administrative procedures "are somewhat deficient in ecclesiastical practice and the administration of justice." It is proposed that court hearings should as a general rule be public, with discretion on the part of the judge to conduct closed hearings for adequate reason. A further step away from the secret-informer techniques normal in curial practice and authorized in the Code would be the provision that "in both judicial and administrative proceedings, all the data charged against the accused or the appellant must be made available to him."*

In modern times, the Church does not normally have executive powers to enforce its decrees. It doesn't send violators to jail or put them in stocks because they come late to Sunday Mass. But it still is in a position to impose certain legal sanctions. It asserts and sometimes exercises the right, for example, to exclude a public sinner from the sacraments. The theological basis for this assertion is not clear to all, for ultimately it is only God who reads the heart of man and knows that his apparently sinful act is in fact a sin. And even the juridic basis is questionable, because canon 2195 of the 1917 Code gives expression to a continuing tradition that no penalty has binding force unless the person on whom it is imposed was guilty of grave sin when he committed the act for which he is sentenced. Without going into the ramifications of this complicated issue, it suffices to note that the 1917 Code distinguished between penalties — or censures, as they are tech-

* See, for example, Canon 1771 (parties may not normally be present at examination of witnesses); Cans. 2186–2194 (suspension of clerics); Can. 571 (dismissal of novice); Can. 970 (exclusion from orders); Can. 1933 (imposition of excommunication, suspension or other penalty without a trial).

nically called — which apply publicly (*in foro externo*) as well as in conscience (*in foro interno*), and those which apply only in conscience. Not a few theologians and canonists have long wanted to do away with the second type (*in foro interno*) altogether and restrict censures to matters dealing with overt acts and consequently applicable *in foro externo*. This might be regarded as a middle position between the two described earlier, those who want a strictly legal formulation of laws, and those who would reduce law in the Church to a rule of faith and morals based on the person and teachings of Christ. The Felici document went part of the way toward this middle position. It agreed that much of the present practice should be eliminated, but the principle itself as reflecting the best traditions of ecclesiastical jurisprudence for centuries "should by all means be confirmed." Similarly, laws declaring juridical actions null or excluding some from rights acknowledged to the generality of Christians — such as the present exclusion of illegitimate children from holy orders — would be limited to grave matters and those affecting the common good (*bonum publicum*) and necessary to Church discipline.

Finally, "the legislative, administrative and judicial functions of Church power should be clearly distinguished, as should the organs to administer each of these functions." This for the Church is a revolutionary principle, a principle in fact established in civil society by two great revolutions, the American and the French. The Church, from the center in Rome to the rural parish, is governed by institutions that combine executive, administrative, and judicial powers, continuing the system of medieval society in which the king both made the laws and administered justice.

It quickly became apparent from the discussion that the Synod Fathers approved of the broad formula for reform of canon law. Many of them, however, indicated their fears that the practical results could easily fall short of expectations, if the task of implementation was left to the same small group who had formulated the principles. They sensed an undertone of formalism and legalism in the document which could result in an extremely restrictive application of the principles.

Cardinal Léger of Montreal was one who expressed this viewpoint forcibly. He regretted profoundly "the too juridic character" of the proposed revision. Every trace of Roman law should be eliminated as radically as possible, he said. In addition, the pastoral purpose of the law should be made more evident. While the law should be formulated in legal terms, it should be brought into line with the pastoral function of the Church, which he described as a combination of the teaching and governing functions.

Cardinal Giovanni Urbani of Venice said that it should not be forgotten that the Gospels, not the law, were the constitution of the Church. The new code should avoid falling into moralism and should leave more freedom to the local Churches. He recommended softening the articles dealing with warnings and with the execution of laws. The code itself should be reduced to some syntheses of constitutional principles, leaving latitude to express their distinctive spirituality.

Cardinal Döpfner, of Munich, Germany, also urged the greatest possible decentralization of the law-making process. There is an important difference, he said, between the relation of the constituent parts of a sovereign state to the state as such and the relation of the local Churches to the universal Church. Each local Church is already an image of the universal Church and it should be able to develop its own character. One consequence of the recognition of this principle would be that reservation of decisions to the Holy See would be reduced to a minimum. Cardinal Döpfner also said that prudence should be observed in formulating principles of divine law, whether natural or positive, because in many cases such obligations were still a matter of difference of opinion among theologians. The canon law has a pastoral purpose, he said, and it should accordingly try to avoid conflict between its prescriptions and the consciences of believers.

The real issue in these and similar interventions was not

what the principles proposed by Cardinal Felici for the reform of canon law said, but rather the purpose to which they would be put. Did reform or updating of the law mean simply to move from one fixed position to a more modern but equally fixed position, or did it mean to change from a static to a dynamic mentality, to create a system which would have built into it the elements needed to adjust itself continually to the changes taking place in the world as a whole and in each of its regions and cultures?

The same question underlay much of the conflict at Vatican Council II, and it is one of the most basic challenges confronting mankind in our times, not only in the area of religion but in regard to all social and political structures. Although the concept of Evolution has been clearly formulated for about a century, it is only gradually being realized as one of the most important elements of the human condition, an evolution not simply of the animal species, but of the mind, spirit, and intelligence of man as well, his concept of his rights and functions, his dreams, aspirations and expectations.

The Catholic Church flatly opposed this profound illumination, for reasons which are today immaterial and can most charitably be passed over in silence. But in the mind of many churchmen, the notion of Evolution has not yet been emotionally integrated. As will be seen in the next chapter, the Congregation for the Doctrine of the Faith still refers to it as a "theory," by which it means an unproved working hypothesis. With this mentality, a man necessarily thinks in terms of a static world, at a moment when the most obvious fact of human existence is movement, constantly accelerating movement destined to continue for the foreseeable future. He does not see that the Church's new legal system, whether it is to be codified or not, must have a fluidity to correspond to the facts of life and the spirit of Vatican Council II. At most, he will seek to make it conform to the letter of the statements of that assembly. He can justify updating merely as a concession to the weakness of modern man, his inability to live as ruggedly as his forebears. But if he starts from the notion of a concession, rather than from that of progress toward a more human and more Christian ordering of life, he is obliged to formulate laws calculated to freeze development at the stage that had been reached precisely at the end of the Council, just as the earlier Code had sought to freeze the life and institutions of the Church in the forms judged by its framers appropriate to the moment at which it was promulgated.

What is missing from such a calculation, of course, is the fact that man is going ahead so fast in this nuclear and cybernetic age that the needs of 1967 are already quite different from those of 1965. This point was made forcibly by Father Maurice Walsh, S.J., Weston College, Massachusetts, a member of the Canon Law Society of America, in a round table discussion in Rome during the Synod, a meeting which — like many others on the periphery of the Synod debates — provided valuable feedback for the Fathers. "What the Commission for Canon Law Reform is now proposing," he said, "would have delighted canonists in the United States two years ago, but we have done a lot of reflection in the meantime and we have seen how the Church has changed and is changing as a result of the Council. In consequence, the current proposals no longer measure up to our expectations and needs."

What this expresses is precisely the fear that the proposed revision will retain the spirit and mentality of the 1917 Code. The changes, however significant, would remain technical. A restrictive application could produce practical results little different from those of the present system. The main thrust of the debate was, accordingly, not directed towards challenging or even refining the principles, but rather toward finding ways to ensure that they would be implemented in the spirit of Vatican Council II. Two main recommendations emerged. The first was that the revised code should be merely a fundamental law, somewhat similar to a written constitution, leaving the formulation of specific and detailed legislation to subordinate bodies throughout the world in accordance with the principles of subsidiarity. The second was that law is too important to be left in the hands of lawyers, and that consequently the fundamental law should be the work of the entire people of God, and the subsidiary laws should similarly be the work of all those to whom they would apply. In each case, the working groups would be chosen strictly for their competence. They would include pastors, theologians, canonists, philosophers, sociologists, psychologists, and specialists in the other ecclesiastical and life sciences.

On the principle of subsidiarity as such there was universal agreement. It could hardly have been otherwise in the light of the teaching of recent popes, and in particular of Pope John's statement that the principle is absolute and applies to every society. But there were wide differences of view as regards its application. Archbishop Joseph Parecattil, of Kerala, India, a prelate of the Caldeo-Malabar rite, and Ukrainian Archbishop Maxim Hermaniuk, of Winnipeg, Canada, for example, urged that there should be a single code for the Western and Eastern Churches, with special applications left to the initiative of the local Churches. Archbishop Parecattil said the general code should deal with such things as the hierarchy and the sacraments, leaving room for adaptation where desirable, for example, on the issue of clerical celibacy in the Eastern rites. Melchite Archbishop Edelby of Antioch agreed that there were points in which the disciplines of all rites could be brought together in a single basic text, but emphasized the practical danger of attempting such an effort within the emotional climate that has long prevailed in Rome. The formulation of a single code, he said, "risked presenting the Eastern Churches with a *fait accompli,* with a further latinization of their practices, and also with the reduction of their quite different ways of life and discipline to a common denominator."

Father Bidagor, Secretary of the Commission, intervened in the discussion of separate codes for Eastern and Western Churches to say that the question was closed, that it had been decided to make a basic code which would permit the formulation of different codes in accordance with the principle of subsidiarity. Just what he meant by this was never fully clarified. One point that was well stressed was that the former official concept of one code for the Western Church and one for the Eastern was based on a total misconception. There are not just two Churches, each with its spiritual and legal traditions. There are many Churches. The way of life of the Syrian rite Catholic is as different from that of the Catholic of the Byzantine rite as they both are from the Latin rite. Underlying all the discussion is yet another issue on which theological investigation has only begun. What distinguishes the Christianity of the West from that of the East? Are we simply in the presence of superficial differences resulting from their distinct historical and cultural experiences? Or are we faced with two ways of transmitting revelation, each with its own profound characteristics? Can they be brought in course of time into a new cultural synthesis, or is it proper and necessary to maintain in separation and juxtaposition the complementary qualities of each in order to achieve the fullness of the body of Christ?

Father Bidagor's observation indicated a willingness on the part of the Commission to allow a generous application of the principle of subsidiarity to the Eastern Churches. A phrase in the Commission's document showed that a much more restrictive application is envisaged for the Western Church. "It seems contrary to the mind and spirit of the Second Vatican Council," it said, "to have in the Western (Latin) Church particular statutes which would amount to a special form for the laws of national Churches." The document added that this did not exclude somewhat wider autonomy of law-making for national episcopal conferences, especially as regards the administration of Church property, and also a more extensive use in Church courts of the procedures practiced in the civil courts of the country in question. The concession regarding administration of Church property is not very significant, because in many countries the local civil law already governs to a considerable extent. Besides, some reservations were expressed about the relaxation of controls on money transactions unless as part of an overall reform of Church finances. Curial supervision is often today the only effective curb on foolish spending by bishops and religious superiors who lack management ability and training. The withdrawal of the controls can only proceed step by step with the development of administrative techniques and procedures in each region and country.

The proposal to adjust to local procedural practice in Church courts, while obviously not an enormous concession, was universally welcomed. The change has long been urged by the Canon Law Society of America, among others. Its purpose is obvious. On the one hand, people expect that the safeguards to which they are accustomed in their civil courts will also be found in those of the Church. On the other hand, it eases the problem of the lawyer who today finds himself representing a client according to procedural rules totally different from those in which he is trained.

Many bishops of the Latin rite, however, envisaged the application of the principle of subsidiarity as something far more radical than the suggestions of the Commission. There must be a profound decentralization of the law-making process, Cardinal Franjo Seper, of Zagreb, Yugoslavia, said, citing as one reason "the exceptional conditions in which the Church can find itself in some countries in times of persecution." Cardinal Thomas Cooray (Ceylon), Cardinal Léon Etienne Duval (Algeria), and Cardinal Owen McCann (South Africa) were among those who agreed. The new code, they said, "should bring out the legal consequences of the Vatican Council's proclamation of the collegial nature of Church government." They also asked for more emphasis on the rights of all Christians as persons, on the rights of the laity, and on the problems posed for the Church by the new status of women in contemporary society as contrasted with the traditional Catholic concept of woman's role.

Another who spoke very strongly in favor of decentralization of law-making was Cardinal Fernando Quiroga y Palacios, of Santiago de Compostela, Spain. "The particular Churches, even in their diversity," he said, "are the true Catholic and universal Church. The principle of subsidiarity should apply not only for the pope and the bishops, but also between the hierarchy and the faithful, and also between members of religious orders in their own internal relations." In a somewhat similar vein, Cardinal Ignatius Gabriel Tappouni of Antioch (Syrian rite) said that the new code should define more clearly the rights and duties of bishops, and not limit itself to listing faculties granted to them. Several other Synod Fathers followed his lead in asking that the new law distinguish clearly between what pertains to the Pope by virtue of his office and the rights which he *de facto* exercises.

Archbishop Adam Kozlowiecki, of Lusaka, Zambia, raised an issue with very basic implications. The practice of speaking of Western and Eastern Churches should be abandoned, he said, because it reflected a geographical division that had ceased to be valid. The Churches of Asia and Africa did not belong in either category. There were, he added, more variations within each of the groups than between the groups as such. It is this last point about the deep cultural differences now hidden by the imposition of a single juridic and liturgical system within what is called the Western or Latin rite Church that there has been most reluctance to face. The post-colonial evolution of Asia and Africa, nevertheless, is such that it cannot be ignored in the proposed revision of canon law.

The procedures at the Synod were not such as to permit a concrete formulation of the consensus. The discussion made it clear, nevertheless, that most of the Fathers favored for the Latin rite Church an application of the principle of subsidiarity similar to that envisaged by the Commission as proper for the Eastern Churches. This would mean that the new code would be nothing more than a brief constitutional law setting out very general principles, something comparable to the Constitution of the United States, with the implementing laws left to national or regional conferences of bishops legislating in terms of the socioeconomic, cultural, and spiritual situations and needs of each area.

Interestingly enough, a similar recommendation was made by a group of scholars meeting at the very same time in New York under the sponsorship of the Canon Law Society of America and Fordham University. They urged a division of power between central and regional governing bodies. Church offices throughout the world, they said, should be able to act independently of the Vatican on various issues, including the selection of bishops. The executive, legislative, and judicial powers should be completely separated. Guarantees of individual rights should be spelled out, this to include due process of law, which would grant legal protection to persons charged with offenses against the Church.

The same idea was being simultaneously expressed in Rome by Father Maurice Walsh, also a member of the Canon Law Society of America, in the round table discussion mentioned above. "The Americans generally want a much greater decentralization of canon law than is currently being planned. We want to see on the universal level only an absolute minimum of law, with any detailed legislation, to the extent that this is necessary, left to the episcopal conferences, so that the vast bulk of the material in the present Code would simply be removed, and the rest of it left to local option. Admittedly, such a vast decentralization of law is not an easy thing, but we think of it as vitally necessary. And as decentralization is now being planned, we would like to be in on the planning of it as well. American canonists in general are very unhappy about the way in which the reform of canon law is being handled, the fact that it is being done in secret, without really a sufficient spread of opinion that goes beyond the Roman mentality. For example, we have truly outstanding canonists in the United States who have no truly active part in the reform process."

Father Walsh's criticism of the way in which the reform is being handled goes to the heart of the issue. It is precisely the point made by several Synod Fathers when they called for a more collegial effort. Cardinal Owen McCann of Capetown, South Africa, was particularly emphatic about the matter. The formulation of the new code, he said, should be preceded by open discussion of the issues in appropriate publications in all parts of the world.

Concepts similar to those of Father Walsh were expressed even more vigorously at the same round-table discussion by a Brazilian professor of canon law who is also one of a group of theological advisers to the bishops of Brazil. "We have suffered in Latin America throughout our entire history," to synthesize the words and thought of Msgr. José Maria Moss Tapajos, "from laws imposed on us by Europe, laws made with a European mentality for European conditions, but utterly unsuited to our conditions and mentality. We are not prepared to have this process repeated once more; and if it is, the laws will not be observed, because our totally different cultural and social situations and needs make the observance of European laws impossible. We can consequently never again accept a law in the preparation of which we have not been vitally involved. And the law itself should simply be a fundamental or constitutional law covering general principles, with everything else left to the local Churches."

The extent of the opinion within the Synod itself in favor of restricting the central Commission for the Reform of Canon Law to drawing up a fundamental law was such that the Commission's president, Cardinal Felici, proposed the creation of a special committee of the Synod to study the issue and make a recommendation. Under the rules of procedure of the Synod, however, the life of a committee could not be longer than the Synod session, and it was quickly agreed that the issues were so vast and complicated that no useful conclusions could be formulated in a few weeks. Instead, at the end of the debate on October 7, each Father was asked to express orally his approval or disapproval of the principles formulated in the document that they had been discussing. The result was quite surprising. The document as a whole obtained only 57 favorable votes, far short of the 124 needed for a two-thirds majority. The other votes, to the number of 130, were all affirmative but with reservations. The two principles which seemed to the Fathers to most need clarification were those dealing with the juridic character of the proposed new code and with the way in which the principle of subsidiarity should be implemented in this new code. Because of the many reservations, three Fathers were named as an informal committee to study them and make a synthesis for submission to the Holy Father as the expression of the Synod's advice. The three members were Archbishop George Dwyer, of Birmingham, England, Archbishop Simon Duraisamy Lourduswamy, of Bangalore, India, and Auxiliary Bishop José Guerra Campos, of Madrid, Spain.

The text of this report has not been made public, but it can be deduced from the statements of the Synod Fathers as already reported in this chapter. What is perhaps most basic is the stress on the fact that it is no longer possible for the central authority of the Church to make detailed laws for the universal Church as it did in the past, that the need for pluralism is as pronounced in the Church as in the world in this period of decline of the West's political and cultural domination and the resurgence of cultures that until recently seemed doomed to proximate extinction. The division is no longer into East and West. We now have the Latin countries, the Scandinavian countries, the situations in Africa and Asia which call for solutions according to circumstances. Everything points toward a fundamental law drafted in general terms, with authority vested in national and regional conferences of bishops to make the appropriate implementing legislation. By taking this direction, canon law will better fulfill its own function, while simultaneously helping to implement the doctrine of collegiality and promote the cause of Christian unity.

It is also clear, as an analysis published by the IDOC information service in December, 1967 pointed out, that a strong desire exists among the bishops that "the text of the future code should be sent to all the bishoprics in the world before the drafting of the final text." In the view of the IDOC editorial board, "the road that has yet to be traveled before the revision can be completed is a long one." It considers that the Synod discussion has made it easier to put the consultation on a wider basis, and also that it has clarified the task that faces the Commission for the reform of the code, a reform that involves "not a mere revision but rather the drafting of a completely new code." It concludes with the hope that the subject will reappear on the agenda of the next Synod. With the work of the Commission in a more advanced stage, it can then be discussed "in greater detail and with greater maturity."

CHAPTER 4

Dangers to the Faith

Cardinal Michael Browne, a native of Ireland and a former Master General of the Dominican Order, remains physically and mentally vigorous at the age of 80. A member of the Congregation for the Faith, he is a faithful supporter of its recently retired 77-year-old head, Cardinal Alfredo Ottaviani. As vice-chairman under Ottaviani of the Theological Commission at Vatican Council II, he could be counted upon to focus all problems within a western juridically-oriented tradition, and in the rigid categories of the scholastic theologian.

Cardinal Ottaviani's blindness had become more total in recent years, causing him to lean ever more heavily on his friend. It was Cardinal Browne, accordingly, who got to his feet on October 4 to present and explain to the Synod Fathers the second agenda item, current dangers to the faith. His *relatio* or oral presentation, simply summarized a document which had been circulated to the bishops' conferences some months earlier. To appreciate its content calls for a brief background.

Shortly after Pope John announced his intention to summon Vatican Council II, he instructed the various curial departments to prepare appropriate documentation. Committees were formed with members drawn from around the world, but with the control of doctrinal opinions and tendencies tightly guarded by the Curia. Among the many drafts readied for the approval of the coming Council were four prepared by the preconciliar commission on theology, of which Cardinal Ottaviani was president. These so-called *schemata* or position papers dealt with the sources of revelation, the moral order (dangers of subjectivism, abuse of psychoanalytic techniques, etc.), the deposit of faith (pantheism, existentialism, modernism, the family and chastity). As a group they purported to deal with the nature and function of the Church. In fact, they constituted a Syllabus of Errors, a litany of beliefs and theories current in the modern world which the authors judged dangerous to faith and morals.

When the Council assembled in October, 1962, the Fathers quickly rejected these four documents. It was not principally because the bishops denied the accuracy of what they said, though even on that issue there were strong dissents on various points. The substantive criticism, as a number of speakers at the Council made clear, was that they were too scholastic, too juridical, too canonical, too centered on morality, and not biblical enough. Some bishops expressed the hope that they would be "given a reverent burial" as not only irrelevant but harmful to the Church in the circumstances of the world of the twentieth and twenty-first centuries. Minds are not won today by denunciations and arbitrary orders, they insisted. They are won by love, by concern, by commitment, by the testimony of lives honorably dedicated to the service of others. The result was the gradual elaboration of the greatest document of Vatican II, the Constitution on the Church, with all Christians recognized as members of a mystery — engrafted in the body of Christ through Baptism — held together by love and dedicated to the service of man as well as the worship of God. That document was the work of a Mixed Commission named by Pope

John in November, 1962, comprising cardinals who were members of the Theological Commission and of the Secretariat of Unity, that is to say, representatives of the two major tendencies within the Council. The important Constitution on Divine Revelation was also a fruitful result of the efforts of this Mixed Commission, after the original draft prepared by the preconciliar commission on theology (presided over by Cardinal Ottaviani) had been overwhelmingly rejected by the Council.

The curial bloc at the Council was unsuccessful in its opposition to the Constitution on the Church. After it was approved, however, a new way was sought to achieve the original objective. No sooner was the Council over than work began on a letter which was sent in July, 1966, over the signature of Cardinal Ottaviani, to the bishops of the world and the heads of religious orders. It was a well-planned strategy. The principal errors contained in the four *schemata* rejected by the Council were reformulated, and the recipients of the letter were asked to indicate which of them currently constituted the most serious threats to the Faith in their respective countries or religious congregations. The use of multiple-choice techniques in correlating the replies would produce a weighty list of errors which, on the admission of the bishops and religious superiors themselves, could be considered current.

The strategy, however, proved too transparent. The French bishops agreed that some errors existed but nevertheless rejected the list outright as irrelevant to the post-conciliar Church, and it was leaked to the press. The bishops of Switzerland, Belgium, Germany, and Austria gave even more optimistic answers than those of France. The Latin Americans said they were concerned about disciplinary problems of the clergy but had no serious worries in the doctrinal area. Spain was mainly serene and positive, saying there was no cause for concern in practices and attitudes. Most of the bishops of Asia and Africa made it clear that they did not share

Cardinal Ottaviani's preoccupations. Their serious problems, they said, dealt with how to relate the Church to a world in rapid change. In addition, some noted that the formulation of various issues, for example, the virginity of Mary and the real presence of Christ in the Eucharist, reflected a Western mentality quite foreign to their ways of thought. A spokesman for the Irish bishops said they had not bothered to reply, on the ground that none of the errors was significant in their country. The bishops of the United States gave an answer which added up to about the same thing. The total result was a worldwide consensus that, even to the extent that dangers existed, only harm could be done by cataloguing and anathematizing them. Whatever value such procedures might have had in earlier times, they did not fit the needs and realities of the twentieth century.

It is necessary, on the contrary, the bishops insisted, to recognize that modern man is different from men of earlier times. Thanks to the impact of electronic means of communication and other elements of our technological world, we are in a phase of evolution characterized by enquiry. The explosion of knowledge was achieved directly in the technological area, but it reaches into all areas, including religion, and its method is the Socratic method of universal questioning. It is consequently both inevitable and proper that Catholics as part of this culture should challenge practices and viewpoints hitherto accepted without much reflection, such as fasting, abstinence, birth control, clerical celibacy, and clerical-lay relationships.

Although Catholics began to discuss these issues in any significant way only during Vatican II, the Council was not the cause of the new public discussion. It merely gave recognition to pressures already building up to explosion point, and it provided a controlled outlet for them. The Council consequently attempted to answer the questions that were in many hearts: what is the Church and what is its relevance? As it tried, it was forced to probe ever deeper. The techniques of enquiry perfected by our technological culture compelled it to distinguish the cultural detritus, the verbal or semantic incrustations in the relation of Catholicism to other religions, as well as in the forms of our worship, the function of the priest, the participation of the laity, the place of communications, the meaning of the religious life, the purpose and achievement of the missions, the cultural elements in our forms of government.

If one reads the signs of the times in these terms, as the Fathers of Vatican II did, it gradually becomes evident that it is meaningless to fight error by the negative approach of sterile condemnation. This the French bishops expressed well in replying to the Ottaviani letter.

"The responsibility of the bishops is primary in doctrinal matters. Accordingly, the French bishops intend to exercise openly, in these years of the implementation of the Council, their duty to watch over the formulation and the expression of the true faith. They know, moreover, that the root of the evil is often in the realm of philosophy or even of metaphysics. But, as has been said before, this mission of the bishops is an essentially positive one. What is needed is to proclaim the word of God, to get the teaching of the Council across to all the people, and to set out precisely the 'fixed points' of the faith, without being afraid of saying the good and the bad, the true and the false.

"In addition, the problems of doctrine underlie all pastoral activity. It is consequently the task of the bishops to evaluate the doctrinal implications of current pastoral initiatives. Particular attention must be given to the methods of teaching the faith, a vital matter in a world marked by unbelief. . . .

"Doctrinal difficulties are loyally recognized and a resolute effort has already begun to overcome them. But these shadows must not make us forget the light projected by the Council on the life of our dioceses. The symptoms of vitality are many and reassuring, among the clergy and the laity alike. If they are not spelled out in this report, neither can they be left out of the calculation. The pastoral orientation of the Council, the opening to the world it achieved in all fields, have been welcomed with deep gratitude by the Catholics of France. They have aroused a missionary impetus and a spiritual hope which are far more significant than the reasons for concern."

One pastor who also expressed this dynamic viewpoint well is the Melchite Archbishop Neophyte Edelby, "In the Church there will always be people with a nose for error, who find heresies everywhere," he stated in a lecture in Rome in February, 1967, while the debate provoked by the Ottaviani letter was still warm. "One should look ten times before declaring a doctrine is heretical. Moreover, it is not enough for a thoughtless person to say something stupid in order for him to receive the honor of condemnation. Heresy only merits revelation when it starts to spread, when it constitutes a risk to the Christian people, threatening the fundamental unity of the faith. Often in the history of the Church, the extreme heresy hunters have by their abuses done as much wrong to the Church as the heretics themselves. The latest enquiry of the Congregation for the Doctrine of the Faith has shown that . . . there was no real danger of heterodoxy in the Church . . . The Church currently needs greater freedom rather than greater repression. We therefore wish the coming Synod of Bishops to say no more on doctrinal matters than the Council said. Neither would I like it to undertake interpretation of the Council's doctrinal affirmations. It has neither the competence nor the grace."

At the time Archbishop Edelby spoke, it was known that an item about dangers to the faith figured on the upcoming Synod's agenda, but it was not known how the Congregation for the Faith would formulate it. Having urged the Congregation not to repeat a third time the twice-committed error, the Archbishop outlined an approach in keeping with the Council spirit and the expressed mind of many national hierarchies.

The Synod, he said, "should reassert confidence in the Holy Spirit, encouraging pluriformity as against the recent tradition of absolute uniformity, including dogmatic theology, theological methodology, biblical research, and patristic tradition. The Synod's doctrinal task is to create mutual confidence in the Church, to favor freedom of expression, while interesting the greatest possible number of people in the life of theology."

In preparing its documentation for the Synod of Bishops, the Congregation for the Faith tried to take these criticisms into account. It presented in objective terms such issues as demythization of the Bible, the crisis of authority, and the causes of atheism, offering arguments for and against various solutions without laying down a prefabricated conclusion. In presenting the document to the Synod, Cardinal Browne also agreed that times had changed, and that the Church should explore for herself the new spiritual culture of the world by means of an exchange between the magisterium and theologians, between the center and the periphery, between the Holy See and particular Churches, between pastors and their people.

The Fathers were, nevertheless, not satisfied. They found the whole approach still too negative, still too academic. They continued to fear that any encouragement by them would be used to promote a new catalogue of errors. In addition, it was noted that a basic issue was already resolved without being examined, namely, the nature of the Church's magisterium or teaching authority. The opinions of a curial congregation were being set over against the thinking of theologians, as though these latter did not form a part of the magisterium, with the conclusion that, *a fortiori,* lesser Christians most certainly did not. Actually, while the pope is the supreme teacher in the Church, aided and supported by the bishops, his personal opinions are open to challenge. Even his official decisions, though they are binding on the consciences of Catholics, cannot be made without taking into account the mind of the universal Church, what is technically known as the *sensus fidelium*. As Vatican II's Constitution on the Church indicates, the same Holy Spirit directs the pope, the college of bishops, and the whole body of the faithful, ensuring agreement on matters of teaching and belief. While most Catholics, including theologians, do accept papal pronouncements as authoritative, many have come to resent the finalization of decisions regarding faith and morals by the Roman curial offices. They believe in the pope's authority and recognize what Vatican II called "the charism of infallibility" conferred by his office. But they stoutly deny that this prerogative belongs to the members of the pope's official family. However, in the preparation for the Synod, some responsible organization had to be entrusted with the formulation of the position papers. It was quite legitimate to ask the Congregation for the Faith to prepare the document on doctrine to be submitted to the Fathers. What is at issue is merely how well it read the signs of the times in performing its task.

The doctrinal document splits dangers to the faith into eight neat categories, with a chapter to each. They are labeled respectively: Basics; Christology; Ecclesiology; Anthropology; Basic Morality; Special Morality; Sacraments; and the Present World and the Life of the World to Come. For those who successfully hurdle these eight major obstacles, each strewn with minor theological booby-traps and metaphysical antipersonnel devices, Atheism is served up as a dessert or afterthought.

Basics are biblical revelation and the knowledge and objective expression of truth. Here we are warned in particular against "the modern fascination for the theory of demythization," against the failure of some to give adequate historical value to the Gospel, against the temptation to deny that man can achieve some real knowledge of "those things which are absolute both in the natural and in the supernatural order, as well as an objective recognition of truth and the ability to express it." Finally, the principle is affirmed that "our dogmas are to be understood in the same sense and in the same words, as they have already been formulated."

In all this we are indeed in basics, though perhaps not in the sense meant by the authors. It presents a static understanding of creation and salvation contrary to the observation and understanding of the modern man in his natural and supernatural perspectives. It is quite alien to current thought in the Church, as presented by a man like Father Yves Congar, O.P. Long under a cloud in Rome, Father Congar was "rehabilitated" by Pope Paul in 1964 and hailed by him as a major influence in shaping the course of Vatican Council II.

"Who claims to have a satisfactory explanation of the homogeneous development of dogmas," Father Congar recently asked. "Today we recognize better the historicity of man and therefore also the historicity of the Church, of her institutions and of the pronouncements of her magisterium. We know this better in principle, but in fact we often talk as though words covered and always will cover the same content — which to be sure they do not. . . . What is and what is not liable to be affected by historic conditioning? Vatican II reopened the question of the historicity of the pronouncements of the magisterium, since more than once the Council said *something other* than had been said by the same magisterium previously. People trained in historical studies and used to historical thinking will not find this disquieting. Others with a monolithic, monarchic, and wholly divinized view will find it disturbing. Their view is a fallacy."

Under Christology, the Browne document shows its distaste for the direction taken by modern biblical studies regarding the meaning to be ascribed to the Gospel narratives dealing with miracles and other aspects of Christ's life, and it repeats the insistence already expressed under Basics on the importance of the wording of dogmatic formulations. In the light of the broad freedom given to scholars in the formal documents of recent popes and in the statements of Vatican II, however, it is forced to nuance its warnings. What perhaps stands out most clearly here is a resistance to the current stress on the true humanity of Christ, in line with the equal stress today on the entire human phenomenon, without so much as a hint that heretofore much modern Catholic theology had gone to the other extreme by stressing only the divine attributes to the ignoring of the human ones clearly delineated in the Gospels.

Under Ecclesiology, the document attempts to deal with the relation between the institutions and charisms in the Church, a subject on which its authors were badly out of their depth. This is understandable, because the theology they learned regarded charisms as something that had existed in the early Church but had long since died out as unnecessary when the institution was solidly constructed. Vatican II squashed this notion, insisting that the Church needs and enjoys both the hierarchical institution and the personal charism given by the Spirit to those he chooses, to be used for the good of the Church. The Council did not give much guidance for correlating these two seemingly contradictory dynamic forces within the Church, nor has sufficient time elapsed for significant theological meditation.

The meaning of the magisterium is taken up again in this chapter, but in terms of the same question-begging assumption as in the Introduction, namely that of a Church teaching and a Church taught. The opening reflection does give some hope by stating that the Holy Spirit leads the Church of Christ "in all truth" by exercising influence on *the whole people* hierarchically constituted. This is followed by practical concessions imposed by the Vatican Council (freedom of enquiry for both the clergy and laity) and by John XXIII's insistence that the deposit of faith is one thing and the way it is expressed another. All of this, nevertheless, leads up to the old oversimplified conclusion that the function of the magisterium may not be reduced to simply following the religious conscience of the community, since it has the direct duty to teach and interpret the deposit of faith, this especially nowadays "because of the trend to challenge everything and to downgrade authority."

The problem about this concept of the nature of the Church and of its way of operating is that it overlooks the extraordinary advance in self-understanding achieved by the Church at Vatican II. Ironically, while it decries the upgrading of the human element in religion, its defect is that it gives undue stress to the humanly organized institution. It portrays the Church as ruled like other human societies, rather than as a mystery in which the Spirit so inspires that the magisterium is not in fact faced with the artificial dilemma of either having to dictate to the community from outside or to follow its religious conscience from within. It sees revelation as a formulation rather than as a fact. It attributes to Christianity a message instead of a mission.

The next chapter dealing with anthropology is similarly disappointing. Everything about man is changing: his attitudes, his aims, his goals, his interpretation of reality. He is evolving, developing, becoming more conscious of his own power, more reluctant to concede the intervention of any outside mover in the daily events of his life than was his ancestor who knew little about the operation of natural laws. Pope John XXIII recognized and welcomed all of this as evidence of a much more sublime and all-embracing design for creation than man's small mind had previously been able to divine. He understood, as historian Gerhart Ladner of the University of California recently summed up his thought, that man seems to be on the verge of a far-reaching Christian integration of his total dynamic being, what the Greeks called *bios,* comparable to the twelfth- and thirteenth-century integration of reason accomplished by St. Thomas and his followers. But whereas Pope John welcomed the leap in faith into the dark which is involved, the document concentrates on the terrors and uncertainties of the way.

There is, as Ladner also points out, a historical reason for this reluctance. The new challenge is a logical evolution from concepts at one time firmly enshrined in Christian thought. Subsequently, however, they were disassociated from it, and today, they are offered to man in a framework that prescinds from or positively opposes Christianity. "The ideas of freedom, justice, peace and love," he writes, "had indeed long been Christian ideas, but their new realizations in our time were not primarily initiated on specifically Christian grounds. These new realizations can hardly be separated from the libertarianism of the American and French Revolutions, from Marx's radical reassessment of social justice, from Gandhi's uncompromising pacifism, and from the re-evaluation of sexuality by Freud. The situation of Christians today might be compared . . . to that of the great scholastics of the twelfth and thirteenth centuries, who encountered the tremendous intellectual challenges of a pre-Christian Aristotle and an extra-Christian Averroes, yet the great challenges of today must be met not only in the realm of thought but also and even more so in the whole arena of life."

Emotionally and intellectually boxed in by a concept of man and of creation as something accomplished once for all in six days, the drafters of the document have nothing meaningful to offer those who seek guidance. It is necessary to steer one's way, they urge, between the Scylla of materialism, determinism, and human self-sufficiency, and the Charybdis of total withdrawal from the world into a false spiritualism that would cling to the old for its own sake and reject the new, no matter how necessary. Actually, the logic of the document compels the latter choice, but since the Council rejected it so explicitly in the Constitution on the Church in the Modern World, it is not possible to sustain it openly.

Neither is the document helpful on the subject of original sin. The traditional explanation was based on a literal understanding of a Bible narrative which, in the light of today's universal recognition of the evolutionary process in the entire known universe, has to be demythized just as surely as the Tower of Babel, the story of Jonas and the Whale, and the marriage of the daughters of men with the sons of angels. But much earlier, the document had already closed tight and locked this door by declaring that demythization is "contrary to tradition and the magisterium."

Perhaps the basic problem is a misunderstanding of the way in which people get to know each other's positions. As recently as a few years ago, the Holy Office was still insisting that it was unnecessary to hear the author's explanations before condemning his book. Our experts study the book most conscientiously, it was explained, and they judge the objective meaning of the words.

The value of dialogue rather than warning was one of the keynotes of the discussion that followed Cardinal Browne's introduction. The general view was well summed up by Cardinal Garrone. Seminarians, he said, should be taught how to speak later as priests to lay people who are highly informed and consequently not prepared to accept a superficial answer to a serious question. "The bishop should keep himself well informed on doctrinal issues. The extent to which he does so is a measure of his effectiveness as a pastor. The magisterium is as necessary to the soul as bread is to the body."

Our times have a much better understanding of the function of speech and of its extension in writing than our forefathers had. Its purpose is to establish communication between persons, to enable each to learn what the other wishes to express to him. This purpose can be effected only through dialogue, a continuing process of projection and feedback through which each gradually approaches the significance of the words and other signs used by the other in the total existential context of the culture, intelligence, awareness, prejudices, and emotional pressures of both parties. As the common sense of mankind (affirmed by various Fathers at the Council) understands, the condemning of a book without dialogue with the author to find out what he means is no way to do business.

Not infrequently, the document contains valuable insights.

The chapter on basic morality, for example, notes that it is very hard to weigh the psychological and social elements in human decisions, and that the human act is integral as conditioned by all the factors causing the person to act, even those of which he himself is not conscious. But when it immediately adds a condemnation of erroneous views which deny objective validity to moral precepts, or which downgrade the natural law while overstressing the importance of the personal conscience, one recognizes that the opposing view is being presented in caricature. The real issue is what each side means by such words as "objective," "natural law," and "personal conscience." Without dialogue, that information cannot be exchanged, and all we have is a conversation between the deaf.

The same comments apply to the other chapters. It is correct to say (as the document does) that moral concepts should not be limited to the religious and spiritual life, overlooking the link of the virtue of religion with charity, justice, and a recognition of freedom, but that neither should the Christian moral concept be reduced to a natural ethic. What is wrong is the false dichotomy here implied between a man's religious and spiritual life and the natural ethic through which it is expressed. Vatican II, by contrast, affirmed clearly that a man's apostolate is his work and a man's work is his apostolate. Similarly, in attempting to provide guidance on the extremely live issue of the meaning of the real presence of Christ in the Eucharist,* the argument proceeds without the least indication of awareness of what twentieth-century man has learned about the constitution of physical matter. A presentation assuming an objective validity to the culturally conditioned explanation of matter in terms of substance and acci-

* The current theological debate does not concern the reality of the presence of Christ, body, blood, soul and divinity, in the Eucharist. At issue is simply the "how" of the presence. Theologians are groping for words that will, at our present level of knowledge of the nature of matter and in consonance with our current understanding of what a person is, convey a meaningful concept of what is in itself a profound mystery and consequently by definition beyond the grasp of any created intellect.

dents is meaningless to people who know matter primarily as an accumulation of tremendous energy poised in vibrant tension.

What is probably the most satisfactory part of the work is the final chapter on the future of the race. Here, evolution is no longer a "theory." On the contrary, the daily growing awareness of the evolution of the human race and the interdependence of all men, with the consequent realization of a universal vocation to help make the world a better place to live in and a universal duty to stand shoulder to shoulder with all men, is presented as a good thing. As in the preceding chapters, the contrasting dangers of too much or too little of this good thing are next set out. Some Christians wrongly lock themselves in a code of individual salvation, neglecting their fellow-Christians and fellowmen. Others are unduly fascinated by the call to serve the neighbor, to the point of neglecting the love of God, denying the value of asceticism and contemplation, or the value of a life consecrated to virginity. Some even go so far as to project the future of the world in purely naturalistic terms, denying the Second Coming of the Lord and taking lightly the gospel teaching on a last and irrevocable judgment. At this point, however, when we seem to be teetering on the edge of an anathema, the subject is prudently dropped with the observation that Vatican II had set the proper tone and indicated the course to follow between these extremes, in its Constitution on the Church in the Modern World. And with equal prudence, the document tiptoes over the issues of the future life. The Church should insist on the resurrection of the body, it says, without inquiring too deeply what the transfigured man will be like. It should stress union with God as the characteristic of the life to come. And while insisting on the last judgment, it should preach with reserve on hell and heaven, "which are outside the order of the visible world and known only through revelation."

The debate that followed Cardinal Browne's presentation of the viewpoints of the Congregation for the Faith showed that all parties were agreed that the core of the Synod's business had been reached. A total of 81 interventions were registered between October 4 and 10. Pope Paul underlined the seriousness of the discussion by attending the opening and closing sessions. "One may presume," commented *Informations Catholiques Internationales,* "that if the Synod had approved the position paper, then this document as drawn up by the ex-Holy Office would have served as the starting point for the preparation of a papal statement, almost certainly an encyclical, which would have recalled all too well Pius IX's encyclical, *Quanta Cura,* and its annex, the 'Syllabus of Eighty Erroneous Propositions.' "

From the outset, it was clear that the possibility of any such approval by the Synod was nonexistent. The Fathers readily admitted the presence of dangers to the faith. Instead of approaching them in "a perspective of error," however, the vast majority insisted that they had to be placed in "a perspective of truth." Rather than wholesale condemnations, they demanded an objective evaluation of each situation in a spirit of calm confidence.

One who helped to set the tone was the circumspect but very open Archbishop of Paris, 54-year-old Cardinal Pierre Veuillot. One must look at the positive side, he insisted. Modern man is asking for the truth, and there is a big advantage in the fact that modern trends of thinking are "essentially honest," because they plead for freedom and inquire sincerely about humanity. In such trends, there is "a deep desire for God and for religion."

Reflecting the views expressed in the reply of the French bishops to the Ottaviani letter, Cardinal Veuillot denied that Vatican Council II had caused the present difficulties. Rather, he said, they are a sign of modern man's thirst and quest for truth. At the Vatican Council, the Church asked what she thought about herself. Now the world was coming back with an equally serious question. Tell us, it is asking, what do you think of your God? How can the Church make intelligible to men who daily acquire greater control of their material environment a creating and history-making God? To try to answer that question involves risks for the believer, but to refuse to try to answer it is to deny the mission of the Christian to the world. It is therefore necessary to open a dialogue with contemporary thought, to climb down out of the ivory tower, and to talk at a mutually agreed level and in a mutually agreed language about our beliefs, our philosophy of life and our moral codes. All of this can only be done by theologians truly dedicated to the service of the Church, and it can be done by them only if the Church accords them the necessary confidence. "We should," he summed up, "have much closer contacts between the Holy See, represented by the Congregation for the Faith, and the bishops, and equally between the bishops and theologians, even here in the Synod."

Cardinal Veuillot's statement carried additional weight from the fact that it continued a line of thought he had long been expressing. During the Vatican Council, he was particularly concerned with the need to speak to the world, to establish a dialogue between theology and contemporary thought, to proclaim that the Church does not merely tolerate science but seeks to foster it positively. He had, for example, criticized an early draft of the Constitution on the Church in the Modern World for failing to answer "the growing anguish of modern science in the face of the smallness and fragility of man confronted by the immense and unfriendly universe, and in the face of an ever-increasing number of discoveries whose direction and finality are unknown and disputed." It is one of his favorite ideas. "Contemporary philosophy, psychology and psychoanalysis force us to rethink various basic problems and enrich our vision," he stated in a press interview in October, 1966. "Our doctrinal function should be exercised in a positive way. Far from blocking research, we should support it."

Bishop Mark McGrath of Panama pursued the same point with his typical lucidity. Only 43 years old, he is one of the world's best known and respected bishops. Panama-born and U.S.-educated, he is absolutely bilingual in Spanish and English, at his polished ease in several other languages. A brilliant theologian fervently committed to Pope John's *aggiornamento,* he made contributions in committee to the principal Vatican Council documents, his diplomatic moderation helping him to reconcile opposing views and conflicting personalities. At the time of the Synod, he was on leave of absence from his diocese as Secretary General of the Council of Bishops of Latin America (CELAM), in Bogotá, Colombia.

Bishop McGrath spoke at the Synod on behalf both of CELAM and of the Secretariat for Non-Christians. Theology, he said, has become too abstract. It had to be brought closer to the reality of the world and take more account of pastoral reality. The approach recommended by Cardinal Browne was too negative and in no way suited to the needs of Latin America, where there was more indifference toward the Church than opposition, and where there was no real atheism. The problem in Latin America was not an ideological but an existential one, namely, that spiritual and material development were out of step. Even those who opposed the Church as an obstacle to social development as they conceived it had an enormous goodwill and deep faith in the future. These were very positive elements and should be evaluated as such.

What was necessary, Bishop McGrath concluded, was to draw the logical conclusions from the documents of Vatican Council II, and particularly from the Constitution on the Church in the Modern World. Although this last-named Constitution is officially described as "pastoral" to indicate that it is not a formally doctrinal statement, its substructure is solidly theological, and Bishop McGrath's point is that the theological implications should now be explored. That would mean, for example, that the faith should no longer be discussed behind ecclesiastical doors as of concern only to the Church and its members. The world is always present and involved, and decisions must serve the vital needs of all.

Cardinal Owen McCann, of Capetown, South Africa, agreed. Apparently the drafters of the document submitted to the Synod wanted to see the Church develop in a way different from that of the world in which we live, but "that is impossible and against the will of God."

It quickly emerged that a basic underlying issue was the role of the theologian in the Church. Both sides agreed that the Council had released a theological dynamism long bottled up, so that currently there existed in the Church an intellectual elite which was going too far, too fast, for the Catholic in the pew. During the period of the late Scholastics, theologians had lost contact with the people, as well as with the sources of the faith. Unaccustomed for hundreds of years to involvement in the technical problems of the theologians, many of the Catholic people were shocked by the sudden and total exposure which has occurred as a result of Vatican Council II on the one hand, and of the communications explosion of our electronic age, on the other.

There is only one way to solve this dilemma, argued Bishop Paolo Muñoz Vega, administrator of Quito, Ecuador. There is no going back but only forward. What the Church needs is more theological study, with its corollary of more freedom for theologians in their investigations, in order to establish the truth about the many currently disputed issues. This viewpoint made a deep impression on those who recalled the evolution it represented for the speaker. At the Vatican Council, Bishop Muñoz Vega had opposed the declaration on religious freedom as calculated to encourage the spread of Protestantism in Latin America.

Bishop Muñoz Vega ended with a concrete proposal, namely, that a commission of theologians should be created. The ambivalent English prelate, Cardinal John Carmel Heenan, unexpectedly gave him a strong endorsement. It is not easy in our time to state with assurance what is and what is not true, he said. Instead of an attempt to provide definitive answers, we need a document outlining the evolution of Christian teaching. Instead of general condemnations, we should "have the humility" to admit that we don't know too much.

The focus was further sharpened by Cardinal Leo Joseph Suenens of Belgium, aged 63, a major architect of Vatican Council II, a man who combines traditional piety, a gentle manner, and a progressive and optimistic vision. In what was generally agreed to be one of the most incisive and constructive contributions to the debate, he paid tribute to the efforts of the authors of the document to understand contemporary thought. But, notwithstanding their efforts, the result was negative, and the atmosphere of the document was one of "feverish anxiety." It presented the Church as a city under siege, fearful of enemies attacking from all sides, enemies so poorly identified that it was hard to distinguish between them and one's friends. Thus, for example, no clear line was drawn between real errors and some unhappy expressions used by theological enquirers, and that was unfair to honest theologians. Similarly, "secularization" was condemned without adequate definition of the term. If it meant the exclusion of all religion, it was certainly condemnable; but it could also mean the legitimate autonomy of worldly values recognized by Vatican Council II. The documents of Popes John and Paul recognized new developments, and the distinction between faith and theology had always to be kept clear. The great truths of Christianity were the concern and the object of faith, while theology dealt with the interpretations given by specialists to those truths. At the present time, it was often difficult to know where to draw the line between the true and the false, between the basic certainties and the area of free opinion, between the unchangeable and the things that can and should change.

Rather than a decay of spiritual values, Cardinal Suenens summed up his thought, the Church is today witnessing a crisis of growth, a development which we should follow with sympathy and confidence. The proper course is to give credit to the theologians who have the courage to work on new problems and to thank them for their positive contribution, remembering that the studies of Father Marie-Joseph Lagrange, now reverenced as classics, upset many when they first appeared.

Cardinal Suenens next turned to Bishop Muñoz Vega's proposal of a commission of theologians and dramatically proposed carrying it a step further. The new body, he said, should be similar to an academy of physicians, nuclear scientists, or other professionals, its moral authority derived from the stature of its members. It should be representative of all schools and tendencies in theology and of all parts of the world. It would not act as a judge and jury on theological views, but as a scientific evaluator of the significance of new theories in its area of competence.

The response both within the Synod and outside was as electrifying as that to some of the great interventions which plotted the course of Vatican Council II. Even the special secretary of the Synod for the subject, Father Edward Dhanis, S.J., a consultor of the Congregation for the Faith, indicated in a nuanced speech that he was not by any means in full agreement with Cardinal Browne and the document. He repeated his reservations in a talk, outside the Synod, to African bishops and theologians.

To those in touch with the contemporary confusion and concern about religion, the Suenens comments make immediate sense. The man of today issues a basic challenge to the believer. What does it mean to believe, he asks. How can your claimed communication with God through losing yourself in Christ help to develop and expand my intelligence and my heart? The emptying of the churches has resulted in large part from the lack of a theological effort to answer these questions, and from the lack of a pastoral technique to convey such answers as exist. This is true of all Christians, but Roman Catholicism is particularly underdeveloped in the area. It is short on answers and even shorter on language to express them. In such a situation, a new syllabus of errors would be a gigantic error itself. All it could achieve would be a hastening of the exodus from the Church in search of truth elsewhere.

A series of interventions that followed Cardinal Suenens showed a convergence from many starting points toward his conclusions. Melchite Archbishop Edelby said it would be wrong to think that errors were as widespread as the document suggested. What was largely at issue were "individual deviations of third-rate theologians."

"Rome is not necessarily the best place for the proposed academy or commission to meet," commented Cardinal Paul Emile Léger, of Montreal, Canada. Now 63 years old, the Cardinal made himself known at the Vatican Council not only for his significant part in forming its spirit, but in particular for his open criticism of the antiquated mentality of the Curia. Just before leaving Canada at the end of September, 1967, for the Synod, he had another joust with it on the secrecy issue. "A badly informed conscience is a badly formed conscience," he told the press in an interview which sought to follow up the unsuccessful plea of the Conference of Canadian Bishops for an open Synod. In the debate, he offered a long and detailed criticism of the report. "Truth can never be imposed like a law. It is a mystery into which we must search. In this respect, the document is not in agreement with Vatican Council II. Its main defect is that it confuses errors with inadequacies of formulation of the truth. For example, when treating of atheism, it should not condemn anything, but should rather speak in a positive way about human dignity. Of course, there are difficult questions in the Church, but the basic question is what is the truth and what is the mystery still to be explored. It is not by a document of this kind but by an exploration conducted by the entire Church, with all its trends and at all its different levels, that we can hope to resolve the crisis."*

---

* Some days after the end of the Synod, Cardinal Léger announced that, with the Pope's agreement, he had resigned his office as archbishop, so that he could fulfill a long-standing desire to devote the rest of his life to work in a leper settlement in Africa.

Archbishop Denis Hurley, of Durban, South Africa, added an interesting suggestion. To ensure its professional independence and integrity, the proposed academy of theologians should not be organized by the hierarchy but should form its own structures in accordance with the law of liberty which is necessary for research.

Cardinal Bernard Jan Alfrink, of Utrecht, Holland, also pleaded for an atmosphere of freedom for theologians. "The official magisterium should encourage the men who dedicate their lives to this work," he said. "It would be appropriate to draft a document to express thanks to the theologians. That would be more useful than to draw up a catalogue of errors or even a list of the truths of faith." The Secretariat for Unity and the Biblical Commission should be represented on the proposed new commission or academy of theologians, he added, and "it is by no means necessary that it should meet in Rome." This was one of Cardinal Alfrink's few interventions at the Synod. The Dutch bishops kept in the background as much as possible. Under constant fire from the Curia since the Vatican Council as the instigators and propagators of dangerous theological theories, they felt it prudent to leave the initiatives to other bishops whose orthodoxy was unchallenged.

First reactions outside the Synod to the news that many favored a commission or academy of theologians was that the Fathers were simply trying to eliminate the Congregation for the Faith by leaving it with nothing to do. The reality is rather more complicated. What they were seeking was an answer to a dilemma which has been in the background of much of the conflict in and around the Church during and since Vatican Council II. How does an institution achieve self-criticism? Is not institutionalized criticism almost a contradiction in terms? It is a dilemma with which civil society has been faced since the coming of democratic forms. The answers have been varied and not always fully successful. They include the auditor general independent of the administration whose budgets and expenditures he revises, reporting to the legislature; the checks and balances of division of the executive, legislative, and judicial powers, with particular stress on the independence of the judiciary; the institution of the ombudsman, an official first introduced in Scandinavian countries and now being copied with various modifications elsewhere. He is the defender of the little man, his job to see that administrators do not abuse their discretion.

All such protective devices have long been absent from the practice and mentality of the Catholic Church, and only recently are we becoming conscious that the institution has suffered greatly from their absence. It is historically noteworthy that the ombudsman concept is a return to the institution known as *defensor civitatis* (protector of the town) first exercised by the pope and bishops in the sixth century, when Rome's imperial structures were breaking down. In the year 554, Emperor Justinian issued a pragmatic sanction authorizing Pope Virgilius to supervise the military and civil rulers, particularly in regard to levying taxes and administering justice. The direct purpose, in keeping with the concepts and needs of the period, was to protect the social order, but the indirect effect was to safeguard the rights of the citizen.

It was a role which the Church did not play for long. On the contrary, as seen from today's vantage point in the light of history, she has usually been counter-revolutionary, resentful and nagging in her relationship with the societal world. She has hesitated to speak out or waited until it was late, appearing to those who needed and were entitled to her words, as the ideological superstructure of the aggressor against the weak. The contrast between profession and reality has in recent centuries become so great as to prevent critical reflection within the institution, leading us to the current situation of theological reflection that sometimes ignores the institution, and an institution that often ignores theological reflection. It is a recognition of this deep defect that urged the Synod Fathers to support an independent body of theologians, not to replace the institution dealing with threats to the faith, but as a counterweight to its previously unchecked authority.

Noteworthy was the agreement of bishops from the third world with their colleagues from the more developed countries. Auxiliary Bishop Edward Pironio (47 years old), of La Plata, Argentina, confirmed Bishop McGrath's assertion that the document was quite incomprehensible to a Latin American mentality. The modern way of speaking, he said, is much more positive, and besides the document does not apply to the contemporary situation. In this age of secularization, he advised, the Church should preach the mystery of Christ, especially his humility and his poverty.

"Our people in Chile don't want to follow atheism, but they do want to do something against injustice," declared Bishop Bernardino Piñera Carvallo, of Temuco. "Marxism is not followed in Latin America because of its ideology but because of its practical approach to existing structures. Unfortunately, the Church has not done enough to change these structures, or even to change the mentality of its own members."

Archbishop Jean Zoa (aged 43), of Yaoundé, Cameroon, pointed out the danger of retaining traditional expressions deriving from European culture and practice when proclaiming the faith elsewhere. To describe the sacraments as achieving their effect *ex opere operato* (by the efficacy of the action itself), a phrase dear to the Scholastics and retained in many books of instruction, was very dangerous in Africa. Superstition was widespread in the old religions, and such a concept would inevitably carry it over into Christianity. Adaptation should accordingly be directed not only toward modern man but also toward emerging man. The proposed academy should undertake both these tasks, and it should also draw clearly the distinction between theology and faith and indicate what really belongs to the faith and what is merely theological opinion. This suggestion would seem to be very much in keeping with Vatican II's statement in the decree on Ecumenism, Article 11, that there is an order or hierarchy of the truths of the faith.

Cardinal Léon-Etienne Duval, of Algiers, at 64 one of the most world-minded of the Church's leaders, added an important new dimension to the discussion. The document, he said fails to reach a synthesis, and it does not understand the true mentality of today's Christians. They expect the Church to be visible to all as a sign of justice and charity in the world, and they want it to repudiate the self-centeredness of so many believers. "The Gospel seems today to be imprisoned by protocol," he added. "It is the whole Church and not merely the Pope that is called on to work for justice in the world. We must end the dispersion of forces that wastes our energies." Some read into these words a criticism of the continuing practice of placing the Pope apart as expert in his own right on all matters in his public pronouncements, as in the recent encyclical on world development, *Populorum Progressio,* instead of as the spokesman expressing the synthesis of the beliefs, the knowledge, and the wisdom of all Roman Catholics. A statement presented to the world by the Pope after dialogue with the faithful and expressing their active consensus would carry more weight today than the traditional encyclical conceived in conspiratorial secrecy, no matter how excellent its contents.

Cardinal Adrian Djajasepoetra, of Djakarta, Indonesia, said the document suggested that the magisterium was something existing outside the people of God and imposed from above on the community, an approach totally at variance with the teaching of Vatican Council II. "We should only formulate what is absolutely essential and say nothing negative about today's revolution in theology."

Bishop Paul Yoshigoro Taguchi, of Osaka, Japan, agreed. He praised the distinction made by Cardinal Suenens and others between faith and theology. Only the fundamental matters clearly pertaining to the deposit of the faith should be precisely formulated, leaving freedom for evolution in all other areas. He criticized the presentation of atheism as not describing accurately the kinds of atheism found in Japan.

Bishop Edward Nécsey, Apostolic Administrator of Nitra, Czechoslovakia, was also unhappy with the comments on atheism. The prime need for Christians, he said, is not only to preach but to practice charity and love. The classical proofs of God's existence are no longer acceptable to many, and a better approach is from the moral sense of man. Many atheists live in good faith. As for Catholics, while they have beautiful encyclicals, many fail to put their teaching into practice. Social justice is more effective than humanitarian efforts. Finally, as far as his country was concerned, such encyclicals as *Pacem in Terris* and *Populorum Progressio* were more beneficial than any doctrinal statements.

The absence of theological experts (*periti*) from the Synod made itself felt during this debate, especially when it touched on such complicated issues as secularization, demythization, atheism, and the death-of-God theology. In general, the bishops avoided being led into a theological discussion in which most of the professionals would be on the other side. In this way, the debate avoided becoming lost in technical details. Instead, the lines of cleavage were clearly drawn. What is the function of the magisterium and of authority in the Church? How free is the theologian in his work?

As already indicated, the consensus of the residential bishops was clear. The curial group did not, however, give up without a fight. It was able to count not only on most of the curial cardinals and their advisers but also on substantial support from the hierarchies of Italy and Spain, as well as from some African countries and some of the Uniate Churches of the East. It was obviously a small minority in comparison with the rest of the universal Church, but it remained sincerely convinced that warnings and condemnations are demanded by the circumstances of our times, and that the Church should have the courage to speak unpopular truths.

Under the rules of procedure, the first speakers were those who expressed the views of the episcopal conference which had elected them. Those who wanted to express personal views followed. The result was that the first days of the debate on the dangers to the faith heard mostly criticisms of the document, while on the final day there was a strong rally in its support. One who had supported it earlier was Cardinal Giuseppe Siri, of Genoa. His support surprised nobody. At Vatican Council II, he had been a leader of the minority on almost every issue on which the consensus of the Fathers had proved it to be out of touch with the mind of the Church. In addition, he was credited with having formulated the phrase with which the intransigents consoled themselves when the Pope promulgated the Council documents: "They are not definitions; they will never bind us."

Rallying now to the support of Cardinal Browne, he told the Synod that it was its duty to denounce the perils of the times, subjectivism, materialism, Pelagianism, and the rest. He warned in particular against "an idolatry of apostolic works," which he called a secularization of the Church. The magisterium is in crisis, he asserted. People should accept not only the solemn magisterium but also the non-infallible magisterium, because all doubts would be removed if everyone was sure about what Rome was saying. The irony of his position was apparently lost on himself, though hardly on those who recalled his reactions to the "non-infallible" statements of Vatican Council II. The logic of his position gives more weight to the statements of curial officials than to those of the bishops of the Church assembled in Council under the leadership of the Pope.

Father William Bertrams, S.J., elaborated on the deviations of theologians and their disrespect for the magisterium. A professor at the Gregorian University, Father Bertrams acquired a certain reputation at Vatican Council II as theological adviser to a small group of bishops opposed to the proclamation of collegiality. He is a consultor to the Congregation of the Council, to the Congregation of Religious, and to the Commission for the Revision of Canon Law. The Church, he said, is a supernatural society founded entirely on revealed doctrine objectively indicated. It is today suffering from a crisis of this "institutional character of the faith," a crisis that can be overcome by re-establishing the concept of the authority of the magisterium and the value of law. Father Luigi Ciappi, O.P., remembered for the extravagant Marian articles he used to publish in *L'Osservatore Romano* until Pope Paul cooled off the exuberances of that newspaper some years ago, deplored the disintegration of the historicity of the Bible. Father Ciappi is a consultor to the Congregation for the Faith, theologian to the Secretariat of State, Master of the Sacred Apostolic Palace, and an official of three other curial units. Bishop Donal Raymond Lamont, of Umtali, Rhodesia, a native of Belfast, Ireland, urged the introduction of a new publication to replace the recently suppressed Index of Prohibited Books. He thought the Commission for Social Communications would be the right body to run this blacklisting service.

Another who supported the curial position was Bishop Carlo Colombo, head of the theological faculty of Milan's major seminary, and reputed to be highly regarded by Pope Paul as a theologian. At the Vatican Council, he was a staunch supporter of collegiality, but on other issues he tended to be conservative or ambivalent. At the Synod he spoke at length of the dangers of "an anthropological rationalism" which overemphasized man's virtues and forgot the supernatural order. To combat this, he said, the magisterium should continually reaffirm supernatural faith. Theological study should be directed to showing that man's genuine dignity is not in the "humanization" of Christ but in the "divinization" of man. He proposed three rules to fix the relationship between the magisterium and theologians. The ordinary magisterium should be seen not as an obstacle to free research but as a light to guide the minds of the faithful. Proper academic freedom should be distinguished from the hasty publication of personal studies that could create astonishment and confusion. Bishops should learn how to exercise their pastoral office of calling theologians to order when they overstep themselves.

On October 7, the third day of the debate, Cardinal Juan Landážuri Rïcketts, of Lima, Peru, recommended the creation of a synodal commission to prepare a report synthesizing the views of the Synod on the situation. It was the first such commission requested under the rules of procedure, which provided for eight members to be elected by the Synod and four to be named by the Pope. It was in effect a vote of no confidence in the document prepared by the Congregation for the Faith, and a further assertion that the authors of that document could not be entrusted with the task of formulating the Synod's objections to it.

Cardinal Ottaviani took the microphone almost immediately to assure the Fathers that his Congregation was fully sensitive to their wishes and had in fact already absorbed the spirit and adjusted itself to the mind of Vatican Council II. It was a conciliatory speech, and one could not doubt the good faith of the old man. From his point of view, he had in fact made tremendous concessions. "We are all agreed that we should embark on a positive road," he said. "We are trying to establish a regular dialogue not only with the bishops, but with the professors of different schools of theology and universities. We have abolished the Index of Prohibited Books. We have brought back the profession of faith to the old formula of Nicea-Constantinople, with just some additions on the primacy of Peter, the magisterium and the sacraments.* Finally, we have eliminated the anti-Modernist oath." For some fifty years, all priests before ordination and bishops before consecration had to take an oath rejecting explicitly a long list of "Modernist" errors, and they had frequently to repeat it on assuming various offices. It had become to many a symbol as humiliating as the anti-Communist oaths demanded in various circumstances of holders of public and academic office in the United States.

Sensing the strength of the opinion in favor of the creation of a commission of theologians, as proposed by Bishop Muñoz

* See text p. 213, below.

Vega on the opening day of the debate, a proposal later endorsed and enlarged into an academy of theologians by Cardinal Suenens, Cardinal Ottaviani as a good politician chose what was for him the lesser of the two evils. "The proposal to set up a 'doctrinal commission in Rome' rather than a 'theological academy' is deserving of very careful consideration," he said.

He was to win on this point, but he did not divert the Fathers from their plan to create a synodal commission. The initial reaction to this proposal had been unenthusiastic, principally because nobody was sure how the voting would go. The overall tone of the debates had shown that there were two "parties," as there had been at the first session of Vatican Council II. The Synod debates had, nevertheless, indicated a much less marked separation of the two sides than at the Council, and there was so much flexibility in the presentation of viewpoints that neither side was anxious for a showdown. They had compromised, when dealing with the first agenda item, by informally agreeing to a committee of three members to sum up the debate. Gradually, however, it became obvious that the views on the second item were too contradictory to follow that precedent, and in consequence the rules of procedure were invoked.

Balloting on October 11 did not bring an absolute majority for any of the candidates. Those in the leading positions, however, were almost all critics of the Ottaviani-Browne thesis, and the trend was further confirmed the following day with the definitive election of Cardinal Franjo Seper (Yugoslavia), 140 votes; Bishop Carlo Colombo (Italy), 128; Bishop John Wright (U.S.A.), 110; Cardinal Julius Döpfner (Germany), 95; Cardinal Leo Josef Suenens (Belgium), 71; and Archbishop Neophyte Edelby (Syria), 69. It was a group clearly progressive yet basically moderate. Cardinal Seper was a member of the Theological Commission at Vatican Council II, and his interventions on atheism at the Council were widely commented. "Christians who defend the established order and the unchangeableness of social structures too stubbornly," he had said on one occasion, "are partly responsible for modern atheism." Bishop Wright of Pittsburgh, also a middle-of-the-roader, is publicly committed to the ideas of Teilhard de Chardin. Cardinal Döpfner was one of the nineteen cardinals who signed the historic letter to the Pope on religious freedom in October, 1964. Archbishop Edelby is famed for his blunt speech. "We must at all costs defend full freedom of theological expression," he declared in a recent conference in Rome.

Even more surprising, yet perfectly logical, were Pope Paul's choices to complete the commission. When election of a commission at Vatican Council II produced an overwhelming majority for the progressive side, the Pope eased the sting of defeat for the minority by naming some of its candidates as a counterbalance. On this occasion, by contrast, Pope Paul did not name a single member of the Curia. Instead, he ranged around the third world and came up with four excellent representatives. They were Bishop Muñoz Vega of Quito, Ecuador, a former rector of the Gregorian University, Archbishop Joseph Cordeiro, of Karachi, Pakistan, a specialist in relations with Islam, Cardinal Paul Zoungrana, of Ouagadougou, Upper Volta, and Bishop Paul Yoshigoro Taguchi, of Osaka, Japan. The choices were logical, but they also proclaimed an amazing displacement of power from the Roman center to the four corners of the globe. They announced that the Catholic Church had become catholic.

The commission, with Cardinal Seper as president, was given ten days to synthesize the debate and to formulate the principles and proposals to which it had given rise. All felt the time was very short, but it was necessary to complete the report quickly for evaluation of the results by the Synod, and in view of the pope's health, nobody was anxious to extend the life of the Synod beyond its projected 4-week duration.

The commission did in fact complete its task with laudable thoroughness and objectivity in the allotted time. Its report*

* See text p. 214, below.

contains three parts: a description of the current doctrinal situation, guiding pastoral principles for dealing with it; concrete suggestions.

In the effort to reformulate truth in terms meaningful today, as urged by Pope John and Vatican Council II, some "unwarranted innovations, false opinions and even errors in the faith" have appeared, the report states. Some call into doubt such truths of faith as "those concerning the knowledge we have of God, the person of Christ and his resurrection, the Eucharist, the mystery of original sin, the enduring objectivity of the moral law, and the perpetual virginity of the Blessed Virgin Mary." These problems, however, cannot be explained or resolved on an intra-Church basis, as — for example — by blaming the efforts of theologians or the failure of the magisterium to act. Their origin is to be sought rather in the nature of our civilization and the forward movement of culture, in "man's ever-increasing awareness of the evolution of the universe and of his own life and history."

Recalling the positive spirit of Vatican Council II, the report then formulated six principles calculated to remedy the dangers; continual preaching of the faith; exercise of the authentic magisterium by the bishops, both individually and collegially; a positive and pastoral stress in exercising the magisterium; free but responsible activity of theologians in cooperation with each other and with the bishops; prudence in diffusing new formulations of doctrine; and joining the witness of a Christian life to the witness of teaching.

Not only should preaching of the faith be richer and more generous, the report urged, but its presentation should be in the context of the specific advances in all fields of knowledge and taking into account the special problems of our times. This task "belongs first of all to the bishops, with their helpers in the priesthood, aided also by members of religious orders. But it also belongs to laymen engaged in teaching the faith and in catechizing; it belongs, in fact, to all the faithful, and in a special way to parents in regard to their children. All the children of the Church, therefore, each according to the charism given him, must be aware of their responsibility for passing on the holy gift of faith to the men of our time."

The Christian example urged in the final principle was presented as particularly important in the area of social and international justice and charity, so that the Church may be truly "a sign lifted up among the nations" (Is 11:12). Here reference was made specifically to Pope John's encyclicals, *Mater et Magistra* and *Pacem in Terris,* and to Pope Paul's *Populorum Progressio.*

Finally, the report formulated two proposals for submission to the Pope. One concerned the creation of a theological commission; the other, drawing up of a declaration on questions of faith. It proposed that the six principles already listed should be submitted as a unit for Synod approval, and that the two proposals be voted on separately.

The first proposal was in two parts, one concerning the composition and functions of the commission; the other, the method of selection of its members. Its membership would embrace "theologians of diverse schools, named for a definite term, of outstanding ability and recognized scholars, living in various parts of both the Western and Eastern Churches." It would be their task, "acting with proper academic freedom, to give their help to the Holy See and especially to the Congregation for the Doctrine of the Faith, principally in regard to doctrinal questions of major importance." As regards the method of selection, the Synod was asked if it approved the naming of the members by the Pope from lists drawn up by conferences of bishops after consultation with universities and theology faculties in the territory of each.

Finally, the Synod was asked if it wanted the Holy See to consult with the conferences of bishops and then draw up "a positive and pastoral declaration concerning questions involved in the contemporary doctrinal crisis, in order that the faith of the people of God be given sure guidelines."

Although some of the bishops were unhappy with a procedure which gave them no opportunity to consult the episcopal conference which had elected them, they gave overwhelming approval to the work of the synodal commission. The six principles were approved by 143 votes to 4, with 31 conditional approvals (*placet iuxta modum*). The creation of a commission of theologians was approved by 124 to 14, with 39 conditional approvals. Most of the conditional approvals included a request for an internal reform of the Congregation for the Faith by introducing theologians of all tendencies to participate in the discussions which precede its decisions. The point had been made by Cardinal Garrone during a discussion of the report the previous day that such a reform was urgently required. The naming of the members of the theological commission by the Pope on the recommendation of the bishops' conferences was approved by 137 to 18, with 23 conditional approvals; the "positive and pastoral declaration," by 139 to 8, with 31 conditional approvals.

An unanswered question is whether the Congregation for the Doctrine of the Faith will be given the task of drawing up this declaration. A strong indication, however, has been given that it will not. In reporting back to the Synod on the work of the commission he headed, Cardinal Seper stated: "It remains for us only to express the hope that a Catechetical Directory, as already requested by many of the Fathers, be prepared as soon as possible." The following day, Cardinal Jean Villot told the Synod that the Pope had asked him to say that his Congregation was about to do so. Cardinal Villot, formerly Archbishop of Lyons, was earlier in 1967 named head of the Congregation of the Council, the competent office for everything connected with catechetics. Explaining the nature and limits of his work, he said that catechetics is the ordinary instrument by which the Church carries out her mission of evangelization and salvation. It contains unchangeable revealed truths, as well as elements which can and should change according to the needs of the times. And even the unchanging truths must be presented in living fashion, effectively, in a manner conformable to the mentality of each age. The Congregation, he said, would prepare only a "general directory" to formulate and define the content of catechetics, giving particular attention to the part dealing with faith, and it would have to be supplemented by national or regional directories to apply the principles to local conditions. Moreover, the Congregation would have to do its part of the work in cooperation with bishops' conferences, so that it would be "a fruit of the collegiality of bishops proclaimed so solemnly by Vatican Council II." He asked for suggestions from all bishops' conferences by Easter, 1968. The suggestions would he said, be studied by a small group of experts to be named by the bishops' conferences, and the results would be incorporated into an outline which would again be sent to the bishops' conferences for further comment before publication.

The resulting document could very well become "the positive and pastoral declaration concerning questions involved in the contemporary doctrinal crisis." If not, it must almost inescapably determine the tone and direction of that document.

CHAPTER 5

Seminaries Open Their Windows

Cardinal Gabriel Garrone is the new man in the Curia. As Archbishop of Toulouse, France, he became known for his progressive positions. At the Council in November, 1964, he created a sensation by attacking the Congregation of Seminaries and Universities, then a citadel of conservatism, in terms recalling those used a year earlier about the Holy Office by Cardinal Frings. He urged decentralization, an increase in the authority of episcopal conferences over seminaries, a change in the rights and duties of the Congregation. "It must take more account of the needs of local countries. . . . It must no longer be behind the times or negative in its approach. . . . It should have as members men from all over the world. . . . It should be more open to progress and change in the sciences which pertain to seminary training. . . . Finally it should use the experience of men who are true experts in every field of higher learning."

In February, 1966, Pope Paul brought him to Rome in circumstances which few men would have had the humility and courage to accept. He was called to reform the Congregation he had criticized. But he was put in the number two spot, with the whole of the administration he had challenged still intact. Above him the 88-year-old Cardinal Pizzardo was still at his desk and insisted on signing everything. Below him, the permanent officials held to their attitudes and methods. Yet even in that sticky situation, he managed to do some significant things. Thus, he stopped the practice under which Italian Seminaries submitted every routine problem to the Congregation, even the issue of dismissing a student. "If his superiors can't decide," he insisted, "on what possible basis can we?"

Bit by bit, Pope Paul opened up the situation for him. He transferred Archbishop Dino Staffa, the secretary, to the innocuous Apostolic signatura (one of several Curial tribunals) on the death of Cardinal Ciriaci, then made him a cardinal in compensation. Bishop Joseph Schröffer, of Eichstätt, Germany, came in as secretary of the Congregation of Seminaries. In June, 1967, Archbishop Garrone reached a position of real power by being made cardinal. Although Cardinal Pizzardo remains technically the head as prefect, Cardinal Garrone as proprefect makes the decisions and sees that they are carried out. It is he who attended the Synod as rapporteur for the agenda item on seminary reform. He not only presented but signed the report introducing the discussion.

Another Frenchman, Cardinal Jean Villot, Archbishop of Lyons, was persuaded to become head of the Congregation of the Council. The double blow to Roman domination of the Curia was too much for the Roman neo-Fascist weekly *Il Borghese,* known equally for its *Playboy*-type color photos and its intransigent opposition to the memory of Pope John and all he stood for. It ran several articles denouncing "the escalation of the French Soviet" in the Vatican, renaming the building near St. Peter's which houses the two Congregations "Avignon," in mock tribute to the French city in which the popes were "exiled" in the fourteenth century.

As part of his apprenticeship, Cardinal Garrone in 1966 and 1967 traveled widely in Europe and in North and South America, visiting seminaries and discussing their problems with bishops, rectors, professors, and students. If his travels omitted Africa and Asia, that resulted neither from lack of energy nor lack of interest. Seminaries in mission territories come under the Congregation for the Missions and are thus excluded from his jurisdiction. Similarly, those of religious orders and congregations come under the Congregation of Religious. This tripartition of seminary training was severely criticized at the Council, and many expect it to be corrected soon.

At the Congress for the Renewal of Theology in Toronto, in August, 1967, Cardinal Garrone made a rather negative impression at a press conference. He was apparently being overcautious as a result of European misconceptions about the ways of the press in North America, so that his answers tended to be unduly noncommittal. He did, nevertheless, make one very clear and significant statement. Asked what concrete measures he planned for seminary renewal, he said he really had none. It was not his job, he explained, to work out plans for seminaries all over the world. That was the job of the local conferences of bishops. They were the only ones who knew the situation, and consequently only they could take the right steps. His job was mainly to spur the conferences to action, and to help them by interchange of ideas.

The similarity of this program to what he proposed during Vatican II is evident. It brings into the open what is perhaps the most profound of the philosophic issues dividing the Church today. The efforts to decentralize Church government are often presented as primarily a struggle for power, a new attack by the barbarians on the majesty of Rome. Since human beings are involved, one cannot eliminate vested interests. But that is not the crux of the matter. The real issue concerns the nature of creation.

In the traditional Catholic view, a view acceptable in a primitive and medieval society in which man's control of his environment was marginal, God created the world in a single act, in six days, as Genesis puts it. At that time, he gave to each thing its nature and functions, with man at the highest pinnacle of creation, lord of everything else, but himself subject to a series of rules established by God. The next step, also reasonably logical, was to see the central government of the Church as the definer and interpreter of these rules, with the Roman Congregations as the operating structures for that purpose. From there it was a short jump to the situation in which the Congregation of Religious was presumed to be a better judge of the vocation of a young man whom none of its members had ever seen, than the seminary superiors under whose guidance he had lived for years.

During the past four centuries, man's control of his environment has grown steadily as a result of forces which the Catholic Church had played a major part in setting in motion. The Church, however, resisted the change it had induced. In particular, it fought the idea of evolution, the theory developed in the nineteenth century which sees creation as a continuing operation, in which all men are called to participate actively, a process destined to continue to the end of history. Thanks to the initiatives of the French Jesuit Teilhard de Chardin, a significant part of progressive Catholic thought learned to absorb this interpretation of creation. The so-called Roman theology, nevertheless, continues to resist it, as was seen at the Council and as had become still clearer at the Synod. If Cardinal Garrone wants the conferences of bishops to take the initiative in training the seminarians in each country, it is because he sees the entire Church, and not simply the Congregation he heads, as involved in perfecting this portion of the world.

When his turn came to present his ideas as rapporteur for the third item of the agenda on October 11, Cardinal Garrone quickly transformed the mood of bishops who had been somewhat distressed by the negative stance adopted by the final brace of speakers of the previous debate on doctrine. He did not gloss over the seriousness of the situation facing seminaries but he did not have to delay over it either. Everyone knows how deep the seminary crisis is, he averred, and all agree that there must be a different kind of seminary training, both to answer the pastoral needs of the people and to take care of the spiritual, intellectual, and emotional problems of the young celibate himself.

Let us start from the facts, he said. The first fact is that we have a mandate from Vatican II, which "daringly decided a true change" of seminary methods, and decided it unanimously. The next fact is the character of today's youth. "It is clear to see," he said, "that the ways of being, the qualities and the tendencies of youth, even if they sometimes upset us, are a function of the great changes of our times. Even if the young people themselves sometimes misunderstand them or are imprudent in their ways of putting them into effect, these aspirations express the reality of the world of our times and open it up for us. Educators must recognize the signs of the times."

Building on this exposition, the Cardinal told the Fathers he would appreciate, on behalf of the Pope, their views on two issues: decentralization and the training of seminary directors.

As he read the directives of the Vatican Council, he said, they clearly called for the most extensive decentralization in the matter of seminary regulation. The episcopal conferences should work out the reform of the seminaries in the territory of each, so that local needs and conditions would receive prime consideration. The bishops should stop referring "the most trivial questions" to Rome for solution. Instead, they should engage in dialogue with those in charge of the seminaries and between them work out the programs of seminary study and training.

As for the Roman Congregation, he proposed that it should henceforth conceive its primary task to be one of encouraging and inspiring local initiatives. It might, if the bishops so desired, work out a set of general directives as a framework within which the individual conferences would proceed. He also suggested the creation in each country or region of a technical committee of seminary rectors and professors to be responsible for reform, and an annual meeting in Rome of those in charge of seminary updating in each country.

On the training of personnel, the Cardinal noted that up to now, the main stress had been on training professors, but that it was necessary to take a broader view and train educators capable of "understanding the young and developing them in terms of today's needs by passing on to them the wisdom of the Church." The students, he said, should play a major part in their own training, living as teams and following courses that would bring them into contact with the world outside the seminary. The philosophic and theological content of their studies should be renewed, stressing particularly a broader unity in their theological knowledge. The teaching of doctrine should be oriented toward contact with real life, and avoid a speculative approach that amounted to the satisfaction of intellectual curiosity rather than progress in spiritual insights.

Another suggestion made by Cardinal Garrone was that the teaching staff of seminaries should include laymen, a practice which is already established in some countries, for example, the United States and Japan. Professional schools should, he said, be established to give specialized training to seminary teaching staffs and spiritual directors, who even in the Roman ecclesiastical universities currently receive no significant training in the pedagogic and psychological sciences. The reason for this, he added, is that future priests will need an interior spiritual life based on a fully adult faith that is not imparted by present seminary routines.

The Cardinal summed up by asking the views of the bishops on three points. Should a year of specialized graduate training be made a universal precondition for any kind of work in a seminary, whether as professor, rector, or spiritual director? Should every country establish its own institute to train such personnel? Should they look for the help of specialized institutes, like the Sulpician Fathers, who have for centuries made seminary work their special vocation?

The Cardinal's report, although relatively brief, evoked an overwhelmingly favorable response from the Fathers. A clear consensus favored the formulation of principles on the basis of which the conferences of bishops would draft their own rules, the creation by each country of a technical committee of professors and superiors, an annual congress in Rome, specialized training for professors and spiritual directors, and all possible help from such institutions as the Sulpicians.

Thomas Cardinal Cooray of Ceylon agreed in his comment that current seminary education still followed the principles of the Council of Trent excessively, isolating seminarians from the life of the surrounding civil and parochial community and stifling their personality. He questioned, however, the wisdom of having too many meetings at all levels, especially an annual congress in Rome, on the ground that this would absorb too much of the time of too many of the best people. Alfred Cardinal Bengsch of Berlin agreed on this point, while approving of more contact between students and staff, as well as a better training of spiritual directors, the training to include substantial pastoral experience.

Archbishop Denis Hurley, of Durban, South Africa, urged closer cooperation between diocesan seminaries and those of religious communities. "The seminary training should produce specialists," said Cardinal Suenens of Belgium. "We must rethink the role of the priest radically, and stop envisaging him as a kind of monk. On the other hand, the day of the priest who turns his hand to any kind of work is gone. We must go for top qualifications, specialization, and 'shared responsibility' with the bishop." In a similar vein, Cardinal Alfrink of Holland said that each country's circumstances differed and the training must differ accordingly. "We are in an era of uncertainty and research. The classical methods of information have ceased to be viable. What works today is experimentation."

Confirmation of the need for an approach to meet each situation came from all sides. "In the countries in which the Church is persecuted, the students should learn a trade," said

Joseph Cardinal Slipyi, Ukrainian Archbishop of Lwow. Archbishop Paul Nguyen Van Binh of Saigon, Vietnam, and Archbishop Gilbert Ramantoanina, of Fianarantsoa, Madagascar, urged that seminarians and seminary personnel of mission countries should as far as possible be trained in their homelands "to avoid the uprooting which occurs when they are sent to Europe or America." This nevertheless would not be easy because of the limited facilities for specialized training in mission countries. Bishop Román Arrieta Villalobos, of Tilarán, Costa Rica, agreed on the desirability of steeping the seminarian to the greatest extent in the culture of his own region.

The same point was taken up in a slightly different context by Bishop Joseph Kuo, of Taipei, Taiwan. "Students educated in Rome should return home to complete their studies," he said. The problem here is that the most brilliant students of mission countries spend ten years in a different culture and a different world, at the Palace of Propaganda Fide in Rome and the summer villa at Castel Gandolfo. The impact of this long immersion in an alien culture is so extreme that many never again feel at home among their own people.

Another frequently recurring concern was expressed succinctly by Archbishop Adam Kozlowiecki, of Lusaka, Zambia. "Training cannot be completed in the seminary. It must continue indefinitely afterwards." The need for spiritual as well as professional training was likewise stressed. "Let us be suspicious of activism," said Archbishop George Dwyer, of Birmingham, England. "Let us train students in contemplation." The same point was made by Bishop Fulton Sheen of Rochester, New York, who drew applause when he declared that seminarists must learn once again to understand the meaning of the cross. It was the first intervention of the Synod to be applauded.

Several bishops carried the debate even beyond the projections made by Cardinal Garrone, especially in an area in which considerations of protocol undoubtedly had held him back. It would have been indelicate for him to raise the issue of the seminarians who come under the Congregation of Religious and those under the Congregation for the Missions. The one who did this was Archbishop François Marty, of Reims, France. "We must build a bridge," he said, "between the Congregation of Seminaries and the other two Roman Congregations which are concerned with making regulations for the education of seminarians." One had simply to look round the hall to appreciate the point. Of the 180 diocesan bishops present at the Synod, only 100 come under Cardinal Garrone, and it is no secret that the conciliar updating achieved by his Congregation has not been paralleled in the other two.

Yet another important point was raised by Archbishop Marty, a question to which nobody attempted to give an answer. "How do we involve the whole people of God, including the laity, in the training of candidates for the priesthood?" It was perhaps an auspicious coincidence that at almost the same moment as Archbishop Marty was asking the question, the Synod received a telegram from the Congress for the Lay Apostolate which had just started a week of meetings in Rome. It expressed the desire of the laity to work according to their own special vocation, in close union with the bishops, in the spirit of Vatican II. Archbishop Marty subsequently elaborated his point in a press conference. "Lay people," he said, "should play an important part in the training of future priests. They can help us to discover the characteristics which go to make a priest for today's world, because they know very well the kind of priests they need. We have to establish an active and positive dialogue with them before we ordain candidates." Here it is worth noting that Bishop Fulton Sheen has made a concrete move in this direction in Rochester, New York, by including lay people on boards which decide whether or not to admit seminarians to the priesthood.

The value of minor seminaries was questioned by Bishop Bernardino Piñera Carvallo, of Temuco, Chile. "We get more vocations out of Catholic Action," he said. Another Latin

American prelate, Cardinal José Maurer, of Sucre, Bolivia, raised yet a further issue. "We are very grateful to the Spanish hierarchy for sending priests to work in our continent," he said. "Some of them, however, do not seem to be completely adapted to the situation in my country and consequently sometimes show a tendency to want to change the existing ecclesiastical structures."

After the bishops from around the world, speaking in the name of their respective episcopal conferences, had had their say, came the turn of the Fathers who wanted to express their personal viewpoints. While the overwhelming majority of the former had supported the program proposed by Cardinal Garrone, the latter — on the contrary — tended to be strongly critical, pointing up once more the time-lag between the mind of the Curia and that of the residential bishops.

Cardinal Ottaviani drew some very fine distinctions. The lack of serious formation can lead priests to grave deviation from the right path, he said, and the fact that so many priests are in difficulties today shows that more screening of vocations is required, stressing quality above quantity. Family background is important in his opinion, and every means available — short of psychoanalysis — should be used to get an accurate evaluation of each candidate's character. Spiritual directors should have a training that would enable them to discern whether outside influences rather than a true vocation were keeping a young man in the seminary. But if changes of this kind were desirable, discipline should always be retained in order to control the liberty of the students. And as for "mixed education," that was out of the question.

Cardinal Ottaviani was not by any means alone in his insistence on discipline. Archbishop Casimiro Morcillo González of Madrid, Spain, had earlier provoked a substantial and constructive discussion by saying that "vocations tend to decline in seminaries which open up to modern demands, while on the contrary they become more numerous in those which are more austere." There was general agreement that a seminary requires a degree of discipline and control, but that the continuance of outdated regulations was as sure a way of emptying a seminary as was the absence of discipline. In addition, undue strictness was fatal for the strong personalities most valuable in the contemporary apostolate.

Father Luigi Ciappi, O.P., consultor of the Congregation for the Faith, Master of the Sacred Palace, theologian for the Secretariat of State, and holder of several other curial positions, said he questioned the juridical value of the principle formulated in Cardinal Garrone's report. As master of the Sacred Palace, Father Ciappi is, according to the Vatican Yearbook, "the pope's confidential theologian." Only the Council decree has the force of law he said, and it ordered the preservation of that philosophical patrimony which had a lasting value. The Council decree referred back to Pius XII's encyclical *Humani generis* of 1950, and it was in that doctrinal statement rather than in an exhortation of the Congregation of Seminaries that the bishops should look for guidance. Father Ciappi further expressed regret that doubt was now being cast on the value of classical metaphysics, and he asked if — in the light of *Humani generis* — the insistence on present-day philosophical trends made it lawful to substitute a new metaphysics for the classical form. He also said that the wrong kind of books were getting into seminary libraries and that many lacked volumes encouraging genuine philosophical and theological research. In addition, superiors were not always as prudent as they should be in selecting students to go to State universities for a doctorate of philosophy, while at the same time, the total number of students so trained should be increased in order to provide a more effective defence against modern errors and assure fruitful contact with contemporary culture.

For Father Ciappi, as was evident in this intervention, it was unthinkable that there should be a substantive change in theological thinking; or that the Fathers at Vatican II could really have been serious when they reversed the directives given in *Humani generis* and other papal documents. Yet that is precisely what they did, and the specificity and decisiveness of their action were limelighted by the last-ditch fight to prevent it led by the then secretary of the Congregation of Seminaries, Archbishop Staffa. While it was proper to begin from "a philosophical heritage which is perennially valid," they declared in the Decree on Priestly Formation, it was no longer enough. The students should also be conversant with contemporary philosophical investigations, especially those exercising special influence in their own country, and with recent scientific progress.

The end of the debate, nevertheless, left Cardinal Garrone clearly in possession. Agreeing with Cardinal Garrone and disassociating himself from Father Ciappi's views, Archbishop Marty outlined subsequently in a press conference what were the directives given by Vatican II for the training of seminarians. It called, he said, for a missionary spirit, a communitary spirit, and a priestly and well-balanced life. The missionary spirit would enable them to announce the Gospel to all men within the framework of the human and social milieu of each. The priest being at the service of all men for the work of light and grace, he must authenticate the word of God and apply it to human life. He must serve grace through the sacramental life. The communitary spirit will enable priests to live and work in union with the bishops whose co-workers they are, in sacramental brotherhood with other priests, in authentic and profound dialogue with all Christians and even harmony with those who do not believe. The well-balanced priestly life expresses itself as much in the activity of the ministry as in the priest's own individual life. It enables him to be both open and serene.

CHAPTER 6

Marriages Are Still Mixed

"You might as well try to square the circle as hope to find a perfect solution of the problem of mixed marriages." Such was the conclusion expressed by Cardinal Lorenz Jaeger, of Paderborn, Germany, after several days of Synod debate on the subject. Of the five issues on the agenda, this was definitely the one that caused the bishops most trouble. The range of viewpoints was extremely wide, and few were confident that their opinion was the correct one.

The ambiguity began with the document prepared beforehand for the guidance of the Fathers. It was the joint work of two curial bodies whose divergences are a matter of public record, the Congregation for the Faith and the Secretariat for Christian Unity. The Secretariat has from its establishment by Pope John in 1966 specialized in the study of the theological and pastoral problems raised by the ecumenical movement, engaging in a constructive dialogue with other Christian bodies, and opening up vistas and possibilities previously overlooked. The Congregation for the Faith, however, still claims final jurisdiction over mixed marriages, a reality which had its symbolic expression in the choice of the rapporteur and his secretary, Cardinal Paolo Marella and Msgr. Joseph Tomko, both attached to this Congregation.

Since the Council, tension between Catholics and other Christians has increased on the issue, in spite of important ecumenical advances elsewhere. In November, 1964, the Fathers discussed a proposal that would liberalize significantly the regulations for marriage of a Catholic with a Christian belonging to a body issued from the Protestant Reformation. Only the Catholic party would have to undertake to use all reasonable means to raise the children as Catholics. The local bishop could give a dispensation making a marriage before a Protestant minister valid. A Catholic married before a Protestant minister would no longer be excommunicated. Mixed marriages in a Catholic Church would have the same solemnities as marriages between Catholics. After a debate which showed strong support for the proposal, the Council Fathers voted by 1,492 to 496 to pass the matter to the pope, so that he would "very quickly make a decision, . . . thereby saving time."

The implementing instruction of March 18, 1965, fell far short of the terms of the Council proposal. Though the Protestant partner need no longer undertake to raise the children as Catholics, he must promise not to obstruct the Catholic spouse in his performance of this duty, a promise normally in writing but made orally by permission of the local bishop. And if the Protestant cannot in conscience give this undertaking, there is provision for an appeal to Rome for a dispensation. Dispensation to permit marriage before a Protestant minister is also reserved to Rome. The other two points are substantially authorized.

Protestant reaction was very negative. "The Instruction marks some progress," said Pastor W. A. Visser 't Hooft, then secretary general of the World Council of Churches, "but it falls short of what could have been expected after the promulgation of the Declaration on Religious Freedom, the Decree on Ecumenism, and particularly the discussion of the problem of mixed marriages at the Vatican Council. The difficulties which the previous regulations created for the non-Catholic party to a proposed marriage are eliminated only in very small measure." The Instruction, Dr. Visser 't Hooft added, could not be reconciled with the principle enunciated in Par. 5 of the Declaration on Religious Freedom that "parents have the right to determine, in accordance with their own religious beliefs, the kind of religious education that their children are to receive."

A brief historical background will help to clarify the issues. Up to the sixteenth century, exchange of consent between the parties was all that was needed for a valid marriage. The Council of Trent made the presence of a priest a condition for validity in certain countries, an obligation extended in 1908 by Pius X to all countries except Austria, Hungary, and Holland. These three exceptions were eliminated when the Code of Canon law was promulgated in 1917. The discipline, as established in the Code of Canon Law of 1917 for the Western Church, compelled both parties to undertake to raise the children as Catholics, made the presence of a priest obligatory for validity, and arranged for mixed marriages to be celebrated without solemnity, and normally in the sacristy. In 1949, the presence of a priest for validity was extended to marriage between a Catholic and an Orthodox, but this restriction was revoked, in major part in 1964 and totally in 1967, as a result of initiatives taken at the Council. Cardinal Frings, of Cologne, Germany, suggested at the Council that the Western Church should return to the pre-Tridentine practice, but that proposal then found no serious support.

Thanks to the dialectic interplay of the two teams, from the Congregation of the Faith and the Secretariat for Unity respectively, in the preparation of the document to be studied in advance by the Synod Fathers, the result was a true "working paper" in the sense in which the term is used at the United Nations or other international assemblies. It set out the issues, indicating the possible solutions, but leaving it to the meeting to draw conclusions and make decisions. If there was a problem, it was that it was late in completion and circulated to the bishops' conferences only in August, so that many of them had no time to give it the study it merited. The delay in distribution also resulted from the tension between the two Congregations, a tension that goes back to Vatican II. The Congregation for the Faith had originally succeeded in having itself named as drafter of the working document on mixed marriages to be presented to the Synod. The Secretariat for Unity, which has been in constant discussion with the World Council of Churches on the subject, as on many others, opposed the draft as calculated to undermine its work, and asked to be allowed to prepare a counter-document. Instead, Pope Paul adopted a procedure already used by Pope John in 1962, naming a mixed group of the two Congregations, with the results just indicated, namely, a balanced and objective statement of position.

The statement opened by insisting that the Church today takes its teaching mission as seriously as it always has, and that it recognizes its obligation to defend truth and the faith of its members. It then proclaims the importance of the family, "definitely the breeding ground of the Church, so to speak," and of marriage, "from which comes the family, and which the Apostle assures us is a sign of the union of Christ with the Church."

The Church's different attitudes to different kinds of marriage were then explained. A marriage of a Catholic to an Anglican or a Protestant is not governed by the same legal rules as one between a Catholic and a person who is not baptized. The difference is based on the double fact that the former is a sacrament and that a "partial communion" exists between the partners because of their common baptism and their sharing of other elements of the Christian patrimony, as set out by Vatican II in the Constitution on the Church and in the Decree on Ecumenism.

Marriage of a Catholic and an Orthodox is accorded an even higher status, because of the close identity in doctrine and sacramental practice of their two Churches, a point also stressed by Vatican II.

After this preamble, the document asked eight questions, two dealing with terminology, two with the undertakings (*cautiones*) to be given before marriage, two with the legal form, and two with pastoral aspects. The first question asked if the expression "mixed marriage" should not be changed, because of the ambiguity of the word *mixed*. It can mean people of different sexes or different races, being commonly used in the latter sense in the United States. More importantly, as the document observes, "the term does not express any objective reality and it implies a denial of Christian communion between two Christian bodies." The Orthodox dislike it particularly "because in using it the Catholic Church seems to deny to them that very wide communion of faith and sacramental life which it clearly affirms in other official documents."

Assuming agreement on the need for change, two possible expressions were offered in the second question, "interconfessional marriage" for one between Christians, and "unequal marriage" (*dispar*) for one between a Catholic and an unbaptized person.

The third question contained two parts. To give a dispensation, is it enough that the competent authority is morally certain (1) that the Catholic party is in no danger of losing the faith and is prepared to do everything possible to have the children baptized and raised as Catholics; and (2) that the other party recognizes the obligation in conscience of the Catholic and does not exclude the baptism and education of the children in the Catholic faith? The question is basic, and no satisfactory answer seems in sight. Where marriage is concerned, the ecumenical rule of "equal standing," laid down by Pope Pius XII and observed in the meetings of Pope Paul and Patriarch Athenagoras has not hitherto applied, and even the new document does not concede it. It would transfer the obligation from the legal order to that of conscience, but giving a priority to the Catholic conscience.

The fourth question asked if the canonical prohibition of mixed marriages without a dispensation should be abrogated; the fifth, if the "canonical form" (presence of a priest) should also go. Is it possible to recognize the sacramental validity of every marriage, even a civil one, contracted between two baptized persons? This would be to return to the situation before the Council of Trent, with the difference that Trent was particularly anxious to avoid secret marriages, a matter now handled by the civil authorities. It is perhaps indicative of some evolution in the Catholic attitude that the Congregation for the Faith in June, 1967, authorized a marriage without the canonical form between a Catholic and a non-baptized person professing no religion, subject to the condition that the marriage would be neither private nor secret, and that there would be at least a civil ceremony. The sixth question, subsidiary to the fifth, was that if the canonical form is retained, should the bishop have power to dispense, a power now reserved to Rome. The Council indicated in 1964 its desire for this change.

Finally, the two pastoral issues. Since at present a mixed marriage can be celebrated either during Mass or outside the Mass, would it be desirable to have a special form of liturgical service for marriages between Catholics and Protestants, a form that would fully respect the religious consciences of both parties? And what kind of preparation should the parties have before the marriage and perhaps also after the marriage, to ensure a Christian home in which both would develop and help the other to expand their common Christian faith?

It was a cause of considerable surprise at the Synod on October 17, when Cardinal Marella introduced the discussion with his report on the issues. Unlike the previous rapporteurs, he departed not only from the text but from the spirit of the "working document," coming out forcibly instead for the original position of the Congregation for the Faith and urging a continuation without significant change of the existing regulations. Many regarded his action as a failure to observe the conventions and a political blunder on the part of the Congregation for the Faith. Having collaborated, on the instructions of the Pope, in the formulation of a common document, they had chosen to abandon the agreed position without paying the Secretariat for Unity the courtesy of consulting or even notifying it.

The first major change made by Cardinal Marella was that he started from the abstract principle of the safeguarding of the faith and the "rights" of doctrine, instead of starting with the rights of persons, a change all the more curious since Scholastic philosophy itself recognizes that only persons have rights. He asserted that the only choice is a single and universal legislation for mixed marriages, excluding the possibility of a degree of pluralism in keeping with different local conditions. He came down roundly in favor of retaining the canonical form (the presence for validity of a Catholic priest), as well as the undertaking by the non-Catholic party to raise the children as Catholics. He reintroduced arguments drawn from the Old Testament which by agreement had been dropped from the earlier document. They concerned marriage between a Jew and a pagan, and the Secretariat for Unity had pointed out that they had no bearing on marriages between two Christians. Nevertheless, Cardinal Marella now insisted that they had "an indirect value."

The shift of approach in this report of Cardinal Marella from that of the document sent the Fathers in August was so total that the second speaker in the debate asked outright which of the two should be taken as the basis for discussion. He was Cardinal Justin Darmajuwana, Archbishop of Semarang, Indonesia, and he showed his clear preference for the earlier document. The Church should declare openly that the spouses have a true and common responsibility for their own religious life and that of their children. The Church through its pastors should try to help them to make conscientious decisions and resolve their problems. "It would seem desirable," he added, "to put an end to the *cautiones* or unilateral promises. This is an extremely complex and serious matter, and its resolution calls for clear ideas and formulae which do not seem to exist in the report. Bishops and episcopal conferences should be given more freedom."

Bishop Thomas Cahill, of Cairns, Australia, expressed himself in similar but more limited terms. He urged that the present law be revised, so that moral persuasion would take priority over juridic rules. The canonical form should not be necessary for validity, although he favored forbidding marriage without the canonical form, so that a Catholic who neglected it would be doing wrong. To replace the legal promises he proposed an exhortation. All of his proposals, he explained, had a pastoral purpose, namely, to reduce the scandal caused by the high number of invalid mixed marriages under the present system. And on one point he clearly differed with Cardinal Darmajuwana. Dispensations related to regulations affecting validity should continue to be reserved to Rome. The only dispensation to be allowed to bishops would be to have a second ceremony in a Protestant church.

As this intervention already suggests, the residential bishops are themselves deeply divided on the best way to deal with mixed marriages, their views often lacking internal coherence because based on a variety of special situations which urge one method of solving one problem and a contradictory method of solving another. It seemed clear from the outset of the debate that there was little likelihood of a consensus. Nevertheless, the air was cleared on several matters, and some imporant related issues were also ventilated.

Archbishop Zoa of Yaoundé, Cameroon, thought the canonical impediment could be eliminated, namely, the obligation to get a dispensation to enter a mixed marriage, while noting that it would be advisable to study the steps to be taken in terms of the procedures of the Church to which the other party belonged. In this way, the authorities of both Churches would be in agreement from the outset. He thought the canonical form (presence of a priest) should be retained, but with faculties to the bishop to dispense in his diocese without having to apply to Rome. He further observed that in countries in which polygamy is common, it was far more urgent to give people an understanding of the beauty and goodness of Christian marriage than to make rules for mixed marriages.

Archbishop Adam Kozlowiecki, of Lusaka, Zambia, went all the way down the line with Cardinal Marella. The new code should have precise canonical norms. Young people should have the difficulties of a mixed marriage driven home to them, and they should be told that marriage is a serious matter, not the fulfillment of a dream or the gratification of a passion. The current forms should be retained, especially the undertakings, in the terms of the 1966 Instruction. The present canonical form should not be changed. The faith of the Catholic partner, he said, is endangered both by marriage with another Christian and by marriage with a nonbaptized person. Coadjutor Archbishop Angelo Fernandes of New Delhi, India, expressed a similar viewpoint, though in less extreme terms. "No changes in existing canonical legislation . . . the canonical form should be preserved . . . local bishops should not have authority to dispense."

The above interventions were made on October 16, the first day of the discussion on mixed marriages. Seventeen Fathers spoke the second day, all of them on behalf of their respective episcopal conferences, and the total effect was to confirm the multiplicity of viewpoints, with the speakers breaking down into two broad categories, those favoring the retention of the present legislation, and those seeking modifications which would stress more the common Christianity of all the baptized and recognize more fully the rights of conscience of the non-Catholic spouse.

Those in the first category included Archbishop John Dearden, of Detroit, and Archbishop Philip Pocock, of

Toronto. Underlying their position is the practical argument that the present arrangement has stood the test of time. It is clear, and it is administratively easy to operate. For that reason, Archbishop Dearden said that the United States bishops wanted the matrimonial impediments to be retained in their present form including the canonical form for validity. The only change they sought was that the bishops be authorized to dispense. Archbishop Pocock spoke in almost the same terms, recommending the retention of the present form "because otherwise many marriages will be exposed to grave uncertainties." He also thought that bishops should have authority to grant dispensations, as being in a better position to judge the requirements of particular cases than an authority at a distance. Archbishop Pocock added a personal note. Some of the earlier speakers, he said, had painted a very negative picture of the impact on religion of the growing number of mixed marriages as a result of the increased mobility of modern life. "The picture is not wholly black," he observed. "I am myself the offspring of a mixed marriage." The reference was to one of his grandparents.

The speaker who expressed himself most totally in favor of retention of the present rules was Archbishop John Baptist Theunissen, of Blantyre, Malawi, a native of Holland. Only one satisfactory solution to the problem of mixed marriages exists, he said, and that is "the full restoration of Christian unity." While divisions remained, the instruction issued in 1966 provided sufficiently both for the needs of Catholics and for their relationships with other Christians, subject to some adaptation of the general directives to local conditions. It was necessary, he said, to insist on the obligation of the parents to ensure the Catholic education of the children, and that called for promises in writing. The canonical form should be required for validity because it safeguards the sacred character of marriage and facilitates the Catholic education of the children. All dispensations from the form should be reserved to the Holy See. It would be a cause of confusion for the faithful to permit a non-Catholic clergyman to officiate at a marriage in a Catholic church.

A very different approach was urged by other bishops, many of them from northern and north-western Europe, especially Germany, France, Holland, and Belgium. In their view, the present system is made by lawyers for the convenience of lawyers, rather than by pastors for the benefit of those in their charge. It is concerned more with the marriages that don't work out than with those that do. While achieving an external order, it hides many abuses. Vatican Council II eliminated the application of the canonical form (presence of a Catholic priest) in the case of marriages of a Catholic with an Orthodox "so as not to multiply the number of invalid marriages," and the argument is that the marriage legislation of the Western Church since the Reformation similarly tends to multiply abusively the number of invalid marriages.

The pastoral position was presented at length on behalf of the French hierarchy by Bishop Pierre Puech, of Carcassonne. On the issue of the canonical form, a difference of opinion exists within the French hierarchy. However, the bishops who would like to eliminate the present rule requiring the presence of a Catholic priest for validity of the marriage carry particular weight, Bishop Puech said, because they are the ones in whose dioceses most mixed marriages take place. They would be the bishops in the eastern part of the country, near the borders of Germany and Switzerland. They believe that mixed marriages celebrated in the churches of the major Protestant denominations should be recognized as valid. In France, these denominations — as has been established by recent ecumenical dialogue — give every assurance as regards the indissolubility of marriage.

The second point made by Bishop Puech was that great concern is expressed over marriages between Catholics and Protestants, but not nearly enough over what is much more common in France, namely, marriage between a practicing Catholic and one who is merely nominal. It is well known that in

France, as in other countries which have a high proportion of so-called traditional Catholics, it is common to grant a Church wedding without any assurance that the parties really have the faith, that some priests simply skirt the issue to avoid social embarrassment.

Bishop Puech's final point was that every mixed marriage carries within itself the drama of Christian division, providing the acid test of ecumenical dialogue. The solution for the problem should be sought by dialogue with the other Christian denominations, in order to reach agreement on a common pastoral approach. By abandoning the canonical form laid down by Trent, while bearing in mind that those who are baptized are mutually the ministers of the sacrament, many difficulties would be eliminated, and there would be fewer invalid marriages and fewer divorces. Because of the importance of the ecumenical aspect, Bishop Puech concluded, the matter should be placed under the competence of the Secretariat of Unity. It was a comment made by various other speakers.

Similar views were expressed on the following days by Cardinal Alfrink, speaking for the Dutch bishops, Cardinal Döpfner for Germany, Cardinal Suenens for Belgium, Bishop Johannes Vonderach, of Chur, for Switzerland, and Bishop John Martensen, of Copenhagen, for Scandinavia.

Cardinal Alfrink stressed that the problem was primarily theological, because it involved the divine law which calls for safeguarding and raising the children in the faith, then pastoral, and finally juridic. The form imposed by the Council of Trent was directed primarily against secret marriages, an issue no longer serious. The problem should be restudied today in the light of the documents of Vatican Council II. He thought the canonical impediment should be eliminated, and that the canonical form should either be eliminated altogether or required only for liceity, with power to the bishops to dispense.

Cardinal Döpfner would keep the canonical form for liceity

only, with authority to the bishops to dispense within a framework to be determined for each country by its episcopal conference. The Catholic party should promise to ensure the baptism and Catholic education of the children, and the other party should merely undertake not to stand in the way. Even that condition should not be absolute, because there might be situations in which for serious reasons it would be possible to tolerate the education of the children in a non-Catholic denomination.

Cardinal Suenens favored keeping the canonical form, with authority to the bishop to dispense. He held that this position was not necessarily anti-ecumenical, but on the contrary provided an opportunity for dialogue about the sacraments of baptism and matrimony. He urged a very thorough theological investigation of marriage as a human institution and as a sacrament and sign of the Church.

Bishops Martensen and Vonderach were particularly critical of the *relatio* or introductory statement of Cardinal Marella as being excessively juridical in its approach. Bishop Vonderach said that the mixed marriage problem was more acute in some places than others, and that consequently it was not surprising to find difference of opinion among the bishops. The present situation, however, was not satisfactory either pastorally or from the ecumenical viewpoint. Having described ecumenical talks in progress in Switzerland, he suggested that a study of the nature of marriage was an essential preliminary to discussion of mixed marriages in ecumenical encounters. It was necessary, he said, to keep in mind both the truth of marriage as deriving from revelation and the teaching of the Church, the Christian character of marriage between baptized persons, the pastoral importance of charity, the significance of conscience and responsibility, and the task of formation of conscience. Bishop Martensen said that present legislation did not harmonize with either the ecumenical or pastoral aspects of marriage between a Catholic and a Lutheran. It was no longer permissible to think of all

Protestants as adversaries of the faith of Christ or in the category of the heretics about whom St. John had spoken so sternly. The legislation regarding the promises should be restudied to ensure that it was not more demanding than the divine law.

Another who was strongly in favor of change was Archbishop Edelby. "Current practice is a reflection of the preoccupations of the Church in the Middle Ages, always ready to defend herself against heretics," he said, "but mixed marriages cannot be regarded as everywhere and always an evil. If they imply certain dangers, the proper measure should be taken to anticipate those dangers. But if the door is closed, Catholics cannot go out and others cannot come in. A universal and detailed discipline is not appropriate for a matter so complex and delicate. It would be immoral to ask of the non-Catholic what he cannot give in conscience. The children do not belong to one parent or the other, but to the two together. The parents must consequently find a solution that is just for them and satisfactory to the Churches of both."

Cardinal Heenan of Westminster expressed a middle position on behalf of the English bishops. He recognized that the number of mixed marriages is likely to increase, including the number of those celebrated in non-Catholic churches, and said that the great danger of this trend was an increase of religious indifferentism. It was important to protect both the conscience of the Catholic and that of the non-Catholic party. It should, accordingly, be enough to insist that the Catholic promise to make every effort to ensure the Christian education of the children. The canonical form should be kept in principle, with permission to the bishops to dispense according to formulas to be established by each episcopal conference.

The bishops of Scotland, whose view was expressed by Bishop Francis Thomson, of Motherwell, would go even farther, making marriages valid even when performed without the canonical form, though retaining the form for liceity. The trouble with the present system, Bishop Thomson said, is that most Catholics do not distinguish between validity and liceity. When a marriage is performed without the canonical form, it is usually impossible to get the parties to repeat the ceremony, so that the Catholic simply abandons all religious practice. The proposed change would eliminate the need for a new ceremony. The Catholic party could be reconciled privately and could then return to full religious practice, including reception of the sacraments.

Bishop Michael Browne, of Galway, Ireland, expressed a much more rigorous stand on behalf of the Irish bishops. The 1966 instruction should be continued unchanged, he said, because enough time had not elapsed to give it a fair trial. The promises should be required, or at least the pastor should give the bishop the reasons on which he based his moral certainty that the children would be raised as Catholics. In addition, the canonical form was necessary to save the holiness and indissolubility of marriage.

After a total of 54 cardinals and bishops had spoken on the mixed marriage issue in the name of national conferences, Father Joseph Buckley, superior general of the Marist Fathers, made the final collective statement in the name of the superiors general of religious orders. Religious superiors are only indirectly interested in the problem, he said, but they are nonetheless interested because of the substantial number of priests under their jurisdiction who are engaged in pastoral work. In their view, the level of religious formation and education of the Catholic party in a mixed marriage is of the greatest importance. Where the right education is present, invalidating laws are superfluous, and where it is absent, laws by themselves can provide no solution. The danger to the Catholic party is also influenced by the religious background of the non-Catholic.

The debate was closed by statements from eight Fathers speaking in their own name. The first was Cardinal Ottaviani, and he adopted the intransigent position with which he is normally identified. The terminology in use expresses reality and should be preserved, he said, because it is clear to all. The impediment should also be retained. Pastors should instruct both Catholics and non-Catholics in their respective duties. The canonical form should be preserved because marriage is a social fact and not a secret incident of concern only to the contracting parties. As for the rite of marriage, a "certain liberality" is in order, permitting a non-Catholic clergyman to read his prayers after the celebration of the marriage.

Cardinal Browne of the Congregation for the Faith followed the lead of Cardinal Ottaviani, though in more moderate terms. He recognized that situations vary from one country to another. The faith of the Catholic partner must be protected, as must the Catholic education of the children, but with respect for the views of the other parent, to whom the children also belong. Catholics cannot demand of the non-Catholic party anything that would be against his conscience, nor should demands be made of the Catholic that would endanger the peace and unity of the family. The impediment should be retained as a warning against the dangers of mixed marriages, and the canonical form should be preserved, but with authority for bishops to dispense according to rules laid down by their respective episcopal conferences.

Father William Bertrams, S.J., also of the Curia, returned to the point made by Cardinal Marella in his *relatio*. While the provisions of canon law in general are for the welfare of individuals, he said, those regulating mixed marriages are "for the supreme welfare of the faith." It is necessary to explain to non-Catholics, with charity but in all truth, that the Church cannot yield on principles dealing with "the divine rights of the faith." Those experienced in the pastoral ministry testify that suppression of the canonical form would cause great harm. Bishops should be able to dispense only in exceptional cases and according to principles laid down by the episcopal conferences.

Cardinal John Krol, of Philadelphia, speaking in his personal capacity, agreed. The suppression of the canonical form would not resolve any problem but would rather cause greater ones, he said. It would lead many people outside the Church, where they could no longer profit from the pastoral help of those responsible for them, because there can be no pastoral care of those who are absent. If every marriage was to be regarded as valid without the canonical form, there would be a great increase in the number of applications for dissolution of marriage on the ground of insufficient intention.

Almost immediately after Cardinal Ottaviani had finished his statement, Cardinal Bea made an intervention which carefully avoided a direct confrontation but which nevertheless indicated something of the conflict that had been raging behind the scenes. He noted that the Secretariat for Christian Unity which he heads had not been consulted in the preparation of Cardinal Marella's *ratio,* whereas the document distributed to the Synod Fathers had been the result of a collaboration between the Congregation for the Faith and the Secretariat for Unity. The big difference between the two was that the document had presented arguments for and against change in the present legislation, leaving it to the fathers to decide, whereas the *relatio* had come out flatly in support of the *status quo.* Mixed marriages, he continued, raise practical pastoral problems, to be resolved not by appeals to the past but by evaluating current situations and giving due consideration to the concrete difference from country to country. Every man's natural right to marry should be protected, and it has to be remembered that the children belong to both parents. He thought the impediment should be retained as a way to help the parties to realize the dangers of a mixed marriage, but the Catholic should not bear an obligation calculated to endanger not only the peace but the unity of the family, nor should the non-Catholic be forced to go against his conscience. Because of the great diversity of situations, Cardinal Bea favored retaining the canonical form not only for liceity but for validity, but giving bishops power to dispense according to rules to be set by episcopal conferences. Vatican Council II's rules on ecumenism should always be observed, remembering that the dangers of mixed marriages are not removed by laws but by intensive pastoral care.

Two important related issues not on the agenda were raised during the debate, one by Cardinal Alexander Renard (France) and the other by the Maronite Patriarch of Antioch, Cardinal Paul Meouchi.

Cardinal Renard began by recalling Bishop Puech's comment that a lot was said about the dangers of mixed marriages but that there was not nearly enough thought given to the danger of a marriage between a practicing Catholic and one who had been baptized a Catholic but had lost the faith. We have to think of the further case of two persons baptized as Catholics but neither of whom practice their religion and who have no intention of raising their children as Catholics. Such cases, he said, are becoming increasingly numerous and pose serious problems for pastors, some of whom refuse to marry them in a Catholic ceremony. A theological issue is involved here, namely, whether the marriage of such baptized persons is a sacrament. For such situations, Cardinal Renard thought that, instead of a religious ceremony, three other possibilities could be provided. One would be marriage in the church in the presence of the priest, without any religious ceremony. The second would be marriage in the presence of witnesses known to the priest, with a dispensation from the canonical form. The third would be a civil marriage, with the permission of the bishop and a clear notification to the parties of the indissoluble nature of marriage.

Cardinal Meouchi raised the issue of the possibility of remarriage while a former spouse still lives. Archbishop Zoghby, Greek Melchite Patriarchal Vicar for Egypt, had introduced the same question at Vatican Council II in September 1965, urging that the Western Church should follow the tradition of the Eastern Church in interpreting St. Matthew's Gospel (5:32 and 19:9) on divorce and remarriage. The Eastern interpretation permits remarriage of the innocent partner. Cardinal Meouchi referred to a more limited situation in his Synod intervention. Since the Orthodox Church permits divorce, he asked, should the Catholic partner divorced by an Orthodox spouse not be free to remarry? The Catholic Church accepts the validity of an Orthodox marriage, he said, and yet the Orthodox admit divorce. That being so, how can the Catholic spouse be bound to a greater extent than the Orthodox one? He suggested that there are two different realizations of the sacramental character of marriage in the Catholic and the Orthodox traditions, one excluding and the other permitting dissolution. If that is so, he argued, should the Catholic spouse in an Orthodox marriage not have the benefit of the Orthodox sacramental regime? The Council of Trent, he noted, while reaffirming the Western interpretation, had been careful to phrase its statement so as not to exclude the Eastern tradition.

While leaving for a later chapter a general evaluation of the impact on the Synod of the Congress of the Lay Apostolate, it is appropriate to note here a resolution voted unanimously by that body at its final plenary session on October 18, that is to say, in the middle of the Synod debate on mixed marriages. This Congress session was in the evening, and the Synod Fathers attended it as a body. The resolution asked the Synod to take into account in its deliberation the following views of the Congress of the Laity.

"1. The validity of unions blessed by ministers of the main Protestant denominations should be fully recognized, as has been the case for unions blessed by ministers of the Orthodox Church.

"2. The automatic excommunication of Roman Catholics married in the Protestant Church hurts gravely the charity and the peace which Our Lord has been establishing between us these last years.

"3. The determination of the faith in which the children will be brought up should be left to the choice of parents through the grace of the marriage sacrament and with the help of qualified representatives of the Churches.

"4. Every effort towards a common pastoral, that is, concerted at all levels amongst the ministers of the different faiths, will be welcomed with joy, not only by interfaith couples, but also by all Christian parents whose children may find themselves in the same situation."

Some surprise was expressed at the second point, in view of the fact that the 1966 Instruction put an end to the previous automatic excommunication of a Catholic who went through a marriage ceremony in a Protestant church. The drafters insisted, however, that their purpose was to dramatize the difference between the juridic and the human situation. Although the Catholic party is no longer legally excommunicated, he is not legally married in the eyes of the Catholic Church and consequently is excluded from the Eucharist. What is the difference, they asked, between not being excommunicated and not being allowed to receive Communion?

At the final working session of the Synod on October 28, the Fathers expressed their opinion on the various issues that had been discussed in regard to mixed marriages. The legalists were careful to insist that the procedure should not be called a "vote," because it produced not a decision but merely an indication of viewpoint to help the Holy Father to make his decisions. On the major issues, the Fathers expressed themselves overwhelmingly for the present legislation. In favor of retention of the canonical form were 125 fathers, with 28 conditional approvals (*placet iuxta modum*), 33 against, and 1 abstention. Retention of the canonical impediment — prohibition of marriage without a dispensation — was supported by 128 Fathers, with 29 conditional approvals, 28 opposed, and 2 abstentions.

While seeking to retain the existing structure, the Fathers would like to make it less rigid. Bishops, they said, should be able to give dispensations without having to refer to Rome (105 in favor, 68 conditionally in favor, 13 opposed and 1 abstention). They would prefer a more appropriate ceremony than the Mass for some mixed marriages (153 to 5, with 27 conditional approvals). They favor the introduction of special pastoral efforts for the spouses and children of mixed marriages (171 to 0, with 16 conditional approvals). As regards terminology, the result was curious. The Fathers would like to get away from the present usage, "mixed marriage" for a marriage between Christians and "disparity of cult" for a marriage of a Catholic with a non-Christian. However, they rejected the proposed alternatives. For example, 110 rejected "interconfessional marriage" and only 29 approved it.

The biggest change proposed by the Fathers was to introduce a further degree of flexibility in regard to the promises that the children be raised as Catholics. To grant a dispensation for a mixed marriage, they said, it should suffice to be morally certain that the Catholic parent will do all in his power to have the children baptized and raised as Catholics, and that the non-Catholic party should know that such is the intention of the Catholic party. The vote on the first section of this proposal was 137 in favor, 6 against, 42 conditional approvals, and 2 abstentions; on the second section, 92 to 13, with 72 conditional approvals and 10 abstentions. Although the final result falls short of what the Secretariat for Christian Unity sought, it goes a considerable distance toward implementation of the principles of the Vatican Council Declaration on Religious Freedom.

CHAPTER 7

Is Liturgical Experiment Controllable?

It was Pope John XXIII's personal decision that the project for reform of the liturgy be placed first on the agenda of Vatican Council II. The Constitution on the Sacred Liturgy was the result, and it was the first document completed and approved by the Council. The need for updating was universally recognized. As one bishop expressed it at the time, the liturgy had developed for four centuries "artificially, in a vacuum, with a proliferation of gestures and rituals." In addition to structural reform, the liturgy needed to be freed from a dead and deadly uniformity. This the Council did, not by substituting one set of details for another, but by providing general directives and doctrinal themes calculated to give Catholics a deeper understanding on the basis of which new forms could be created.

Pressures to implement the liturgical reform developed almost immediately. Those who had worked for renewal of the liturgy in the unsympathetic pre-Council climate were understandably desirous to see the concrete results of their efforts. Others were concerned that two sessions of the Council had produced so little tangible progress, and they grasped at this Constitution as something that could demonstrate concretely that all the effort had produced worthwhile fruits. The widespread favorable response to the first tentative efforts to involve the people actively in the celebration of the Mass attracted the support of pastorally-minded bishops. Some began to believe that renewed liturgy would make religion again meaningful for the many Christians who had been or were being alienated from the Church by the conditions of modern urban and industrial civilization.

It was not long, however, until dissatisfaction made itself widely felt. Catholics have had a tradition of uniformity, of concentration on rubrics and of formalism. In countries in which they live among Protestants, they had grown to regard the external forms, including the Latin language, as the features that distinguish the Mass from Protestant forms of worship. Not a few saw the changes, especially when coupled with the Council's plunge into ecumenism, as a movement to "protestantize" the faith.

At the other end of the spectrum were those who considered that the liturgical changes were not going far enough fast enough. Not a few of them simply ignored the official regulations and plunged ahead with their own experimentation. Even in the United States, which in canonical matters has always tended to be conservative and legalistic, many such groups have formed. A typical expression of their devotion is the "catacomb Mass," as it has been called. Held in a private home with the presence of ten to fifty people, it is led by a priest who holds a discusssion with the group after the homily, conducts a eucharistic service without vestments, using ordinary bread, and giving Communion under both kinds, all to the accompaniment of folk music and in an atmosphere more often associated with a revivalist meeting than with a staid Catholic religious ceremony.

In between comes the great mass of the faithful, both priests and lay people, who have accepted the changes with the docility and respect for authority which have particularly characterized the Catholic Church in modern times. But they have often accepted with little understanding. While many of them find the Mass less boring and more spiritually satisfying in its changed form, many others feel not a little cheated when they discover that the promised transformation of themselves and of the community to which they belong has not accompanied their faithful acceptance of the new liturgy. As one change follows another piecemeal, they ask how long is this going to continue, and why.

The conflict and confusion have occurred not only throughout the Catholic world but in Rome itself. Just after the promulgation of the Constitution on the Liturgy, Pope Paul established a new body, the Council for the Implementation of the Constitution on Sacred Liturgy, in February, 1964. It consisted of 11 cardinals and 36 bishops under the presidency of Cardinal James Lercaro, Archbishop of Bologna. A firm believer in the movement for liturgical renewal, Cardinal Lercaro found himself from the outset involved in jurisdictional disputes with the conservative-minded Congregation of Rites, which previously had a monopoly over matters liturgical, and opposed by other powerful members of the Curia.

The most conspicuous expression of this conflict occurred in April, 1967 with the publication of a pamphlet entitled "The Rent Tunic" (a reference to Christ's tunic without seam, for which the soldiers cast lots, rather than tear it into pieces, after they crucified him). Its hundred pages of abuse of Cardinal Lercaro can be judged from a short extract. "It would be improper and unjust, Eminence, to describe you as a termite, although I consider you (leaving aside your intention which has been and which undoubtedly is quite different) a subtle assailant, the one most to be feared since the man of Wittenberg [Luther]. . . . Termites bore while hiding themselves, in silence, in the shade, while in your case on the contrary the thing which is least clear (I don't say that it is obscure) is simply the way in which you have got yourself into the post which is most useful and necessary for your work; I refer to the post of president of the council set up to implement in the right way the teaching of the Council, a teaching good in itself but destined in your hands to be betrayed, violated, destroyed, regarded as a scrap of paper."

The author was a little-known and unimportant writer of edifying novels and lives of saints. Significant, however, was a preface signed by Cardinal Antonio Bacci, a member of the Congregation of Rites. While expressing "some reserves," he praised the work as "due entirely to an ardent love for the Church and the propriety of its liturgy." Its author was "a perfect Catholic." Its pages, "reminiscent of St. Catherine of Siena," might serve to correct some ideas.

Seeing this attack as a further step in a continuing operation calculated to destroy not only himself personally but the work of liturgical reform, Cardinal Lercaro protested in strong terms to Cardinal Tisserant, dean of the College of Cardinals, and to Cardinal Cicognani, Secretary of State, demanding public and adequate reparation. A meeting of the Italian bishops on April 6 condemned the "unjust attack." The clergy and people of the archdiocese of Bologna called for a clear answer to the question whether or not Cardinal Bacci and the author were correct in saying that the Council for the Liturgy and its head had violated the spirit and letter of the teaching of Vatican Council II.

Pope Paul himself gave the answer on April 19. Receiving the Council in audience, he said that he wished to come to the defence of Cardinal Lercaro against "an unjust and irreverent attack." While it was entirely proper to seek to keep Latin in the liturgy, this could not be done in a way that would contradict "the great principle, reaffirmed by the Council, that the liturgy should be intelligible at the level of the people, or the further principle proclaimed today by the culture of the people that they should be able to express their deepest and most sincere feelings in a living language."

Immediately, nevertheless, the Pope went on to deplore "instances of indiscipline" which showed a tendency to desacralize the liturgy. "This new mentality on which the demolition of authentic Catholic worship tends to be based implies such doctrinal and pastoral deviations that we do not hesitate to consider it erroneous."

Such was the general climate of doubt and tension about the progress of liturgical reform which decided the Holy Father to ask the Synod for some additional guidelines. The preparation of the position paper and presentation of the issues to the Fathers were entrusted to the Council for the Liturgy, with Cardinal Lercaro acting as rapporteur and Father Annibale Bugnini as secretary. Father Bugnini is both secretary of the Council for the liturgy and sub-secretary for liturgy of the Congregation of Rites, thus serving as a liaison between the two bodies.

In the three and a half years since its creation, the Council for the Liturgy had held 8 plenary meetings and hundreds of study meetings in which a total of some 200 experts had participated. It had published instructions on the general principles for the application of the reform, on the rite of concelebration and Communion under both kinds, on sacred music, and on the cult of the Eucharist. It had examined more than 12,000 translations of liturgical texts submitted for its approval by episcopal conferences.

The introductory portion of the position paper and of the *relatio* touched briefly on this background and also put the present efforts into a historical perspective. The liturgy of the Western Church had once before gone through a major series of changes in the third and fourth centuries, when Latin replaced Greek as the vernacular and also as the liturgical language, while simultaneously the earlier practice of commemorating the Last Supper in private homes gave way to the celebration of the Eucharist in public churches. On that occasion, it had taken several centuries of free experimentation to produce the full glory of the Latin liturgy, as well as a type of music to match, the Gregorian Chant. The current reform, by way of contrast, had begun on a much more authoritarian and technical level, seeking to provide ready-made answers, often with disappointing results. Against this background, Cardinal Lercaro asked for guidance on two major issues, the basic structure of the Mass, and the form of breviary most appropriate to the needs of the priest engaged in an active ministry.

Since the latter part of the sixteenth century, when Pope Pius V reformed the missal as part of his efforts to implement the decrees of the Council of Trent, the "normal" or "standard" Mass has been the low Mass celebrated by the priest in private with a server to assist him. All other Masses, the low Mass for the people on Sunday, the sung Mass, the High Mass, and the Bishop's Mass, were developed from that basic type. According to the spirit of the Council, Cardinal Lercaro suggested, we need to develop a new basic structure, a Mass in which the people participate and sing. Before the Council, he noted, some considered such a suggestion improper on the ground that every participation of the people tended to minimize that of Christ and to distract from the reality of the sacrifice. But that view, he contended, was quite mistaken, because Christ had established the sacrament for the Christian people, and all should have their active part in it, one of them designated to read the lesson, others as the choir, and all making the responses and joining in the hymns. If such a Mass was established as the norm, the result would be a psychological change. Other types of Mass would still be possible, but they would then be seen as departures from the norm because of special circumstances.

The Cardinal also proposed various changes in the content of the Mass intended to express better the nature of the service and to make it more meaningful. The first called for clearer distinction of the three parts. The introductory ceremony would be reduced to a single penitential action instead of two. The liturgy of the Word or readings from the Scriptures and homily would be made more substantial. The Offertory introducing the eucharistic celebration would be shortened. The prayers and hymns would be restudied to make them more applicable to the contemporary scene, and more modern and less complicated musical forms would be authorized as optional substitutes for Gregorian Chant. A 3-year cycle of Scripture lessons would be introduced for Sunday Mass, with three readings each time, one from the Old Testament, one from an Epistle of the New Testament, and one from the Gospel. As a final point regarding the Mass, the Cardinal made several suggestions about the canon. It should be said aloud, he proposed, and might be said in the vernacular. In addition to the text given in the Roman Missal, three alternative canons might be authorized, all three recently composed and in experimental use for some months.

The breviary or divine office recited each day by all priests began as a form of prayer for contemplatives monks based on Scripture readings and the works of the Fathers of the Church. It was gradually modified to meet the needs of clerics engaged in an active apostolate. Cardinal Lercaro proposed structural changes to make it more functional for the priest today. The nocturnal hours, so called because intended to be sung or recited during the night, would be replaced by "spiritual reading," which was originally the primary content of these hours. In addition, the Psalms would be spread out over a 4-week cycle instead of being read in their entirety each week.

In addition to the questions of the Congregation of the Liturgy, Pope Paul decided to take advantage of the presence of the Synod Fathers to ask their views on four other liturgical questions. On these questions they were called to express a personal opinion, not that of the episcopal conferences which had elected them. They concerned the three new eucharistic prayers already mentioned; the desirability of substituting for the Nicene Creed in the Mass the Apostle's Creed, which is both older and easier to understand; the addition of the scriptural words "given for you" after "This is my Body" at the consecration of the host, as is the practice in other rites; and the elimination of the non-scriptural words "the mystery of faith" from the form of consecration of the wine.

Cardinal Lercaro's *relatio* was greeted with animated and prolonged applause, interpreted as an expression of the repudiation by the Synod Fathers of the charges of which he had earlier been the victim. In the debate that followed, the Fathers who spoke on behalf of episcopal conferences, with few exceptions, approved both what the Council for the Liturgy had done and what it now proposed. Indeed, after nearly thirty speakers had followed each other along the same lines, six Fathers withdrew their request to speak on the ground that their views had been fully covered. Later, however, when the time came for those who wished to express their personal views, some strong dissents were voiced.

A typical speech was that of Archbishop François Marty, of Reims, France, vice-president of the permanent committee of the French bishops. Having praised Cardinal Lercaro for the extent and success of the efforts of the Council for the Liturgy, he gave unqualified approval to the proposal for the new "normal" Mass, adding that appropriate weight should be given not only to the traditions of the early Church but also to contemporary traditions. Signs and symbols used in the liturgy should, he said, be intelligible and appealing to the new mentality created by our technical civilization. The liturgy should have a message for the modern world, even for those who have lost the faith or are not Christians. Special Masses should be developed, he suggested, for children, for teen-agers and for small groups, and the ceremonies could be simplified in places where the level of instruction of the people is low. He expressed approval of the new canons, adding that if it was decided to modify the formula of consecration, the modification should be introduced into all of them.

Bishop Clemente Isnard, of Nova Friburgo, Brazil, urged additional changes, including the use of ordinary bread and wine, and a return to the practice of the early Church when the consecrated bread was taken by each communicant into his own hand before being eaten. The Eastern Churches commonly use ordinary bread whereas the Western Church uses unleavened bread, the kind presumably used by Christ at the Last Supper held during Passover time. Theologians today would not challenge the validity of the consecration of leavened bread made from wheaten flour, and the tendency is toward a less absolute stand regarding the kind of grain and the kind of fruit from which the bread and wine are made. Many theologians in the not distant past claimed that wheaten flour and wine of the grape were essential for validity, but it now seems at least probable that Christ used barley bread, and that the wine was very different from ours, a kind of concentrate, of the consistency of honey, mixed with water before drinking. Bishop Isnard further expressed the hope that the period of liturgical change would not end when the Council for the Liturgy completed its work. The principle should be that the liturgy is always in need of reform he said.

Archbishop George Flahiff, of Winnipeg, Canada, also expressed his own admiration and that of the Canadian bishops for what the Council had done but — like Bishop Isnard — thought the pace of change too slow. "The application of the general principles guiding the liturgical updating is not sufficiently bold and courageous," he said. "One has rather the impression of a timid and inadequate compromise, never getting to the radical solutions needed by priests engaged in the ministry. We still have many traditional elements which today are meaningless."

Archbishop François Ligondé, of Port-au-Prince, Haiti, supported Bishop Isnard's request that the consecrated bread be placed in the hand of the communicant and not in his mouth. Asked at a press conference for his view, Archbishop George Dwyer, of Birmingham, England, said that it would be "a more expressive form of the sacrament, and not against the faith." Noting that this was the practice of earlier times, he said that views today were mixed. "It seems to me that the piety of our countries has been developed in the direction of an extreme reverence towards the Eucharist. Many of the faithful would be upset by the proposed change. But I, personally, am not 'bigoted' on the point."

Greater variation in liturgical forms to suit the conditions of different cultures and civilizations was urged by Bishop Joseph Kuo, of Taipei, Taiwan. This, he said, was particularly desirable in mission countries. The door should also be left open to a freer adaptation of liturgical texts for languages which did not lend themselves to a literal translation. He also proposed that all liturgical prayers be addressed to the first person of the Trinity, to the Father in or through Christ, to use St. Paul's formula.

The plea for more variation in liturgical forms and more freedom in translation was echoed by several Fathers from Asia and Africa. The sense is what is important, said Archbishop Joseph Parecattil (Caldeo-Malabar rite), of Ernakulam, India, and the words must be adapted to the mental capacity of those to whom they are directed. Archbishop Jean Zoa, of Yaoundé, Cameroon, asked that priests be given more latitude in the celebration of the rites, within rules laid down by the episcopal conferences. He also favored having a layman give the Sunday homily at times.

One episcopal conference which indicated some hesitation about the direction in which liturgical experimentation is moving was that of the United States. Speaking in its name, Archbishop John Dearden, of Detroit, said that notable progress had been made in the liturgical field from the days of "sterile rubricism," but that many abuses had been introduced as a result of unauthorized experiments conducted under the pretext of acting in the "spirit" of Vatican Council II. He asked the Council for the Liturgy to draw up a detailed declaration to clarify the real meaning of the word *experiment* and its relationship to ecclesiastical authority. It would be helpful, he added, if things still under study were not made known to the public, and it would be advisable when announcing liturgical changes not to state that they only constitute a step toward further changes. This would serve as a brake on unlawful tendencies and encourage those who, with a spirit of obedience and genuinely pastoral ideals, are seeking changes in keeping with the current needs of the people of God.

Archbishop Dearden spoke on the third day of the debate at a session which had been preceded by an experimental "normal" Mass celebrated for the benefit of the Synod Fathers in the Sistine Chapel. Italian was the language throughout, except for a short section in Latin. One of the new "eucharistic prayers" or canons was used, with the addition of the words "given for you" and the elimination of "the mystery of faith" from the formula for consecration. The double *Confiteor* was replaced by one brief expression of sorrow, followed by a minute of silence and the usual form of absolution. After reading three short texts of Scripture, Father Bugnini, the celebrant, gave a 7-minute homily. The entire service took 45 minutes. Reaction was mixed. One difficulty about the ceremony was that the "normal" Mass should be the Sunday Mass celebrated in the parish church with the participation of the people. The Synod Fathers were not a congregation in that sense. They had come not as a group of the faithful to worship, but as a committee to study the pastoral impact of a new type of service on a typical parish congregation, a congregation that was not present. It was an artificial experiment, as must be all experiments staged by liturgical commissions whether in Rome or elsewhere. It should logically strengthen the argument that unofficial experimentation must be encouraged over an extended period, as in the fifth and sixth centuries, in order to find new meaningful forms.

That was not, however, the reaction of various Fathers, to judge by the day's discussion. Following Archbishop Dearden, several others voiced similar sentiments. Changes should not be introduced without very careful preparation of the people in advance, according to Bishop Donal Lamont, of Umtali, Rhodesia, because the faithful are showing signs of weariness from "a constant stream of changes which cause disturbance and spiritual confusion." It seems opportune not to proceed with further liturgical experiments, or at least not to publish them, added Bishop Edward Mason, of El Obeid, Sudan, in order not to create confusion and encourage criticism. He thought that experiments should be particularly controlled in seminaries and religious houses. Bishop Joseph Bowers, of Accra, Ghana, urged a global reform, "studied with accuracy and promulgated all at once," rather than a continuation of the periodic introduction of minor changes. Archbishop Bernard Yago, of Abidjan, Ivory Coast, said the people were "disturbed and scandalized" by all the changes. Auxiliary Bishop José Guerra Campos, of Madrid, warned against building up a "revisionistic mentality" and a degree of distrust for authority by the periodic issuance of additional liturgical changes.

The debate within the Synod was being paralleled by one on the same subject outside. Professor H. Schmidt, S.J., professor of liturgy at the Gregorian University, Rome, moderated a round-table discussion by Archabbot Rembert Weakland, O.S.B., of St. Vincent's, Latrobe, Pennsylvania, Rev. Adrien Nocent, O.S.B. (Belgium), Rev. B. Neunheuser, O.S.B. (Germany), Rev. George Pinell, O.S.B. (Spain), Rev. S. Marsili, O.S.B. (Italy), and Rev. Mauricio Ferro Calvo (Colombia). The moderator proposed three questions. Should the present state of transition be allowed to continue indefinitely, leading to liturgical anarchy? Should the objective be a freezing of liturgy in new forms, what might be called a "restoration"? Or should the current transition be encouraged to develop into a dynamic-organic evolution, thus producing a true renewal capable of allowing continuous adaptation?

Archabbot Weakland blamed the liturgical malaise in the United States primarily on those bishops and pastors who delayed all action until the period of experimentation should end, combined with a lack of pastoral education of both clergy and laity, and "an uncertainty of what the liturgical experience is exactly about." Such attitudes made underground experimentation inevitable. "We hear more and more often the phrase that there will never be a true liturgical reform in the United States as long as Sunday Mass is obligatory and the Church is full of those who come only to keep from committing a mortal sin." The problem "of rites and books," he concluded, is trivial compared with that of creating "an experience liturgy that corresponds to twentieth century cultural patterns."

"The psychological sciences and those dealing with human life no longer permit us to regard tradition, no matter how loved and venerated, as more than a diving board," according to Father Nocent. "Some experimental pluralism, controlled by the bishop through a liturgical committee, seems necessary to a liturgy which seeks to be an integral part of life." "The so-called new forms are often not very new," Father Marsili added. "Rather, they represent the restoration of ancient forms. Translations should not necessarily follow the Latin text slavishly. We have to realize that the danger of becoming stratified in new forms exists, and the result would be to leave us worse off than before." For us on the other side of the Atlantic, Father Ferro Calvo observed, "the basic problem is to create a *Latin American* liturgy. This liturgy should take into account the physiognomy proper to the Church in the different regions. The concrete solution of many problems will depend on the theoretical solution offered by theology. But the contribution of theology alone is not enough; it needs the cooperation of the human sciences."

Both the speakers and the audience (which included several Synod Fathers) indicated a basic agreement with the program of the Council for the Liturgy, although several sought faster and more basic change. Other voices, however, were simultaneously being raised on the margin of the Synod. The near unanimity of the Fathers in support of Cardinal Lercaro during the first days of the Synod debate provoked a violent reaction in traditionalist circles, and these resorted to a technique frequently practiced in Rome. Obscure writers for Roman publications were fed materials for articles which came to the immediate attention of the Fathers. The most extreme of these efforts appeared in *Il Messaggero* of October 23 under a five-column heading which read: "A great mass of believers moves into action to defend tradition; the Catholic Resistance is coming to life." A subtitle said that "associations and publications of the entire world" were demanding that the Synod Fathers should not allow the "so-called conciliar spirit" to carry liturgical reform beyond the limits fixed by the Vatican Council itself. According to the author, the vast majority of the Catholic people throughout the world is "faithful to tradition," but a conspiratorial minority has seized control of the decision-making processes and is imposing its views dictatorially. He claimed that the "normal Mass" being proposed to the Synod fell under the condemnations of the Council of Trent and of Pius XII's encyclical *Mediator Dei,* and that the proposal to say the entire Mass in the vernacular was not only in violation of the decrees of the Council of Trent but "risks making the entire celebration invalid." All of this led to the conclusion that the Church today is in a situation similar to that in the period immediately following the Council of Nicea, when "the great majority of the bishops had strayed into a more or less openly declared Arianism," so that "it fell to the laity to continue the Catholic tradition in silence and in the shade, bringing that tradition safe through the raging tempest by continuing — with the clergy who had remained faithful — to recite the Nicean profession of faith."

Curial cardinals who took the floor at the Synod after the bishops speaking on behalf of the episcopal conferences, were less violent in their expression, but their intention was equally to block Cardinal Lercaro's proposals. Cardinal Amleto Cicognani warned against "frequent novelties" as tending to lessen the sacred character of the liturgy, to disturb the people, and to fatigue the priest. He said the canon of the Mass should remain in Latin, "at least for those who might prefer it," that the Latin text should be included with all translations of liturgical prayers, and that the Gregorian Chant should always be held in honor. The people of God do not want all these novelties, he asserted. "We have had enough experiments. We have had enough innovations."

Faithfulness to tradition is a basic element in the history of the Church, Cardinal Antonio Samoré said. Care should be taken not to lose our hold on the rich patrimony of tradition, and we should try to carry on the living worship of the past. The alternative would be to risk unleashing "a veritable flood sweeping away everything in its path, without the possibility of saving anything or turning back." In consequence, the only admissible changes were those which did not break the bond with tradition. The possibility of saying Mass in Latin should always be retained, especially for priests and people traveling abroad. National conferences should see that there are always some Masses in Latin, especially in cities visited by many tourists.

Cardinal Angelo dell'Acqua adopted a more conciliatory position. While agreeing with Cardinal Cicognani that the Latin text should be placed alongside translations of liturgical prayers, he described the historical and biblical part of the work of the Council for the Liturgy as "excellent." His closing comment indicated his concern at the pattern — evident throughout the Synod — of consistent opposition by the spokesmen for the major curial bodies to the changes sought by most of the bishops speaking on behalf of episcopal conferences. The Congregations of the Curia, he urged, should not give the impression that they disagree with what has been "legitimately decided" by the national conferences. Neither should they seem, "as sometimes happens," to be quarreling among themselves.

The debate was closed by seven speakers who invoked the right of reply. A few supported reservations made by curial cardinals. Cardinal Heenan, of Westminster, England, for example, said there should be less insistence on music, that there should be some Masses in Latin, and that the Council for the Liturgy was too theoretical because few of its members had "any real pastoral experience." Archbishop Joseph Cordeiro, of Karachi, Pakistan, criticized several aspects of the "normal" Mass and warned against a danger of "a false spirit of collectivism" if adaptability of the liturgy was not kept within defined limits. Most of the replies, nevertheless, were in the other direction. Cardinal Döpfner, in a short but strong statement, rejected various criticisms of the Council for the Liturgy. Bishop Isnard (Brazil) supported more freedom of experimentation and faster progress. The reform had gone very well in Brazil, he said, because the people had been allowed to implement their ideas. Unnecessary problems had been created in some countries by denouncing as abuses what the Council for the Liturgy would a little later approve. Father John Schütte, superior general of the Society of the Divine Word, made a very positive speech. The liturgy, he said, should be missionary in spirit. Nothing belonging to the cultures and traditions of mission countries should be excluded from it, and controlled experiments in cultural assimilation should be encouraged. The people, instead of being dismissed at the end of the Mass, should be sent forth to perform their mission.

Cardinal Lercaro concluded with thanks for all the views expressed and an assurance that they would be given full weight by the Council for the Liturgy. He disagreed with the criticism that the Council was short on pastoral experience. On the contrary, he said, the number of pastors involved as members and *periti* was very great. Agreeing with the objections to the "piecemeal" introduction of liturgical changes, he noted that the Council for the Liturgy was not always to blame, a reference to the jurisdictional conflicts with the Congregation of Rites. The Council prepares the decisions, but they are countersigned and issued by the Congregation.

The subsequent "expression of opinion" confirmed the fact of substantial reservations regarding the "normal" Mass. There were 71 in favor and 43 opposed, with 63 conditional approvals (*placet iuxta modum*) and 4 abstentions. What this means is that the principle of a community Mass as the norm is adopted but that changes must be made in the formula presented to the Synod Fathers in the Sistine Chapel. Many bishops felt that there should have been more advance consultation with them, and that a preponderance of liturgists over pastors in the work had produced a somewhat artificial result. They believe that a satisfactory formula can result only from widespread experimentation on the parish level.

On the proposed change of the penitential act at the beginning of the Mass, 108 were in favor, 23 against, with 39 conditional approvals and 10 abstentions. For three Scripture readings at Mass instead of two, on an experimental basis, 72 for, 59 against, with 41 conditional approvals and 8 abstentions. For authorizing episcopal conferences to substitute appropriate hymns for the Introit, Offertory and Communion antiphons (which would mean a downgrading of Gregorian Chant), 126 for, 25 against, 19 conditional approvals and 10 abstentions.

The four questions regarding the reform of the Breviary won a maximum of 144 and a minimum of 117 approvals, with rejections varying between 25 and 7, and conditional approvals varying between 31 and 20. The earlier discussion had included many references to these questions, but the primary issue was always the Mass, and few strong views were expressed on the proposed Breviary reform. Several urged that the laity as well as the clergy be encouraged to recite the divine office. Bishop Fulton Sheen was the one who dwelt at greatest length on this point, saying it should be obligatory for clerics and a matter of free choice for lay people. Bishop Paul Dalmais, of Fort-Lamy, Equatorial Africa, said that recitation of the office should not be imposed "under pain of mortal sin." Archbishop Hurley of Durban, South Africa, said that Lauds and Vespers should be obligatory, the other hours "strongly recommended." Bishop Marty (France) urged reduction to two hours, one for the morning and one for the evening, with a longer office for days "not marked by great apostolic activity." Archbishop Bernardin Gantin, of Cotonou, Dahomey, thought that a very short office should be imposed on priests "under a grave obligation." Archbishop Francis Arinze, of Onitsha, Nigeria, expressed a definitely minority position. He said the office should remain as before, with the exception of Prime, and that it should be universally obligatory. Auxiliary Bishop Luis Henríquez Jiménez, of Caracas, Venezuela, was in substantial agreement. The changes proposed in the Breviary tend to lessen the priest's spirit of prayer, he said, while adding nothing substantial to his prayer life.

The Synod Fathers also gave affirmative answers to the four questions put them in their personal capacity by the Pope, although in one instance the assent was heavily modified. The three new canons for the Mass were approved by 127 to 22, with 34 conditional approvals. The optional substitution of the Apostle's Creed for the Nicene Creed in the Mass was approved by 171 to zero, with 16 conditional approvals. The addition of the words "given for you" to the formula of consecration of the bread won 110 affirmatives to 12 negatives, with 61 conditional affirmatives. There was, however, significant resistance to dropping a phrase, even though nonbiblical, from the central part of the canon. Only 93 voted to remove "the mystery of faith" from the formula of consecration of the wine, with 48 opposed and 42 conditional approvals, their condition being that the words be spoken by the deacons or by the people instead of by the priest. One thing that is clear is that a thousand-year-old tradition continues to carry weight with the bishops of the Church.

CHAPTER 8

Laity Invite a Dialogue

While the Synod talked its way through its limited agenda, other meetings of world significance blossomed under the shadow of St. Peter's, interacting at least symbolically with the representatives of the Catholic bishops of the world. In addition to the first visit in history of the Ecumenical Patriarch of Constantinople to the Pope of Rome, they included an International Catholic Rural Congress, a Congress of the World Union of Catholic Women's Organizations, a general assembly of the International Secretariat of Catholic Technologists, Agriculturists and Economists, an Assembly of the International Federation of Catholic Men, a General Assembly of the International Movement for the Apostolate in the Independent Social Milieux, a General Council of the World Federation of Sodalities of Our Lady, the second plenary meeting of the *Justitia et Pax* Commission for world development, and the Third World Congress for the Lay Apostolate.

"Like many others, I went to Rome for the World Congress for the Lay Apostolate with little enthusiasm and no high hopes," to quote José de Broucker of *Informations Catholiques Internationales* of Paris. "This massive manifestation, ten years in preparation, seemed to me the closing of a page of the Church's history rather than the start of a new chapter. I was quite wrong. My consolation, for what it is worth, is to know that I wasn't the only one."

Massive the Congress certainly was, with its 3,400 participants from 72 nations.* It was also not calculated to raise great hopes. The first session of the Vatican Council in 1962 had shown that several months were needed for the 2,500 Fathers to find some common ground and establish the ideological and emotional lines of force in the body of bishops, a body highly homogeneous by education, experience, and function of its members. What consensus could 3,000 men and women of diverse background achieve in one week, especially when their very purpose was ambiguous?

Many people, including many delegates, thought of the Congress as a Congress of the Laity, which is what in fact it turned out to be. But juridically it was something quite different. The preposition is "for," not "of."** And the meeting is not for the laity but for the lay apostolate. When Catholic Action was institutionalized in the 1920's and 1930's, the notion of the apostolate was spelled out clearly, on pragmatic grounds, to meet the needs of a special situation, but it was not clarified theologically. Catholic lay organizations were given a "mandate" by the bishop and were directly responsible to him. The duty of the members was to help in situations in which the clergy were unable to perform their tasks either for lack of numbers or from an inability to penetrate certain strata of society. The layman's apostolic work was considered as something separate from his job, a spare-time effort of supererogation as a kind of unskilled laborer or foot soldier under the constant supervision of his clerical officers. He had

* The total was made up of 1,415 national delegates, 261 international delegates, 88 observer-consultants from other Christian bodies, 346 experts, 877 auditors, and 413 newsmen.

** The prepositional relationship is important in curial practice. There is the Congregation *of* Religious, and the Commission *for* Social Communications, but the laity come under the Council *on* — or *concerning* — the Laity (Consilium de Laicis).

no voice in making policy or formulating strategy. His pledge was to obey the decisions of higher authority. This structure, useful in the Italy of Pius XI and Pius XII to maintain a youth movement independent of Fascist Youth, proved quite unsuited to the needs and temper of Europe in the period following World War II. France, for example, went through one crisis after another as dedicated young Catholics plunged into social activities to which the bishops were not prepared to give institutional approval. The theological concept developed by Vatican Council II of a call to all Christians, by virtue of their membership in the Church through baptism, to contribute to the building of the body of Christ, by their own initiative and on their own responsibility, implied the ending of the monopoly of the mandated organizations. The activity by which a man made his livelihood was henceforth established as his primary, if not sole, apostolate.

The Permanent Committee for International Congresses of the Lay Apostolate (COPECIAL), which organized the meeting, made no attempt to clear up the ambiguity, nor indeed had it authority to do so. Under its charter, the national delegations were named by the bishops or by bodies chosen by the bishops of their respective countries, and the international delegations came from the "mandated" international Catholic organizations. Each national delegation was headed by a bishop and had one or more priest advisers. As many as six members could be "non-lay" (priests, seminarians, religious Brothers or Sisters), and even this rule was not strictly enforced. Clerics numbered 8 in one delegation of 17 members, 4 of 7 in another, 1 of 2 in another, and 6 of 13 in yet another. Most countries, nevertheless, complied with the request of the organizers to keep the proportion of clerics low. What was more difficult was to ensure a true cross section of lay opinion. Many delegates were employees of the bishops or involved so long in "official" movements as to reflect clerical more than lay thinking. Even those picked to represent the "non-organized" laity would rarely have won an election.

On the opening day of the Congress, however, Cardinal Maurice Roy, of Quebec, president of the Council on the Laity, took a step which served to establish the meeting as decidedly and decisively a work of the laity. In a talk to the bishops heading the national delegations he stressed that the object of the discussions was "direct and concrete dialogue between laymen." While the presence of the bishops at the meetings was desirable, they should avoid "a too frequent intervention" which might tend to restrict the laymen's freedom of expression. Even if a layman put forward some unorthodox view, he told them, the bishops should remember that they perform the "office of correcting" only in their respective dioceses, whereas at the Congress each workshop had an Ecclesiastical Assistant and the Congress itself had an Ecclesiastical Commission to ensure that the discussions were "doctrinally correct." The Cardinal ended with a request to the bishops "to pass on this message to the priests and religious taking part in the workshops."

A few delegates were chagrined that the Church authorities could not trust so handpicked a body to keep within doctrinal bounds without an Ecclesiastical Commission to measure its words. Most, however, interpreted Cardinal Roy's message as a clearing away of obstacles, an invitation to speak out freely, and the Congress did in fact express itself with a frankness seldom heard in Rome.

The agenda had been framed in very general terms as a study of "God's People on Man's Journey." The program called for discussion in two series of workshops of a total of 16 aspects. The first series dealt with spiritual attitudes of man today, the family in the present evolution of society, cooperation between men and women in the various fields of social life, tensions between generations, social communications as a cultural revolution, social responsibilities for development in a planetary society, peace and world community, and migration; the second series, presenting the Christian message, Christian education, new methods of formation, dialogue within the Church, tasks of laity in renewal of Church communities, updating of lay organizations, laity's place in Church's missionary activity, and finally, ecumenical dialogue and collaboration.

It was a routine program and everything indicated a routine performance. The organizing committee consisted entirely of nominees of the Holy See. They named the 5 presidents of the Congress and the 25-member steering committee, as well as the 80 presidents and rapporteurs of the workshops. The only group outside their control was the assembly of the Heads of Delegations which formulates "all texts issued by the Congress as a whole, such as resolutions, motions and recommendations." But there was no reason why this body should be more radical than the others. Heads of national delegations were chosen by their bishops, and those of international delegations by the Holy See.

From the very first day, nevertheless, the Congress was dominated by a sense of destiny, a spirit of prophecy, demonstrating how deep is the power released in the Church by the second Vatican Council and how universal the renewal of the face of the earth. Unlike the Synod of Bishops, the Congress showed little concern for the institutional problems of the Church, apart from a stress on the urgent need to bring institutions into line with contemporary social forms, focusing instead on those of the world today.

The mood was defined in the opening address by Dr. Thom G. K. Kerstiens, of Holland, general secretary of the International Christian Union of Business Executives. Although many still know little about the teaching of Vatican Council II, he noted, it is today necessary not only to implement its teachings, but to develop and complete them. "There are questions which the Council did not treat, or treated only superficially, which we have to study close up," he asserted to the applause of the plenary session. Our contemporaries are concerned with war and peace, with a world of haves and have-nots, with the increasing alienation of man in an economy of abundance. They seek to end racial prejudice, to understand why young people behave the way they do. They look for a new economic philosophy "neither liberalist nor socialist but directed to man redeemed by Christ and . . . establishing a balance between economic efficiency and the full realization of the human being." They need a new morality of commerce and international exchange, a theology of revolution, a reflection on the field opened to Christians in a secularized world.

Insisting that witness obliges us to develop our religious culture to the same level as our secular education, Dr. Kerstiens said there was "no more sorrowful sight than the layman who has attained a far-reaching specialization in his professional life, but who remains in his religious culture at the fifth grade of primary school." Modern young people, he also said, leave Christianity not because they find it too exacting, but because they find it too middle-class, not capable of galvanizing their generosity for worthwhile causes. "If we don't get down to serious business, we are going to find a steadily increasing number of Christians take the exit to a world in which they will feel more at home. . . . If we don't try to answer the serious questions posed us, we mustn't be surprised that the world looks on us lay Christians as no more useful than the hippies, and our clergy as interesting as the cuckoo in the clock."

The mood was confirmed on that same opening day when the Assembly of the Heads of Delegations rejected a routine prefabricated message of greetings to the Synod of Bishops and directed the preparation of a statement with teeth, a statement presented to the Fathers at a Synod session not only by a Congress delegate, but a woman, Mrs. John D. Shields, president of the U. S. National Council of Catholic Women. Unlike the strictly conventional greetings which the Synod of Bishops had sent the Congress, this reply was substantial and hard-hitting. Having recalled that "the entire people of God participates in the priestly, prophetic and royal office of Christ," it urged the development of "a dialogue in the terms advocated by the Vatican Council texts, this being an indispensable condition for our participation in the life of the Church at every level."

The message deplored the practice of naming from on high the lay members of the new organizations for the laity, particularly the central organization in Rome (Council on the Laity). "Representative structures should be created. . . . The laity should be chosen by elections. . . . These structures should be animated by a spirit of total openness and mutual confidence. They will become fully efficacious only through concrete experiences which must necessarily be tentative."

This insistence on active participation was one of the constants of the Congress. Dr. Kerstiens had already mentioned it in his opening talk. "Modern man seems interested above all in a theology in the development of which we can all take part," he had said. Father Yves Congar, O.P., repeated it in an address which illness prevented him from delivering personally. "An entirely deductive magisterium and theology can be the work of clerics alone," his message stated. "But a theology and magisterium suited to the program we have outlined require the cooperation of all the people of God, clergy and laity, pastors and faithful." The Congress resolutions express the same approach. The laity insisted on voicing their views on the issue of mixed marriages being studied by the Synod, on birth control, on the place of women in the Church, and once more, on the claim of the laity to participate through representative organs in the life of the Church. In its closing resolution, the Congress specifically requested the Holy Father "to enlarge the composition of the Council on the Laity (*Consilium de Laicis*) in accordance with democratic processes, so that it may become truly representative of the multiple cultures, organizations and forms of the lay apostolate in all parts of the world, taking into account a just geographical representation." It urged that the Council on the Laity, so enlarged, should "accelerate the democratic establishment of structures of the laity at all levels across the world." And it called on its own members "to work immediately and consistently for the democratic implementation at all levels of the purposes of the proposed lay councils throughout the world upon their return to their respective countries."*

This is a new sound in Rome, a sound that grates on some ears. The rumblings of high-level displeasure were in fact so vociferous that Pope Paul had felt it prudent at an early stage in the Congress to damp down the ardor. The occasion was a special Mass in St. Peter's on Sunday, October 15, and the statement followed Paul's practice of balancing the pros and cons. "The Church has proclaimed the dignity of the layman," he first said, "not only in virtue of his membership of the human race, but also because he is a Christian. She [the Church] has declared him worthy to be associated with the responsibilities of the Church's life in the way and degree appropriate to him. She has judged him capable of giving witness to the faith. She has declared that she recognizes the fulness of the rights enjoyed by the laity, both men and women: the right to equality in the hierarchy of grace; the right to liberty in the framework of moral and ecclesiastical law; the right to sanctity in conformity with each one's state. . . . The Church sees the layman not merely as a member of the faithful but as an apostle. . . . She places confidence in you and invites you to accept great responsibilities in order to advance Christ's kingdom among your brothers."

So much for "the vast tasks entrusted to the laity in the apostolate." But, added the Pope immediately, does this

---

* Resolutions submitted by the U. S. delegation, but not acted on for technical reasons, went even further. They called for a change of the organizational structure of the Council on the Laity "to create a body truly representative of the laity," its officers and members freely elected by the laity; the creation of truly representative Councils of the Laity at all national, diocesan and parish levels, with officers and members freely elected by the laity; and the restructuring of national and diocesan pastoral councils, consisting of clergy, religious, and laity, "so that lay members be truly representative of the laity and freely elected by the laity."

mean that we have in the Church "two parallel hierarchies, as it were, two organizations existing side by side?" Certainly not, he insisted. It would be "absurd" to suppose that "the people of God are their own interpreters of God's word and ministers of grace," that "they can evolve religious teachings and directives, making abstraction of the faith which the Church professes with authority," that "they can boldly turn aside from tradition and emancipate themselves from the magisterium."

The Pope's words forced the Congress delegates to weigh each syllable of the resolutions they were preparing. Every statement was carefully phrased to clarify that they were not attemping to dictate, but the content was not watered down in the slightest. This is what we think, the delegates insisted, and it is our right and duty to say what we think in so far as it bears on the well-being of the Church. That Pope Paul agreed with that approach was confirmed by a reference he made to the Congress on its closing day. Addressing a group of pilgrims in the Courtyard of St. Damasus, he said it showed that "the laity are not second-class citizens."

Congress procedures called for submission of resolutions to the Assembly of Heads of Delegations by the workshops, by five delegations, or by the Steering Committee. If a two-thirds majority of the Assembly approved, they were presented for adoption in plenary Congress session. The time schedule gave the Assembly just one evening to revise all resolutions, and although it worked far into the night, it completed action on only 8 of the more than 30 texts before it. The texts were numbered in the order in which they reached the Assembly and discussed in the same order. In consequence, some of the most important ones were never reached. The suggestion that behind-the-scenes maneuvers were responsible seems, nevertheless, to be quite unfounded. The blame, if any, attaches to the formulators of a program so vast to be completed in so little time.

The resolution which seems to have caused most controversy both in the workshop which formulated it and in a plenary session on October 13 at which the conclusions of the first series of workshops were presented, dealt with responsible parenthood. "As laymen, we are convinced that responsible family planning is necessary to guarantee the integrity of matrimonial love and of the family institution, in a world where the total population is growing with such an accelerated rhythm," it read. "In the line of this unambiguously moral and Christian perspective, we are of opinion that the choice of the means to prevent a new conception should be left to the conscience of the married couple, with due consideration of medical, psychological, economic and sociological insights." This recommendation found a substantial majority support both in the workshop and at the plenary session, but a minority expressed opposition on the ground that the laity should await the decisions of the Pope with patience and confidence.

Although this text was not reached by the Assembly of Heads of Delegations and consequently did not emerge as a Congress resolution, very similar wording is included in a resolution on world development approved by the Assembly and the Congress. That resolution calls for "a radical transformation of the world economy" because of the "growing gap between rich and poor nations," a gap which "traditional attitudes towards investment and trade cannot lessen." It demands an expansion of government aid from developed countries, "free from political and economic conditions leading to a new form of alienation on the part of the young nations," the level to be raised quickly to one per cent of gross national product "in genuine capital assistance." As regards the attitude of Christians and the Church, it urges a deep theological reflection on creation, on Christ's role in creation, and on the new creation; participation of the laity not only in spreading the Church's social doctrine, but in developing it, according to their technical competence and experience; a spirituality calculated to inspire Christians to struggle for development and for the necessary change of social structures;

a distinction between charitable works in the Church and those directed to development; the encouragement of programs under which committed Christians will "accept a voluntary commitment for a limited period" to train Christians and non-Christians of the developing countries in the skills and techniques they lack; a close cooperation with other Christians and international organizations in these tasks. And to be truly a "sign of unity" (*Lumen Gentium*) among men, the Church should play a prophetic role in man's efforts to achieve international and social justice, fighting to eliminate the contrasts of wealth and poverty within the Church itself; renouncing a standard of living which is often a counter-sign; encouraging active joint works with all other Christian bodies; and the development of Church structures calculated to form a real people of God through "participation and democratic representation of the masses who play a leading role in development."

The mention of family planning came in a section dealing with demographic expansion. It recalled the duty of states to have a policy that is realistic and respectful of man, especially of the responsible freedom of the couple, a policy free from geopolitical intervention of the great powers, and neither an excuse for delaying development nor a substitute for efforts to realize it. Having affirmed the social duty of husband and wife toward responsible parenthood and the duty of Christians to participate in education in this area, it set out "the very strong feeling among Christian lay people that there is need for a clear stand by the teaching authorities of the Church which would focus on fundamental moral and spiritual values, while leaving the choice of scientific and technical means for achieving responsible parenthood to parents acting in accordance with their Christian faith and on the basis of medical and scientific consultation."

The differences of wording between the two resolutions affects neither their substance nor the intention of the Congress. To say that Christians should decide according to their *conscience* or according to their *faith* is simply a choice of words. A Christian's conscience is formed in accordance with his faith. What is clear in both cases is that the spokesmen of the laity, the ones directly concerned, wanted to get the message unambiguously across to the Pope that they believe the question of means is primarily a medical and scientific one.

The circumstances in which the action was taken adds to its significance. From the beginning of the Synod, rumors were circulating in Rome that an encyclical would shortly be issued on family planning and that it would substantially repeat the negative statements on the use of means contained in previous papal documents. To reassure the Fathers, several of whom had informally indicated a desire to raise the issue at the Synod, that no such decision had been made, Pope Paul instructed Cardinal Villot, president of the Synod, to state that the subject could not be discussed on the floor because it was not on the agenda, but that the Fathers were invited to give the Pope their views in writing. That he was still asking views showed that the Pope had not made a final decision. It also became known that he had named yet another "committee of experts" to advise him, a committee composed principally if not exclusively of Italians and consequently less well placed than the earlier commission to reflect worldwide Catholic thinking.

Such was the confused background to the discussion at the Congress. Some of the delegates opposed to a declaration went so far as to question the basic decision in favor of family planning made by Vatican Council II when it said that "parents have the right to determine the number of children they should have." Others, on the contrary, insisted not only that the Vatican Council had resolved this substantive issue but had in addition withdrawn from the previous papal stand concerning means when it said that parents should not use "blameworthy means," without identifying specified means as blameworthy. Footnote 14 of paragraph 51 of the Council document on Family Life refers to the condemnation of artificial means in Pius XI's *Casti Connubii* and Pius XII's *Allocution to the Obstetricians,* as well as to Pope Paul VI's instruction to the special papal commission on population and the family, in which he asked Catholics to follow the norms laid down by Pius XII. The note adds, however, in the same sentence: "This being the state of the magisterium, this Holy Synod does not give concrete solutions to the problem." The solution (condemnation of artificial means) given by Pius XI and Pius XII, which is mentioned in the first part of this sentence, constituted a restriction of the free exercise of the rights of parents. It consequently is neutralized by the statement in the second part of the sentence that the Vatican Council does not give concrete solutions to the problem, since it is a principle of law (as noted in Canon 19 of the Code) that restrictive regulations are to be interpreted narrowly, whereas enabling laws and privileges are to be interpreted liberally.

That such was unquestionably the sense in which the laity interpreted the Vatican Council teaching was confirmed by a "boxed" statement in *L'Osservatore Romano,* the semi-official Vatican newspaper, on October 20. Having quoted the text of the resolution of the Congress, it attributed to Cardinal Roy, president of the Ecclesiastical Commission charged with the doctrinal accuracy of the Congress statements, the observation that the laity had no intention of going beyond the Council's teaching. "This resolution is a factual confirmation of the views held by lay Christians who approach the Church's magisterium with confidence." The *Osservatore* added a further comment. "Specifically as regards the phrase 'leaving the choice of means to parents acting in accordance with their Christian faith,' it is obvious that it should be understood in the sense clearly indicated by Vatican Council II, Nos. 50-B and 51-C of the Constitution on the Church in the Modern World, namely, 'a Christian faith illuminated by the magisterium of the Church.' " Some who had fought for the resolution were at first displeased by the attempt to make it seem nothing more than a vote of confidence in the Pope's handling of the issue, when it was a clear call for a new formulation. Further reflection, however, produced a more positive reaction. Cardinal Roy was recalling his earlier notification that the Ecclesiastical Commission was the only body authorized to rule on the doctrine contained in the Congress' statements, and it had confined itself to saying that the Congress was not invading the field of theology by making known its views to the Holy Father. No gloss by the *Osservatore* could affect the substance of those views.

The workshop devoted to a study of peace produced a set of conclusions which overlapped in part those of the resolution on world development, and only lack of time prevented the two closely-related issues from being consolidated into a single resolution. The principal points were a condemnation of racial discrimination; a call for studies of ways to change the economic system which is widening the gap between rich and poor; support of the peace-making activities of Pope Paul VI and UN Secretary General U Thant; cessation of the arms race and diversion of armaments budgets to world development; a strengthening of the United Nations, coupled with a new attitude toward the Chinese Peoples' Republic and an invitation to it to join the UN; condemnation of the bombing of population centers. The wording of the resolution was softened by the Assembly of the Heads of Delegations. As passed by the Congress, it omitted explicit reference to the bombing of population centers and to China. Instead, it deplored "the scandal of all wars at present in progress," and urged "all possible steps" to end them. It also called on lay people of every country to foster all efforts "to achieve a truly universal participation in the United Nations." A separate draft resolution, which was not reached by the Assembly of the Heads of Delegations and consequently not acted on by the Congress, expressed the belief that the world is standing "on the verge of nuclear war"; condemned the bombing and massacres of civilian populations; called for immediate cease-fire negotiations, on the basis of the Geneva Agreements, in Vietnam, with the cessation of bombing of North Vietnam as a previous step; and the reconstruction of Vietnam under UN supervision.

The Congress also took note of the discrimination against women which is traditional in the Church. Women, it said, should be granted "full rights and responsibilities as Christians," and a serious doctrinal study should be undertaken into their place "within the sacramental order and within the Church." The original draft had been even stronger. It had called for full rights "both as regards the laity and the priesthood." The resolution also asked for the inclusion of women in all papal commissions and said they should be consulted on the revision of the parts of canon law which affect them.

It was a far cry indeed from the lay congresses organized in the late nineteenth century in Italy and France, and subsequently also in Germany, as a gesture of protest against the anticlericalism then rampant. Pope Paul would remember these national and regional meetings better than most, for his father (Giorgio Montini) was one of the early organizers in Italy. While the members could speak freely behind closed doors, they ended up by approving resolutions drafted for them by a tight group of clerics, resolutions which had still to be approved by higher authority before acquiring official status. Such procedures are now decently interred.

The insistence on acting as adults and being treated as adults is undoubtedly the most original of the contributions of this Congress to the life of the Church. The fact is doubly striking because of the quality of the membership, the many priests and high proportion of laymen professionally involved in Church institutions. What such people say cannot be brushed off as the voice of inexperienced malcontents. And if it confirms the existence of serious dissatisfaction with existing Church structures, it also highlights the fact that anti-clericalism is a thing of the past. Not once did workshops or plenary sessions divide along clerical-lay lines.

The Congress did not have the authority to make decisions about the way in which the voice of the laity would in future be expressed in the Church. The subject constantly recurred in both formal and informal discussion. Many wanted regular meetings of the Assembly of Heads of Delegations, particularly in view of the dominant role it played at the Congress. Some saw this Assembly as the desirable means for normal dialogue with the bishops and the instrument for the Church's work of social justice. They doubted that the Commission on the Laity and the *Justitia et Pax* Commission for world development, as curial units with nominated members, could achieve a truly representational quality or long remain free from institutional commitments. The final resolution, however, as already noted, put its trust in updating these and other existing institutions by the introduction of democratic election of the members.

Many members of the *Justitia et Pax* Commission had been delegates or experts at the Congress for the Lay Apostolate, and immediately after the Congress ended, the second plenary meeting of the Commission began. Vatican Council II's Constitution on the Church in the Modern World, Par. 90, recommended the creation of this Commission, but it came into existence only in January, 1967, following a bitter struggle over its control. The professional lay leaders, who were scheduled to become members of the Council on the Laity (recommended in the Council Decree on the Laity, Par. 26), claimed that the organization for world development should come under their jurisdiction on the ground that the temporal order was the special concern of the laity. *Caritas Internationalis* argued that its long experience in helping the poor of the world gave it an incontestable claim. The bishops, priests, and laymen who had originally promoted the idea at the Council opposed both contenders. On the one side they insisted that world development should involve all Christians, not only the laity. On the other, they sought a clear-cut distinction between charitable aid and the work of development, and they wanted a top-level body headed by a cardinal who would guarantee the possibility of operating without curial control or interference. The Solomon-like solution was the creation of two separate bodies with the same president (Cardinal Maurice Roy of Quebec) and the same vice-president (Archbishop Alberto Castelli), while including Msgr. Jean Rodhain, president of *Caritas Internationalis,* as a member of the *Justitia et Pax* Commission.

Under the energetic direction of its American secretary, Msgr. Joseph Gremillion, of Alexandria, Louisiana, the Commission established a clear line of policy and action at its inaugural meeting in April, 1967. Taking as its starting point Pope Paul's declaration to the United Nations that development is the new name for peace, it is seeking to arouse the Christian conscience to the enormity and the folly of the current and growing disequilibrium in the world, and to channel the moral force of Christianity into a concerted effort of mankind to create the conditions for peace by developing the economic and human resources of the poor nations. It will not be an agency for collecting and distributing funds. What it seeks is to establish and coordinate a network of local, national, and regional committees, in liaison with civic organizations and those of other religious bodies, dedicated to publicize and aid projects for worldwide social, economic, and political progress. Its effort will be primarily in the field of propaganda, with its objective the arousing of an awareness on the part of the entire world of the urgency of a total effort toward justice and peace.

The resolution of the Congress for the Lay Apostolate on development was directly in the line of its program, particularly the call to the developed countries to give at least one percent of gross national product to the poor nations in genuine capital assistance. Advantage was taken of the Commission's second meeting to bring its program to the attention of the Synod Fathers. They were told that 12 national committees had already been or were being established, at Brussels, Paris, Washington, London, Manila, New Delhi, Nairobi, Pretoria, Kinshasa, Montreal, Caracas, and Rio de Janeiro;

that in Brazil 13 regional committees were being set up, and that various other regional committees were in the planning stage. They learned about the very extensive program of cooperation worked out with the World Council of Churches (Geneva), covering three major areas; evangelical understanding of justice and love among men; strategies of development; encouragement of new international structures for the organization of peace. And they were informed of the Commission's plans to cooperate in the preparations for the second United Nations Conference on Trade and Development (UNCTAD) at New Delhi in 1968, and in the international year for Human Rights; and also of a 1968 meeting of the Commission itself to be held in Africa. Assurances were received from bishops of many countries that they would take the lead in getting their episcopal conferences to follow up the Commission's initiatives with vigor.

Of the Commission's 14 members 10 are lay men and women. Like the Congress of the Lay Apostolate, it came across to the Synod Fathers as primarily the voice of the laity. The message of both bodies was one calculated to impress both the bishops from all over the world and the resident advisers of the Holy Father. The Pope himself made it clear that he was touched by the sincerity and attested loyalty of the spokesmen of the laity to the Church and his own person. Many around him freely predicted that the views of the laity would carry weight when episcopal conferences met again to choose representatives for the next session of the Synod. Some even looked farther ahead to a single Synod with representatives of all the people of God instead of separate parallel meetings of bishops and the others. But that is still some distance in the future.

One who helped to bring it closer, however, was Ecumenical Patriarch Athenagoras, whose visit — arranged to coincide with the Synod of Bishops — was the first in history of a patriarch of Constantinople to Rome. In greeting him, Pope Paul stressed the symbolic meaning of the Synod as a step by the Catholic Church back toward the synodal tradition always retained by the Orthodox Churches, and while they did not meet in a session of the Synod, the Synod Fathers formed the guard of honor.

Since the presence of lay people is normal in the synodal government of the Orthodox Churches, their inclusion in the Synod of Bishops would represent another step toward the unity which Paul and Athenagoras alike seem to see as almost within grasp. During this meeting, even more than previously, it was stressed that such gestures of friendship and adjustment to each other are more important for completing the already substantial union than theological discussions and assemblies of experts. The prayer in common, which followed exactly the form of a Mass without the consecration of the bread and wine, was designed to encourage hopes of and prepare minds for the full communion which follows logically from the teaching of Vatican Council II on the Christian faith and sacramental life in Christ of the Orthodox. Here the presence of the Synod Fathers becomes doubly significant. For, in the actual historical circumstances, the organic reunion of the two "sister Churches," to use Pope Paul's own expression, can occur only within a synodal framework, a type of supreme synod which will incorporate something from that of the East and something from that of the West. Had there been no other purpose, this alone would have justified the creation of the Synod of Bishops.

Postscript

Two incidents which occurred on the afternoon of the final working session of the Synod of Bishops, October 28, made me clearly conscious of the desirability of two distinct interpretations of the event, one from the viewpoint of the institutional Church, the other from that of the contemporary world. One of these incidents further brought out for me the different emphasis given by Father Murphy and by me to the importance of each of these two viewpoints. That a difference should exist is hardly surprising. A priest professionally involved in the institution will tend to lean in one direction; a layman whose professional survival rests on his sensitivity to world opinion, in the other. Whether surprising or not, the fact of this divergence of opinion came into focus in the following manner.

I had arranged for use of Vatican Radio's facilities to tape an hour-long discussion: "Was the Synod of Bishops worth the effort?" The program was to be used by Vatican Radio itself and by several hundred radio stations in the United States, and also to be distributed for class discussion in seminaries and theology schools. Participants were Father Edward Heston, C.S.C., English-language press officer for three sessions of

Vatican Council II and for the Synod, Mr. James O'Gara, editor of *Commonweal,* Father Francis X. Murphy, and myself.

The diverse points of departure were not long in emerging when we started to evaluate what the Synod had really achieved. On one side were the two priests — content with the entire performance. "It has been worth the effort," said Father Heston. "That has been clearly reflected in the mentality of the bishops and the others who took part. It has had an awakening effect on the Church, made us realize the presence and gravity of certain problems. The effect on Catholic and world opinion was good. It shows a Church less monolithic than before. The bishops had the opportunity to speak out. They realized that they count for more in the structures of the Church than just as individual agents."

"The Synod must be seen as the development of a structure," Father Murphy added in the same vein. "The issues were perhaps not so important, but what is significant is this new way of exercising papal authority. The former primary dependence of the Pope on the Curia for advice is being transferred to residential bishops who know or should know what's going on."

Jim O'Gara saw the same facts in a significantly different light. "It did not do what the proposers suggested when the idea was put forward originally at the Council. It was a terribly churchy agenda. There was grave disappointment at the absence of such items as birth control, a burning concern for millions of Catholics all over the world, and clerical celibacy which many priests of many countries petitioned to have included. . . . The whole idea of the Synod cannot be counted a success in the life of the Church until the opinions and reflections of the people come up from the grass roots. . . . Normal times permit an organic growth. But today people are making critical decisions about whether they belong to the Church, how they relate to the Church, whether the Church has meaning for them. They won't wait twenty or thirty years."

I found myself in full agreement with Jim O'Gara, and I said so. I then suggested that there was a reason why the agenda had been so "churchy." Those who prepared it, I suggested, did not necessarily consider these the most important issues, but rather procedural points that had to be resolved before getting down to substantive problems. It is an explanation which I believe to be true. But if it is, its implications for the credibility of the Church are startling.

Before I develop the point, I must mention a letter which by an extraordinary coincidence reached me that same day. It came from a young man who teaches theology in a Catholic college in the United States, and it shouted what Jim O'Gara and I had been whispering. Jim and I, it must be remembered, are over 30. What do you people over there in Rome think you are doing, he asked in effect. Have you no understanding of what are today's concerns and how urgent they are for those who live them? Let me quote a few typical extracts.

"Stuffy, removed from the world of living and loving, the crying and laughing of the world in which God is present today — sort of clubbish like the New York Athletic for old gentlemen. I haven't talked to two people in the last week that even *read* the *few* scanty lines in print on the Synod. The reaction was: 'Oh, those churchmen are playing around again — probably saying we'll have to go back to eating fish on Friday.' Once they struck clerical celibacy from the agenda, once they maneuvered not to take up the birth control issue responsibly, it seems the world I know just realized that to continue in the old ecclesiastical line meant to call off the whole damn human effort. Now we are sure that we must go on without the Church leadership. That's the way I read it here. Wait until you come home and see what is or isn't in your world.

"The problem of our day is the problem of God: to validate human experience, here, now; the world of I or me in situation; the context of relationships of living and loving. This is where God exists, where he is, where he is present. It's an old problem. In fact, I think it may be the only problem, but today we see it more clearly. Faith can no longer be understood as an act, an exclusively cerebral thing, when the world of man has advanced to a total environmental modality of life and love. Faith is a mode of life, to live so that living and loving are one. That and no more. It is man's image of the world, his standing out. God is in no way like man, but man is in some way like God. We know that God is he whose living and loving are one. If *man,* role-centered that he is, has any goal, it is to become like God: making his living and his loving one. . . .

"The role the Church plays today, as evidenced to all in the Council and in this Synod — the drawer of lines of correct and incorrect, the formulator of obligations and rules — is a false role. She must become instead the prime stimulus to the increase and extension of human capacities, for this is the only place where God is present — in human, interpersonal relations. . . . The problem of Church has been so conveniently truncated in our cultural-ecclesiastical determination of what is acceptable and what is not, the line being so biasedly drawn as effectively to exclude the majority of men, the good men, those who live and love and hurt . . ."

Quite a blockbuster! Yet it is the unvarnished expression of the thought of a highly intelligent young man, well acquainted with the workings of the Catholic Church, professionally trained in Catholic theology, motivated to devote his life to sharing his theological knowledge with his fellow Catholics. If the writer has been, let us say, a Protestant historian or an agnostic scientist, the criticism would probably have been harsher, but the viewpoint would have been precisely the same. That is how people today think about the Church; and as Jim O'Gara said, they are not prepared to wait twenty or thirty years to get action.

Some may be tempted to reject the evaluation as unfair. The Synod was a purely internal matter of the Church, no more subject to outside judgment than are (for example) the internal decisions of a sovereign state subject to question by the United Nations. Pope Paul made the point when explaining why observers of other Christian Churches had not been invited. It is, he said, "a meeting which in both method and purpose is directed to internal questions of the Catholic Church."

The Church has, of course, every right — juridically speaking — to tell the world to mind its own business. But if it does, it has to take the consequences. It must ask itself whether or not it wants a partnership. Vatican Council II said most explicitly that it does. "We feel ourselves responsible towards the entire human family," was how Pope Paul summed up the Council's thinking during the final session. "We are under obligation to all. The Church in this world is not an end in herself. She is at the service of all men. She must make Christ present to all, both to individuals and to peoples, as widely and as generously as possible."

Credibility and relevance. They are the issues. I do not need to dwell on relevance. The difference between the concerns of the Synod and those of the Lay Congress speak for themselves. Those Catholic laymen, like my theologian friend, are concerned with war and peace, wealth and poverty, justice and love, freedom and dignity and equal rights.

Credibility, more difficult to tie down, is no whit less important. Paradoxically, the Church's increased relevancy as a result of Vatican Council II has widened the credibility gap by accentuating the contrast between what the Church proclaims and what churchmen do. Members of the institutional Church are quick to point out that officeholders in the Church are human, that one cannot expect them to change their ways overnight, that they have given a lifetime of service and are entitled to the rewards. It is a dangerous argument. It overlooks the fact that the world expects more of officeholders in the Church than it does of those in business or government. It does so because the Church proclaims that its leaders are men who have offered themselves selflessly from supernatural motives to special service, men whose only concern is the good of the community, men ready to sacrifice themselves if they are blocking the general welfare.

In addition, it is often a specious argument, used not to protect the legitimate rights of the faithful servant but the usurped privileges of one whose abuse of office actively violates the rights of a dozen people or a hundred. This is not the place to insert a long litany of such abuses. The published accounts of Vatican Council II abound with examples. An informed observer, known for his moderation of expression and passion for accuracy, Henri Fesquet, of *Le Monde* (Paris), could write in September, 1964, that members of a Roman Congregation were "trying to retrieve their prerogatives by something approaching gangland tactics." The record of the Synod of Bishops contained in the preceding chapters shows that similar goings-on still go on. All the denunciations of abuses made by the Fathers of Vatican Council II, combined with the subsequent publicity and the exhortations to reform of Pope Paul, have undoubtedly effected an improvement in the statistical picture. The officials today are more careful. Violations of human rights per month are fewer and less glaring. The insertion of new men by Pope Paul into the Curia, men like Cardinal Garrone and Cardinal Villot and Canon Charles Moeller who are in touch with contemporary reality, has helped. The record of the Synod shows that, too.

It would be naïve, however, to think that good men can substitute for institutional reform when the forms have ceased to be viable. It is the error of the United States in setting its face against social change and supporting military dictatorships in Latin America. The men in the Curia are good men. No breath of scandal touches them. Cardinals Ottaviani and Browne are the epitome of benevolence, of personal charm, of simple living. But the whole of history, ecclesiastical and civil, shows that the institution is stronger than the man.*

* In June, 1967, Pope Paul published an encyclical on clerical celibacy in which he assured the priest who was determined to leave but showed

Cardinal Garrone may momentarily decentralize the operations of the Congregation for Christian Education. But if the institution remains untouched, it is only a matter of time until it reasserts itself. The same is true at all levels of the Church, not merely in the central administration. In all of this, the Lay Congress was more realistic than the Synod of Bishops. It stressed institutional change, not mere treatment of symptoms.

What about the major changes introduced by the curial reform of August, 1967? As Father Edward D. Vogt, of the University of Bergen (Norway), a specialist in the sociology of bureaucracy, has established, they were confined to the technical area. The formal structures in a bureaucracy are often a façade to hide the real but unacknowledged mechanisms of decision. The reform stripped away the façade. It not only eliminated baroque survivals, like the Secretariat for Latin Letters, but regraded the other offices according to current power. The Secretariat of State was first in power but last in canon law. Now its power is recognized.

The introduction of a 5-year term of tenure for high officials strengthens the position, not of the pope, but of the less than a dozen cardinals who form the inner circle, each holding some six top curial positions. "Before deep structural changes have taken place," says Father Vogt, "the pope will have to confirm these cardinals after each 5-year term, leaving it to the same inner-circle cardinals to decide what changes they will like to see among the peripheral curial members." The institution of formal meetings of the Prefects, to be convened by the Cardinal Secretary of State, he adds, "seems to give legitimation to the present oligarchical rule of inner-circle

---

"serious and good dispositions for leading the Christian life of a layman," that he could expect dispensation from the obligation to chastity imposed by Canon 132. Five months later, unless he had a friend in the right place, he still had only one practical way to get the dispensation, namely, to "attempt marriage" in violation of Canon 1072, thereby incurring the penalties (and involving the other party in the penalties) prescribed in Canon 2388. This curious first step toward leading the Christian life of a layman is cynically justified by benevolent curial officials with the explanation that one must sin in order to be forgiven.

cardinals. It seems to come dangerously close to the reduction of the pope to a figure-head constitutional monarch, with the Cardinal Secretary of State as the head of his government, ruling in his majesty's name."

All of this is not to deny the value of the reform but simply to put it in perspective. The organization remains pyramidal and consequently can function only for secondary routine activities. The primary functions — legislation, policy-making, decision-making, allocation of resources, control — must, as Father Vogt also points out, be a social process, a common undertaking of the governor and the governed. "If the leader refuses to include the group in his decisions, at least through informal consultation, he thereby suspends his own leadership." Such is equally the message of the Lay Congress: "truly representative . . . at all levels . . . across the world."

In this perspective, also, one can see why the world is so disturbed by what churchmen describe as secrecy but what is actually an organized manipulation of the news. Bureaucracy in the Church, as bureaucracy in general, has always been conscious of the value of knowledge. Historically, the paternalistic system of exercise of authority characteristic of the functioning of the modern Roman Catholic Church, goes back to the Middle Ages when knowledge was the preserve of the few, leaving the many with no viable choice other than to accept their judgment. Information has always had a value and a price in Rome. Long before Marshal McLuhan shrieked it from the housetops, it was known there that information is the ultimate commodity. Naturally, one does not give away for nothing what has a value, which explains the long-established Roman tradition of selling news to promote institutional, ideological or personal objectives, or some combination of the three. The article in *Il Messaggero* insinuating that the "simple faithful" are rejecting the erroneous leadership of their bishops* is a typical example of the working of the system.

---

* See p. 154, above.

Today, however, two factors are missing from the equation. It assumes that the information is the private property of an individual or of a group of officials. And it assumes that the technical conditions for maintaining secrecy can be assured. Nobody questions the right of a pope or of a president to consult in secret with his advisers before formulating and announcing his policy. But we would think it very naïve if the President of the United States imagined he could keep out of the newspapers a series of position papers he distributed to several thousand officials as a preliminary to a policy-making session. It would be only slightly less naïve to imagine there would be no leaks from a session attended by 200 advisers representing a range of views on the issues. The experience of the Synod of Bishops demonstrates that it is equally naïve in Church matters. To compound the folly, the news manipulation is not even a technically good job, and in consequence it does not promote the desired objectives. At the Vatican Radio discussion just mentioned, the comment was made that the Synod debates — as reported — sounded very legalistic and formalistic. Father Heston, who was present at the debates but was not responsible for the content of the handouts, agreed that these gave a misleading impression. "The summations in the official press bulletin," he said textually, "did not represent the complete discussion."

The second missing factor is that such secrecy overlooks the right of the people to know, a right based not merely on their dignity as persons, but also on the need of the society to which they belong. The teaching of the Church on the point is crystal clear. Pope Pius XII saw public opinion as inherent in the social nature of man, a necessary element in every normal human society, including the Church. "Something would be missing in the Church's life," he told the World Congress of the Catholic Press in 1950, "if public opinion was lacking, and both pastors and people would be to blame." But the practice of the Church continues to contradict its professions. Even when the bishops of Canada went on public record that the Synod *needed* the feedback of public opinion, they were ignored.

What more need I say? Is it any wonder that the world, including a growing number of Catholics, regards this institution as low in relevance and credibility? Father Murphy says in effect that the Synod of Bishops we have just had is the best we are currently capable of. I fear he is right. If he is, we have a long way to go from our present five percent or fifteen percent Synod. And a lot of people aren't prepared to wait twenty or thirty years.

Gary MacEoin

APPENDIX 1

*The Motu Proprio, Apostolica Sollicitudo**

Observing attentively the signs of the times, we are making every effort to adapt the orientations and methods of the apostolate to the growing needs of our time and the evolution of society. Hence our apostolic solicitude calls upon us to consolidate by ever closer ties our union with the bishops "whom the Holy Spirit has placed to rule the Church of God" (Acts, 20, 28). We are drawn to this not only by the respect, esteem, and gratitude which we have for all our venerable brothers in the episcopate, but also by the very heavy burden of our office of universal pastor which obliges us to lead the people of God toward the eternal pastures. In these times of ours, so troubled and critical yet so open to the salutary call of grace, daily experience shows us how useful for our apostolic charge is this union with the bishops. We wish to do everything in our power to promote and develop this union, "in order to have around us" — as we said on another occasion — "the comfort of your presence, the support of your counsel, the weight of your authority." (Allocution at close of third session, 21 November, 1964; AAS 56–1007).

It was appropriate, therefore, especially during the Second Vatican Council, that we should be deeply aware of the importance and necessity for us to call more and more upon the cooperation of the bishops for the good of the universal Church. The ecumenical Council was in fact the cause of our resolve to establish a consultative body of bishops on a permanent basis, for in doing so we desired that after the Council the Christian people would continue to enjoy the abundant benefits which our close union with the bishops brought them during the Council itself.

Now that we are approaching the end of the Second ecumenical Council of the Vatican, we think the time has come to put into effect this plan long since resolved upon. We do it the more willingly for being clearly aware how favorable the bishops of the Catholic world are to this proposal, as is shown by the numerous wishes which they expressed on the subject during the Council.

---

* This translation taken from *Canon Law Digest, Supplement 1965,* by T. L. Bouscaren, S.J., and James T. O'Connor, S.J. (Milwaukee: Bruce).

Accordingly, after mature deliberation, because of our esteem and respect for all the Catholic bishops, and that they may have a more manifest and effective share in our solicitude for the universal Church, of our own motion and in virtue of our apostolic authority, we erect and establish in this city of Rome a permanent consultative body of bishops for the universal Church subject directly and immediately to our authority, and to be known as the Synod of Bishops (*Synodus Episcoporum*).

This Synod, which like all human institutions may be perfected in the course of time, is to be governed by the following general norms.

I. GENERAL CHARACTERISTICS

The Synod of Bishops, that is, of the bishops chosen in the various countries of the world to give effective aid to the supreme Pastor of the Church, shall be so continued that it is: *a*) a central ecclesiastical organism; *b*) representing the entire Catholic episcopate; *c*) of a perpetual character; *d*) of such a structure that its function shall be exercised temporarily and occasionally.

II. GENERAL AND SPECIAL ENDS

From its very nature the Synod of Bishops has for its purpose to give information and counsel. It may also have deliberative power when this is given to it by the Sovereign Pontiff, to whom it shall pertain in such case to ratify the decision of the Synod.

1. The general purposes of the Synod of Bishops are: *a*) to maintain close union and collaboration between the Sovereign Pontiff and the bishops of the entire world; *b*) to see that direct and true information be given on situations and questions relative to the internal life of the Church and to the action which the Church should take in the world of today; *c*) to facilitate the concordance of views, at least on essential points of doctrine and on the modalities of the life of the Church.

2. Its special and proximate purposes are: *a*) to establish an exchange of useful information; *b*) to give advice on the questions for which the Synod has been convened.

III. THE AUTHORITY OF THE ROMAN PONTIFF

The Synod of Bishops is directly and immediately subject to the authority of the Roman Pontiff, to whom it belongs:

1. To convoke the Synod whenever he judges it opportune to do so, indicating the place where it is to meet;

2. To ratify the election of the members mentioned in numbers V and VIII;

3. To determine the matter of the questions to be dealt with, if possible at least six months before the meeting of the Synod;

4. To see that the matter of the questions to be treated be sent to those who are to take part in the examination of these questions;

5. To establish the program of the questions to be discussed;

6. To preside over the Synod, in person or through others.

IV. THREE TYPES OF MEETINGS

The Synod of Bishops may be convoked as a general assembly, as an extraordinary assembly, or as a special assembly.

V. THE GENERAL ASSEMBLY

When it meets as a general assembly, the Synod includes in the first place and of its very nature:

1. *a*) The patriarchs, the major archbishops and metropolitans who do not form part of the patriarchates of the Catholic Churches of the Oriental rite.

b) The bishops elected by each of the national episcopal conferences as provided in n. VIII;

c) The bishops elected by the episcopal conferences of several countries, constituted for countries that have no conference of their own, according to n. VIII;

d) And moreover ten religious representing clerical religious institutes and elected by the Roman Union of Superiors General.

2. Those Cardinals who are at the head of the various dicasteries of the Roman Curia also form part of the general assembly of the Synod of Bishops.

VI. THE EXTRAORDINARY ASSEMBLY

When it meets as an extraordinary assembly, the Synod of Bishops comprises:

1. *a*) The patriarchs, the major archbishops and metropolitans who do not form part of the patriarchates of the Catholic Churches of the Oriental rite;

b) The presidents of the national episcopal conferences;

c) The presidents of the episcopal conferences of several nations constituted for nations that have no conference of their own;

d) Three religious representing clerical religious institutes and elected by the Roman Union of Superiors General.

2. Those Cardinals who are at the head of the various dicasteries of the Roman Curia also form part of the extraordinary assembly of the Synod of Bishops.

VII. THE SPECIAL ASSEMBLY

When it meets as a special assembly, the Synod of Bishops comprises the patriarchs, the major archbishops and metropolitans who do not form part of the patriarchates of the Catholic Churches of the Oriental rite, the representatives of the episcopal conferences of one or several nations, and those of religious institutes as stated in numbers V and VIII. But all must belong to the regions for which the Synod has been convoked.

VIII. THE REPRESENTATIVES OF EPISCOPAL CONFERENCES

The bishops who represent each of the national conferences are elected in the following manner:

a) One for each national episcopal conference that has not more than 25 members;

b) Two for each episcopal conference that has not more than 50 members;

c) Three for each national episcopal conference that has not more than 100 members;

d) Four for each national episcopal conference that has more than 100 members.

The episcopal conferences that are common to several nations elect their representatives according to the same rules.

IX. NECCESSARY QUALIFICATIONS

For the election to the Synod of Bishops, of representatives of episcopal conferences of one or several nations and of religious, particular account should be taken not only of their knowledge and prudence in general but also of their theoretical and practical acquaintance with the questions to be treated in the Synod.

X. SUPPLEMENTARY MEMBERS

The Sovereign Pontiff may, if he wishes, augment the number of members of the Synod of Bishops by adding to them some Bishops, some religious representatives of religious institutes, or some expert ecclesiastics, in a proportion not exceeding 15 percent of the total number indicated in numbers V and VIII.

XI. CESSATION OF POWERS

When the session for which the Synod of Bishops was convoked is terminated, by that very fact both the assembly of persons composing the Synod and the functions and charges belonging to each member as such come to an end.

XII. SECRETARIES

The Synod of Bishops has one perpetual or general secretary, who is assisted by the desired number of collaborators. Besides, each session of the Synod of Bishops has its special secretary, who remains in charge until the end of the session.

Both the general secretary and the special secretaries are appointed by the Sovereign Pontiff.

Thus We have decided and decreed, all things to the contrary notwithstanding.

Given at Rome, from Saint Peter's the 15th of September, in the year 1965, the third of Our Pontificate.

APPENDIX 2

*Procedure for the Meeting of the Synod of Bishops**

REGULATIONS ISSUED BY THE CARDINAL SECRETARY OF STATE, WITH PAPAL APPROVAL

Ut Generales Normae *December 8, 1966*

The General Norms providing for the establishment of a synod of bishops for the universal Church were set down by His Holiness Pope Paul VI in his *motu proprio* of September 15, 1965. In order that they may be properly carried out, the August Pontiff has approved the present set of procedures for the meeting of this synod, and orders that they be duly observed. These procedures govern everything that was set down in the above mentioned *motu proprio*.

Given at Rome, December 8th, the feast of the Immaculate Conception of the Blessed Virgin Mary, 1966.

AMLETO Cardinal CICOGNANI
Secretary of State

PART ONE: THE SUPREME POWER AND THOSE WHO TAKE PART IN THE SYNOD OF BISHOPS

CHAPTER ONE: THE SUPREME PONTIFF

ARTICLE ONE: THE POWER OF THE SUPREME PONTIFF

The Supreme Pontiff alone will have power to:

1. Call together the Synod of Bishops, as often as it seems timely

* From *The Pope Speaks,* Vol. 12, No. 1 (1967).

to him, and to designate the place where the meetings shall be held.

2. Ratify the election of the members or participants.

3. Determine topics for discussion.

4. See to it that this subject matter is communicated to those who are to take part in the discussion.

5. Determine the agenda.

6. Preside over the synod either personally or through representatives.

7. Deliberate on the opinions voiced.

CHAPTER TWO: THE PRESIDENT-DELEGATE

ARTICLE TWO: APPOINTMENT OF THE PRESIDENT-DELEGATE

§ 1. The president-delegate presides over the meeting of the synod of bishops in the name and with the authority of the Supreme Pontiff.

§ 2. The president-delegate is appointed by the Supreme Pontiff himself. His office ceases after the session for which he was nominated is completed.

§ 3. If the Supreme Pontiff should appoint more than one delegate, these will succeed each other in office in the order set down by the Supreme Pontiff himself.

ARTICLE THREE: DUTIES OF THE PRESIDENT-DELEGATE

The duties of the president-delegate are:

1. To act as moderator for the synod in accordance with the faculties given him in the letter of delegation and with the agenda order already established, following, of course, the procedural norms prescribed in the present set of arrangements.

2. To assign specific duties to one or another of the synod's participants whenever this will prove helpful in facilitating the work of the synod.

3. To undersign the official acts of the synod. In cases where there is more than one president-delegate, all of them undersign the official acts.

CHAPTER THREE: THE MEETINGS OF THE SYNOD

ARTICLE FOUR: INDIVIDUAL MEETINGS OF THE SYNOD

The Synod of Bishops is convoked:

1. For a *general* meeting if the matters to be treated are of such nature or import that the doctrinal belief, prudent advice and expressed desires of the entire episcopacy of the Catholic world should be sought.

2. For an *extraordinary* session if the topics involve the good of the universal Church and require speedy resolution.

3. For a *special* session if the important matter to be discussed concerns the good of the Church in one or more specific regions in particular.

CHAPTER FOUR: THE MEMBERS OR PARTICIPANTS

Article Five: Participants in the Synod

§ 1. The following are members of a *general* session of the synod:

1. a) Patriarchs, major archbishops and metropolitans outside the patriarchates of Eastern rite Catholic Churches.

b) Bishops who have been elected by their national episcopal conferences, according to the norms set down in Art. 6, para. 1, no. 3.

c) Bishops elected by episcopal conferences set up by several nations jointly for those nations which do not have their own conference, according to the provisions of Art. 6, para. 1, no. 4.

d) Ten religious men to represent clerical religious institutes, elected by the Roman Union of Superiors General.

2. Cardinals in charge of the dicasteries [departments] of the Roman Curia.

§ 2. The following are members of an *extraordinary* session of the synod:

1. a) Patriarchs, major archbishops and metropolitans outside the patriarchates of Eastern rite Catholic Churches.

b) Presidents of the national episcopal conferences.

c) Presidents of the joint episcopal conferences of nations which have no episcopal conference of their own.

d) Three religious men, representing clerical religious institutes, elected by the Roman Union of Superiors General.

2. Cardinals in charge of the dicasteries of the Roman Curia.

§ 3. The following are members of a *special* session of the synod:

1. Patriarchs, major archbishops and metropolitans outside the patriarchates of Eastern rite Catholic Churches, as well as those who represent individual or joint national episcopal conferences or religious institutes (as stated in para. 1 of this article, in Art. 6, para. 1, no. 4, and, as concerns the number of religious, in Art. 6, para. 2, no. 4). All these must, however, belong to the region or regions for which the special meeting of the Synod of Bishops was convoked.

2. Cardinals in charge of the dicasteries of the Roman Curia which have competence in the matters to be treated in a special session are members of that session.

§ 4. Those are also members at individual meetings who have been chosen by the Supreme Pontiff in accordance with the norm laid down in the apostolic letter *Apostolica Sollicitudo* of September 15, 1965.

ARTICLE SIX: THE ELECTION OF MEMBERS

§ 1. 1. Bishops elected by secret ballot by their own individual or joint national conferences gathered together in plenary session are to be considered members.

2. These elections shall take place according to the norms of Canon Law. If more than one is to be elected, each is to be elected on a separate ballot, one after the other.

3. Bishops who represent individual episcopal conferences are to be elected as follows:

a) One for each national episcopal conference having no more than 25 members.

b) Two for each national episcopal conference having no more than 50 members.

c) Three for each national episcopal conference having no more than 100 members.

d) Four for each national episcopal conference having more than 100 members.

4. Joint national episcopal conferences are to follow the same norms for electing representatives.

5. In electing bishops, consideration should be given not only to their general knowledge and prudence, but also to their thorough understanding of both the theoretical and practical aspects of the matters to be treated by the synod.

6. The presidents of episcopal conferences shall report the names of the elected to the secretary-general through the papal legate of their own nation at least two months before the meeting is to begin.

§ 2. 1. The election of religious mentioned above in Art. 5 should take place, with suitable applications where needed, according to the norm of para. 1, no. 2 of this article.

2. In the election of religious men, consideration should be given not only to their general knowledge and prudence, but also to their thorough understanding of both the theoretical and practical aspects of the matters to be treated by the synod.

3. The president of the Roman Union of Superiors General will communicate the names of the elected to the secretary-general at least two months before the synod convenes.

4. Not more than two religious members are to be chosen by the Roman Union of Superiors General to represent the religious

institutes as experts at *special* meetings of the synod. These men should be acquainted either with the matter to be treated or the region involved in the calling of the session, though they need not actually come from that region.

§ 3. The names of bishops and Religious who have been elected are not to be publicized until the Pope has ratified their election.

Article Seven: Delegates' Credentials

At the beginning of any meeting of the synod, the elected delegates shall show their delegate credentials to the Supreme Pontiff through the secretary-general. These credentials must be signed by the president and secretary of their own respective conference or, in the case of religious, by the president and secretary of the Roman Union of Superiors General.

CHAPTER FIVE: STUDY COMMISSIONS

Article Eight: The Establishing of Study Commissions

If the matter treated by the synod needs further elucidation, it is up to the president-delegate, with the consent of the Supreme Pontiff, to set up various study commissions among the participants.

CHAPTER SIX: THE COMMISSION FOR DISPUTED MATTERS

Article Nine: The Establishment and Role of the Commission for Disputed Matters

At the beginning of each session, the Supreme Pontiff will set up a commission composed of three members whose duty it will be to duly examine disputed matters and to refer them to the Supreme Pontiff.

CHAPTER SEVEN: THE PERMANENT SECRETARY OR SECRETARY-GENERAL

Article Ten: Appointment of the Secretary-General

The permanent secretary or secretary-general is appointed by the Supreme Pontiff. He will carry out his office in accord with the wishes of the Pontiff.

Article Eleven: Duties of the Secretary-General

§ 1. The secretary-general is to follow the orders of the Supreme Pontiff and report to him everything concerning the Synod of Bishops.

§ 2. The secretary-general himself participates in the meetings of the synod, acts as moderator of the general secretariat and undersigns all official acts of the synod.

§ 3. It is also up to the secretary-general:

1. To send the letter convening the synod, once he has received orders from the Supreme Pontiff; also to send the agenda as well as any other documents, instructions or announcements pertaining to this particular meeting of the synod.

2. To communicate to all interested parties the names of those members whom the Supreme Pontiff himself has decided to send to the synod, in accordance with the norms of the apostolic letter *Apostolica Sollicitudo,* of September 15, 1965; also to report the name of the one chosen by the Supreme Pontiff to be special secretary of the session.

3. To prepare the agenda for each session, submitting the same to the Supreme Pontiff as well as a list of the members for his ratification.

4. To send a written report of the proceedings of each session to the cardinals in charge of the dicasteries of the Roman Curia, to patriarchs, major archbishops and metropolitans outside the patriarchates of Eastern rite Catholic Churches, to the presidents of the episcopal conferences and to the president of the Roman Union of Superiors General.

5. To execute whatever mandates the synod has laid on him.

6. To collect, arrange and preserve the official acts and documents.

Article Twelve: Assistants of the Secretary-General

§ 1. Assistants of the secretary-general are to be named by the secretary-general and are subordinate to him. They are subject to the approval of the Supreme Pontiff.

§ 2. These assistants are chosen from among ecclesiastics who are knowledgeable, prudent and suited for this task.

§ 3. If the situation demands, experts or technical advisors can be chosen by the secretary-general, with the approval of the Supreme Pontiff.

CHAPTER EIGHT: THE SPECIAL SECRETARY

Article Thirteen: Appointment of the Special Secretary

§ 1. The special secretary is to be named by the Supreme Pontiff for a particular session when the matter to be treated falls under his special expertise.

§ 2. If several matters are to be treated in a session, a special secretary is named for each topic.

§ 3. The office of special secretary ceases once the session is over.

Article Fourteen: Duties of the Special Secretary

The special secretary is meant to be of service to the president-delegate, to the assembly itself and to the secretary-general in the preparation of documents and reports, as well as in providing explanations and clarifications that might be requested. He is also to be of service in the compilation of the official acts.

PART TWO: GENERAL NORMS

CHAPTER ONE: CONVOCATION OF THE SYNOD OF BISHOPS

ARTICLE FIFTEEN: MANNER OF CONVOCATION

§ 1. The Synod of Bishops is convoked by the Supreme Pontiff at the time and in the manner deemed advisable.

§ 2. It is the president's duty to announce the day and hour of the next meeting, as well as the matter to be discussed, according to arrangements prescribed above.

§ 3. Individuals will be notified only if the president judges it necessary.

CHAPTER TWO: CLOTHING TO BE WORN

ARTICLE SIXTEEN: CLOTHING TO BE WORN AT MEETINGS

In meetings of the assembly, participants to whom it applies should wear their ordinary attire without mantelleta; others should wear their normal public dress.

CHAPTER THREE: PRECEDENCE

ARTICLE SEVENTEEN: ORDER OF PRECEDENCE

§ 1. The prescriptions of Canon 106, no. 3 (CJC) and of Canon 37, no. 3 (CJC-*De Personis*) regarding precedence, are to be followed.

§ 2. If one of the members should by chance take his seat out of due order, put forth an opinion or do anything else out of order, he acquires no special right thereby, nor does he establish any kind of precedent.

CHAPTER FOUR: THE SECRECY TO BE KEPT

ARTICLE EIGHTEEN: THE OBLIGATION OF MAINTAINING SECRECY

All who take part in the synod are bound to maintain secrecy both as regards the preparatory business and the work of the assembly. This applies particularly to opinions and votes of individuals, and to the decisions and conclusions of the assembly itself.

CHAPTER FIVE: THE LANGUAGE TO BE USED IN THE SYNOD

Article Nineteen: The Language To Be Used in the Meetings and in the Official Acts

In the congregations of the synod, and in the compilation of its official acts, the Latin language is used.

CHAPTER SIX: COLLECTION AND DISTRIBUTION OF THE OFFICIAL ACTS AND DOCUMENTS

Article Twenty: Manner of Collecting and Distributing the Official Acts and Documents

§ 1. All the official acts and documents are collected and distributed by the secretary-general.

§ 2. An index of the questions to be treated by the synod is sent, if possible, six months before the meeting begins. This will allow time for the convocation of episcopal conferences so that opinions may be solicited.

CHAPTER VII: SOLICITING OPINIONS FROM THE EPISCOPAL CONFERENCES

Article Twenty-One: Manner of Soliciting Opinions

§ 1. Matters which the Supreme Pontiff has ordered to be treated in the synod should be carefully studied beforehand by each episcopal conference or meeting of Eastern rite bishops.

§ 2. Each episcopal body should give its common opinion on how the matter should best be handled.

§ 3. These opinions are expressed by the individual members of the synod in the actual meeting of the synod.

CHAPTER EIGHT: VOTING

Article Twenty-Two: The Taking of Votes

After the members have expressed their opinions (cf. Art. 21, no. 3), the matter is put to a vote, if the Supreme Pontiff so decides.

Article Twenty-Three: Voting Procedure

§ 1. Votes in the synod will be cast according to the formula "*placet,*" "*non placet,*" or "*placet iuxta modum*" when the vote taken involves the approval of a schema in whole or in part; but in votes concerning emendations or modifications or in any other type of vote, the formula "*placet*" and "*non placet*" will be used.

§ 2. Whoever casts a *"placet iuxta modum"* vote will be expected to explain his reservations clearly and concisely in writing.

§ 3. Votes will be cast on the ballots provided for that purpose unless the president indicates another method as, for example, standing or sitting, raising or not raising the hand.

Article Twenty-Four: Majority Vote

§ 1. As regards the required majority vote, if the approval of a given matter is at stake, a two-thirds majority is required, whereas in the case of the disapproval of a given matter an absolute majority is required.

§ 2. The norm of para. 1 is to be followed both in cases where advice is to be offered to the Supreme Pontiff and in cases where the synod is to render a final decision on some matter, after the Supreme Pontiff has given his permission.

§ 3. Should a procedural question arise, it should be resolved by an absolute majority of the voting members.

CHAPTER NINE: ABSENT MEMBERS

Article Twenty-Five: The Obligation To Report Absence

Anyone who is unable to be present at a meeting should give his reason to the secretary-general.

CHAPTER TEN: DISPENSATION FROM THE OBLIGATION OF RESIDENCE

Article Twenty-Six: Gaining Fruits From a Benefice

Anyone who is bound to attend the synod, or who devotes himself to its work in any way, is excused from the obligation of residence during the time of the meeting and while he is present at or working for the synod. He is also entitled to receive any returns or daily revenues from his benefices with the exception of those specifically allotted to those in actual residence.

Part Three: PROCEDURE

CHAPTER ONE: SACRED RITES

Article Twenty-Seven: The Opening and Closing of a Session

§ 1. A meeting of the synod is opened by the celebration of Mass and the solemn chanting of the hymn *Veni Creator Spiritus.*

§ 2. Likewise, the session is closed by the celebration of Mass and the solemn chanting of the hymn *Te Deum.*

CHAPTER TWO: THE REPORT

Article Twenty-Eight: Preparation of the Report

§ 1. A detailed report dealing with the matter to be discussed in the synod is prepared by the bishop who was assigned this task by the Supreme Pontiff at the time the session was called.

§ 2. The special secretary should be at the disposal of the one preparing the report.

ARTICLE TWENTY-NINE: DELIVERY OF THE REPORT

The text of the report, which is to be read in the synod, must be handed in to the secretary-general at least 30 days ahead of time. The latter shall have copies printed for the members.

CHAPTER THREE: THE TAKING OF OFFICE BY THE PRESIDENT-DELEGATE

ARTICLE THIRTY: THE WAY IN WHICH THE PRESIDENT-DELEGATE IS TO TAKE OFFICE

At the first meeting of the synod, if circumstances permit, the secretary-general reads the complete text of the papal document appointing the president-delegate. The president then assumes office immediately.

CHAPTER FOUR: ACTUAL PROCEDURE DURING MEETINGS OF THE SYNOD

ARTICLE THIRTY-ONE: EXPOSITION AND ILLUSTRATION OF THE TOPIC

The president announces the question to be taken up and calls for the one who prepared the report. This speaker proceeds to read the paper he has prepared beforehand, with the help of the special secretary if this is necessary.

ARTICLE THIRTY-TWO: DISCUSSION

§ 1. The president, following a list drawn up by the secretary-general, calls the names of those members who have indicated their wish to address the assembly.

§ 2. After addressing the assembly, speakers should hand in the text of their remarks to the secretary-general.

ARTICLE THIRTY-THREE: REBUTTALS

§ 1. Some members may wish to make a comment or register an objection after hearing the remarks of one of the speakers. He can seek permission from the president to do so.

§ 2. It is up to the president to give permission for such a response, and to determine the time at which it will be given.

§ 3. When he has set the day, and taking into account the list drawn up by the secretary-general, he notifies those Fathers who have requested permission to make responses.

§ 4. Unless the president sets a time limit, speakers should make their responses as brief as possible.

§ 5. One member may speak in the name of several members. If he does so, he should indicate those in whose name he is speaking.

§ 6. Responses are then to be turned in to the Secretary-general in writing.

Article Thirty-Four: Study Commissions

§ 1. If debate shows that a particular question needs further study, the president-delegate can, with the permission of the Supreme Pontiff and according to the rules set up by him (Art. 8), establish a special commission to examine the matter further.

§ 2. In the meantime, the synod proceeds to the examination of other matters.

§ 3. 1. Once the study commission has reached its conclusions, they should be presented to the members by a speaker of the commission's choice.

2. If the members request it, the president may allow a very brief discussion of these conclusions. The discussion must be in keeping with the norms set down in Art. 32.

Article Thirty-Five: Formal Expression of Opinions

§ 1. Once the discussion has been completed, each member makes known his mind on the question, expressing the opinion which was mentioned in Art. 21, para. 2. It is then put in writing and handed in to the secretary-general.

§ 2. If the Supreme Pontiff calls for a vote, it should be taken in accordance with the norms of Art. 22–24.

CHAPTER FIVE: REPORT TO BE GIVEN AFTER WORK HAS BEEN COMPLETED

Article Thirty-Six: Making the Report

When the business has been finished, the secretary-general, with the help of the special secretary, will give a report describing the work on the matter or matters which were examined and stating the conclusions reached by the members.

Article Thirty-Seven: Submitting This Report to the Supreme Pontiff

The president-delegate and secretary-general will submit the report spoken of in Art. 36 to the Supreme Pontiff.

APPENDIX 3

Pope Paul's Address at Official Opening of Synod of Bishops, September 29, 1967

Venerable Brothers,

Grace to you and peace from God our Father and the Lord Jesus Christ. In greeting you, we express our great esteem for you, our joy in welcoming you and our happiness at seeing you gathered around us once again. In the Episcopal Synod, whose first meeting we are beginning today, we see you as the chosen representatives of the whole Hierarchy of the Catholic Church as Pastors of the entire People of God. We greet you, dearly beloved Brothers; we greet the Churches you come from; your presence here and your charity is the noble sign of the wonderful union they have with one another, which truly forms in a mystical manner the bond of God's holy Church. We thank you for giving expression to the feelings they all have, for showing as chosen representatives of the Hierarchy your devotion and affection for us, and for declaring your resolve to work at all times with one accord for God's glory and the world's salvation. This expression merits our acclaim and our gratitude, it matches your goodness and your awareness of your mandate. Our blessing goes with it.

You know the task we are about.

We have celebrated together the eucharistic sacrifice which for its excellence is called *mysterium fidei* and *mysterium caritatis.* No other name can be given to this wonderful sacrament whereby we, pilgrims in time, have Christ's real presence in our midst in the bloodless representation of His redemptive sacrifice. No knowledge other than belief in His word gives us certainty of such a lofty reality; no explanation gives us any adequate understanding of such a great gift save the unbounded charity of Christ Who instituted it and our own humble charity which tries to answer His in all it implies of love bringing union and spreading to others without limit. It is the Mass, this celebration of our repeated good fortune enabling us to have an encounter with Christ not only by way of commemoration, symbol and promise, but principally by way of true living communion also, though this is hidden and expressed in sacramental signs; it is our strength, our food and happiness; it is our joy, lowly yet blessed, which allows us in the wearying vicissitudes of earth to have an inexpressible foretaste of life in heaven; it is our daily encounter in the sign of His cross with Christ glorious at the right hand of the Father; it is Christ's power at work, bringing together in the unity of His mystical body those who partake of Him, the one bread of the multitude of the Faithful.

Why are we saying all this when it is already so familiar and dear to you?

The reason is that we think it can be and should be uppermost in our minds in circumstances such as these which call us to a full lively profession of faith and love.

Now, two years after the termination of the Ecumenical Council, we are, as we promised, gathered once again in this sacred building for a twofold purpose: to honor by the offering of our faith the centenary commemoration of the martyrdom of Saints Peter and Paul, and to enkindle our charity in view of an auspicious first meeting of the Synod of Bishops. These purposes of ours are not without manifest reference to the Council itself. While not possessing the Council's solemnity and power, this gathering of so eminent and authoritative a number of Bishops with the humble successor of Saint Peter, has nevertheless some principal objectives of its own. Foremost among these is the preservation and strengthening of the Catholic faith, its integrity, its strength, its development, its doctrinal and historical coherence and the acknowledgement of the faith as the indispensable foundation of the christian life which is the cause and raison d'être of the Church. We cannot forget the solemn words with which our Predecessor of venerable memory, John XXIII, opened the Second Vatican Ecumenical Council and determined the lofty and essential aim to which it was committed:

' . . . the Twenty-first Ecumenical Council, which will draw upon the effective and important wealth of juridical, liturgical, apostolic and administrative experiences, wishes to transmit the doctrine, pure and integral, without any attenuation or distortion, which throughout twenty centuries, notwithstanding difficulties and contrasts, has become the common patrimony of men. It is a patrimony not well received by all, but always a rich treasure available to men of good will. . . . Now it is necessary for all the teaching of the Church in its entirety to be accepted with a fresh enthusiasm by all, with serenity and tranquillity, in the precision of language and formulation handed down to us which is to be seen most clearly in the acts of the Council of Trent and the First Vatican Council . . ." (A.A.S., LIV, 1962. pp. 791–792).

The solicitude for doctrinal fidelity, which was so solemnly declared at the beginning of the recent Council, must therefore direct our post-conciliar times. More watchfulness is required on the part of those who in the Church of God have from Christ the mandate to teach, to spread His message and to guard the 'deposit' of faith, in proportion as the dangers which today threaten Her are more numerous and serious; immense dangers caused by the irreligious orientation of the modern mentality, and insidious dangers which even from within the Church find utterance in the work of teachers and writers, desirous, it is true, of giving new expression to catholic doctrine but frequently desirous rather of adapting the dogma of the faith to secular thought and language, than of adhering to the norm of the Church's magisterium. Thus they allow free rein to the opinion that one may forget the demands of orthodoxy and select from among the truths of the faith those which instinctive personal preference finds admissible, rejecting the others, as if the rights of moral conscience, free and responsible for its acts, may be claimed in preference to the rights of truth, foremost among which are the rights of divine revelation (cfr. Gal 1, 6–9); and to the opinion that one may subject to revision the doctrinal heritage of the Church to give christianity new ideological dimensions, far different from the theological dimensions outlined by genuine tradition with immeasurable respect for God's own thought. Faith, as we know, is not the result of an arbitrary or merely naturalistic interpretation of the Word of God, as it is not religious expression arising from the collective opinion without authoritative guidance, of those who claim to be believers, not, much less, acquiescence in the philosophical or sociological trends of the passing historical moments. Faith is adherence with our entire spiritual being to the wonderful and merciful message of salvation communicated to us by the luminous yet hidden ways of revelation; faith is not only search, but also, and principally, certainty; and more than the result of our inquiry faith is a mysterious gift which demands docility and responsiveness to the majestic dialogue of God which speaks to our souls if they are attentive and trustful.

For this reason we considered the safeguarding of the faith so imperative after the close of the Council that we invited the whole Church to celebrate a 'year of faith' in honor of the two Apostles, the chief teachers and witnesses of Christ's Gospel. The purpose of this year is to meditate on the very faith handed down to us and to assess in the modern context the decisive function this fundamental virtue has for the stability of our religion and the vitality of the Church, for building up God's kingdom in souls, for ecumenical dialogue and the genuine contact for renewal that Christ's followers intend to make with the world of today. We want in this way to strengthen our own faith as teachers, witnesses and pastors in God's Church, so that Christ her sole and supreme Head, Christ living and invisible, may find it humble, sincere and strong. We want also to strengthen the faith of our children, especially those who pursue the study of theology and religion, so that with a renewed and watchful awareness of the Church's unalterable and certain teaching they may give wise collaboration to furthering the sacred sciences and to upholding the sacred aim of catholic teaching, giving life through light.

This, Venerable Brothers, is the reason for our invitation to you to join us in celebrating the *mysterium fidei* over the tomb of Peter the Apostle, beside his unworthy but true successor, to experience once again the secret inspiring charism of the faith and see its demanding obligations which are a source of strength.

Then from the *mysterium caritatis,* the radiance from the eucharistic sacrifice, we must reach the spirit and try to penetrate the inner meaning of the second purpose which has brought us together here, a purpose of great significance, since it is something new and has repercussions on the life of the Church, we mean the opening of the *Synodus Episcoporum.*

It is not our intention to speak now of this new institution; we have already stated its nature and purpose in our Motu Proprio *Apostolica sollicitudo* of 15th September 1965 (A.A.S. LVII, 1965, pp. 775–80), and tomorrow we shall have occasion to add some account of the canonical aspect. Here today we need only indicate its spiritual source and the moral value it intends to assume. On this point we said that this new instrument of the Church's visible government must be seen as deriving immediately from the recent Council. It was during the Council that we instituted it and the Council virtually brought it into being. In the Council the need was seen for the Catholic Episcopacy, whose collegiality was made plain in the Council's constitutional document on the Church, not merely to be united more closely but to be united more closely in action; just as we had already seen the evident pressing need of making wider and more systematic use of the cooperation and counsel of our Brothers in the Episcopacy for the pastoral government of the Church Herself, made more easy nowadays when travel facilities are so vastly improved.

Accordingly this *Synodus Episcoporum* aims to be a *ministry of charity* within the Church. Its true foundation is in the *mystery of charity,* as we choose to call the eucharistic sacrifice. This is shown, we think, by the fact that it was during His last paschal meal that Our Lord Jesus Christ spoke those memorable words, which form the synthesis of His Gospel: '*A new commandment I give to you, that you love one another; even as I have loved you, that you also love one another. By this all men will know that you are my disciples, if you have love for one another*' (Jn 13, 34–5). To these divine words we can add, as a commentary, those well-known striking words of Paul the Apostle: '*. . . we who are many are one body, for we all partake of the one bread*' (1 Cor 10, 17).

This reminds us that the Church is a communion, a society based on faith and on charity. We have spoken about faith. What do we have to say about charity in relation to the topic that concerns us now? We shall say that it is always opportune to remember that charity — love which is from God and which spreads in the hearts of believers enabling them to love as Christ has loved them is a vital and constitutive principle of holy Church, which is held together interiorly not by bonds of blood, of territory or culture, not by political ties or by interests, but by love. And we would add one question: Can this love increase in the Church of God? We answer immediately recalling the many vicissitudes of such love in the history and institutions of the Church: Certainly it can; and it must. The Church needs to love Herself from within, to love Herself more. Let us put it this way: those who make up the Church, and much more those who represent her and direct her, must feel that in these days they are more firmly united among themselves with that intangible but powerful bond which is the love taught, commanded and given by Christ. '*Let the bounds* of charity be widened' (Aug. Sermo 69, P. L. V, 440). If that was well said we may also add: let *the bonds* of charity be drawn tight.

For the problems of every kind which the Church encounters in our time, and for the increasing effort which She feels she has to make generously for the spread of the kingdom of God and the welfare of humanity, the Church should give Herself this remedy, this strength: grow in the love which designates Her as Christian and which makes of her members 'one heart and soul' (*Acts* 4, 32). What a wonderful thing it is, if it is so in fact, that those whom the Holy Spirit has placed as Bishops to rule the Church of God (cfr. Acts 20, 28), should be concerned to allow themselves to become more active channels of the charity of Christ, to give to their profession of charity a new expression and assume a new institutional pattern.

This is what the *Synodus Episcoporum* is to be. May God help us then to make it in practice what it aims to be in its intention and inspiration — as we have said — the ministry of Charity flowing from the mystery of Charity.

APPENDIX 4

Pope Paul's Address at First Working Session of Synod, September 30, 1967

Let us give thanks to God our almighty Father, through Jesus Christ His Son, Our Lord, in the Holy Spirit the Paraclete, for allowing us to celebrate this first meeting of the *Synodus Episcoporum* for the glory of His most holy name, the benefit of the Holy Catholic Church and the support of Her mission of salvation in the world.

Venerable Brothers, we welcome you once again and, for the encouragement of all, repeat our wish that this new institution, the *Synodus Episcoporum,* may serve to strengthen and reinforce the bonds of faith, charity and pastoral action between our apostolic office and that of the entire Catholic Episcopacy, and likewise between bishops and religious Families. The first purpose in establishing this new instrument of the Church's pastoral government is unity and solidarity in the Catholic hierarchy. Another purpose is the help, advice, and opinions that we hope to have in greater measure from the Episcopacy in the exercise of our ministry. If this is advantageous to the office of primacy which Christ, for the benefit and service of the universal Church, committed to Peter the Apostle and after him to his lawful successors in this Roman See, it serves no less to do honor to the College of Bishops which in this way is associated to a degree with the Roman Pontiff in the care of the universal Church.

For this reason the *Synodus Episcoporum,* while it cannot be considered an Ecumenical Council, since it does not have the membership, authority, and aims proper to it, does nevertheless resemble a Council to some extent; it reflects its spirit and method and, please God, obtains the Council's own charisms of wisdom and charity.

We say this, because you, Venerable Brothers, are representatives in more ways than one: you represent your own individual Churches, of whose unity you are the prime source, as we are by God's will in this Church of Rome, and at the same time you represent the universal Church, the entire Episcopacy and all the Faithful (cfr. Lumen Gentium, n. 23); and to you as 'angels' (cfr. Apoc 2 and ff.) of your Churches we extend a warm welcome. Then you represent (most of you) the Episcopal Conferences which have elected you as members of this Synod; as their elected representatives you give them a canonical presence here, echo their aspirations and voice their experience; your role as their representatives assumes the importance and authority of these ecclesiastical bodies* to which the Ecumenical Council gave greater prominence and a part to play which makes as much for a relative and practical juridical decentralisation and a certain diversity of expression in the Church, appropriate to the tradition and character of the local Church, as it does for the organic strengthening of the Catholic Church's own structure based on unity. So we shall take account of the opinions expressed by your own Episcopal Conferences. It is for you to interpret them here, without prejudice, of course, to the higher duty you all have of following at all times the authority of Holy Scripture, the true tradition of the Church and Her authentic magisterium; and this will not prevent us from evaluating in the Synod's discussions the opinions and reasons adopted. Lastly, you represent the whole hierarchy of the Catholic Church, which in its turn represents Christ Our Lord, the one, supreme, invisible Head of Holy Church from whom every grace is given to us, from whom all our power is derived. And in a certain sense you represent, as you know, the Christian people, not that the mandate you have received derives from it, but because, as Christ's representatives among the people, you know its needs and wishes and work for its spiritual welfare and Christian salvation.

So, Venerable Brothers, although your normal role in this *Synodus Episcoporum* is consultative. (cfr. Motu proprio *'Apostolica sollicitudo,'* art. II), it is, nevertheless, one of great authority, both for ourselves, who have called you to this present consultation and will, in particular cases, give deliberative force to your opinions; and no less so for the entire Church, which acknowledges you as leaders, witnesses, and pastors of the People of God who are at a moment of significance and importance in your exalted ministry.

It will be good for all of us to bear these simple considerations in mind as we set ourselves to the work of the Synod, without delaying to seek a more precise and detailed definition of the Synod's nature than the description given in the Statute we have referred to. There are not a few scholars and publicists eager to analyse the juridical aspects of this institution and to determine, as far as they can, its form and function, according to certain new concepts of the Church's constitutional law. But it is enough for us to reflect how this new organ, at the very heart of the Church, is in harmony with that spirit of union and collaboration between the Apostolic See, the

---

* The Episcopal Conferences.

Catholic Episcopacy, and the Major Superiors of Religious Families, which the Council experienced and fostered, and to observe that it is the intention of this Synod to further the exchange of information and experience concerning the life of the Church, affording the heads of the Roman Congregations and the representatives of the different ecclesiastical bodies the opportunity of meeting and of discussing certain subjects of general interest. Finally it suffices for us to note that it aims at arousing in all who have the responsibility of teaching and of pastoral government in the Church of God the spirit of watchfulness and diligence the preesent time requires.

We might at this point set the work of the Synod in motion without further delay, were it not for a number of preliminary remarks that we think should be made. . . .

The first concerns the absence of some members of the Synod. Some were detained by reason of sickness. Others were prevented from attending because they had not obtained due permission of the civil authorities. To the former we send our best wishes and greetings. They are in our thoughts. To the latter, and especially to Cardinal Wyszynski, Archbishop of Warsaw, and with him to Cardinal Wojtyla, Archbishop of Cracow, and to the Polish Bishops, who in solidarity did not want to come to Rome without their Primate, we send cordial and special greetings. This we do, not without expressing our strong sense of regret because of the obstacle put in the way of such a harmless voyage and because of the unjust conditions imposed on the Church in various countries, where legitimate freedom is still denied her, where the Church is the object of unjustified suspicions, of moral and legal pressures, and an ever fierce antireligious opposition. You know, Venerable Brothers, how much Catholic life in some nations is restricted in its vital needs, both organizational and functional, and deliberately reduced to hardship and to danger of gradual extinction. The hour of trial, of a long and painful trial, weighs heavy on many a Christian community. It indicates to the world how the basic principles of justice and freedom, proper to modern civilization, have not been applied sincerely in some nations where forms of government that are authoritarian, frequently totalitarian, and in practice hostile to religion, have the upper hand. All the more should we appreciate those societies in which the presence and the work of the Church can be affirmed freely and openly. Thus we should feel all the more closely united with our brothers who cannot profess their faith in freedom, but who, in silent patience and with Christian fortitude, at times heroic, persevere in their adhesion to Christ and His Church. We shall not forget them in our prayers.

In the meantime may the thoughts and wishes of this present assembly go to these brothers of ours.

The second observation looks to the Christian Brothers still separated from us. The canonical and, as it were, internal character of the Synod of Bishops, that is, a meeting which in both method and purpose is directed to internal questions of the Catholic Church, has not allowed them to be invited, as they were during the Ecumenical Council, to be present at the sessions of the Synod of Bishops. But let us make two points immediately. The first: the consideration of the effects which our forthcoming meetings will have upon these same Christian Brothers is not, and should never be, absent during the course of our labors. In fact, the calling of the Synod has of itself great ecumenical importance, in proportion as the Synod, following the lines of the Council, gives testimony that in the life of the Catholic Church there is active the time-honored synodal institution, which has been so well utilized in the oriental tradition, and which will strengthen, in a new way adapted to our time, the bonds that exist between the Church of Rome, 'which holds the primacy of charity' (St. Ignatius of Antioch), and the various local churches.

Furthermore, some Christian churches and church communities which are not in full communion with us are watching us with interest and hoping that deliberations of this Synod, the manner in which they are held and the conclusions reached, will open new possibilities for further progress in the ecumenical dialogue already begun.

We are sure, Venerable Brothers, that remaining constant in the 'faith once for all delivered to the saints' (Jude 3), and drawing from its treasures what is new and what is old (Mt 13, 52), you will live up to these expectations.

For this reason, the Synod will consider that each of the subjects included in the order of the day important not only for the internal life of the Catholic church, but also for the holy cause of Christian unity.

And the second point is this: the wish, ever respectful, ever cordial, ever Christian, that we address at the opening of this *Synodus Episcoporum* to all the Christian churches and all the Christian communities with whom, though not yet bound by the perfect communion we wish for, we are united spiritually and substantially by so many bonds of great value — the wish that we may be able to go forward toward one another to full unity, in faith and charity, as Our Lord Jesus Christ exhorted us. This going forward is well under way. Recently, as you know, the first part of our Ecumenical Directory was published; significant ecumenical dialogues are taking place between designated representatives of various Christian denominations with representatives designated by us; with great emotion and great hope last July we journeyed to Istanbul to meet with His Holiness, the Orthodox Patriarch Athenagoras . . . In fact, We are able to tell you that this venerable Patriarch has announced his return visit, which is planned for the end of this next month of October: you, Venerated Brothers, will be able to be present at this new meeting, which fills the Eastern Church and the Western Church with exultation and inexpressible hope.

Finally, one last observation: peace in the world. A subject of such great and all-embracing importance as world peace cannot escape the attention, the interests and prayers of this gathering, cannot but halt its first important considerations. . . .

We are prepared to support every available genuine initiative for peace, and we voice our encouragement to all who are striving by wise and positive mediation for the harmony and solidarity of peoples and for the peaceful establishment of civilized humane peace in the world.

We are certain, Venerable Brothers, that you are convinced, as we are, of these ideals and that, in the faithful recollection of the noble charity of Christ, you share with us this lofty, unstilled yearning for peace among all men.

But the time is now come for us to declare open, in the name of Our Lord Jesus Christ, this first Synod of Bishops; and for us to begin by calling on the Dean of the Sacred College, Cardinal Eugene Tisserant to speak.

APPENDIX 5

The Profession of Faith Proposed by the Congregation for the Doctrine of the Faith, October, 1967

Ego N. firma fide credo at profiteor omnia et singula quae continentur in Symbolo fidei, videlicet:

Credo in unum Deum Patrem omnipotentem, factorem coeli et terrae, visibilium omnium et invisibilium et in unum Dominum Iesum Christum, Filium Dei unigenitum, et ex Patre natum ante omnia saecula, Deum de Deo, lumen de lumine, Deum verum de Deo vero, genitum non factum, consubstantialem Patri per quem omnia facta sunt qui propter nos homines et propter nostram salutem descendit de coelis, et incarnatus est de Spiritu Sancto, ex Maria Virgine, et homo factus est; crucifixus etiam pro nobis sub Pontio Pilato, passus et sepultus est; et resurrexit tertia die secundum scripturas, et ascendit in coelum, sedet ad dexteram Patris, et iterum venturus est cum gloria judicare vivos et mortuos, cuius regni non erit finis; et in Spiritum Sanctum Dominum et vivificantem, qui ex Patre Filioque procedit; qui cum Patre et Filio simul adoratur et conglorificatur qui locutus est per Prophetas; et unam sanctam catholicam et apostolicam Ecclesiam. Confiteor unum baptisma in remissionem peccatorum, et expecto resurrectionem mortuorum, et vitam venturi saeculi. Amen.

Firmiter quoque amplector et retineo omnia et singula quae circa doctrinam de fide et moribus ab Ecclesia, sive solemni iudico definita sive ordinario magisterio adserta et declarata sunt, prout ab ipsa proponuntur, praesertim ea quae respiciunt mysterium sanctae Ecclesiae Christi, eiusque Sacramenta et Missae Sacrificium atque Primatum Romani Pontificis.

I (name) believe with firm faith and profess the totality and each part of the contents of the Symbol of Faith, namely:
(Here follows the so-called Nicene Creed, as found in Roman Missal)

I also firmly embrace and uphold the totality and every part of teachings concerning faith and morals which are either defined solemnly by the Church or asserted and declared by her ordinary magisterium, in the manner in which they are proposed by her, particularly whatever concerns the mystery of the holy Church of Christ, her sacraments, the sacrifice of the Mass, and the primacy of the Roman Pontiff.

(Translated by Gary MacEoin)

APPENDIX 6

Report of the Synodal Commission on the Dangers to Faith

Taking into consideration the intervention of the Fathers with regard to the document of the Sacred Congregation for the Doctrine of the Faith and to the exposition of His Eminence, Cardinal Browne, the Synodal Commission, in the brief time allotted to it, following the directions of the Cardinal Presidents as to the function of this Commission, has worked at preparing a faithful synthesis of those things which were said by the Fathers in the hall of the Synod. The Commission particularly noted that the Fathers spoke especially of the difficulties regarding the integrity of the faith of the Church and its presentation in modern circumstances, and that not many of them treated explicitly of the problem of atheism, although all were conscious of a certain atheistic mentality and of its influence on the modern world.

Leaving aside particular observations, in the present report we intend to submit to the Venerable Fathers of the Synod three points: First, there will be a brief report of what was said by the Fathers about the crisis in which the People of God find themselves today in what pertains to preserving unimpaired and setting forth their faith. Second, principles will be proposed which in this crisis should inspire the manner of acting, especially of Pastors of the Church and of theologians. Third, proposals will be presented which seem to us, in accord with the thinking of the Fathers, more likely to meet the present difficulties.[1]

I. The current crisis concerning Catholic faith and doctrine.

Very many Fathers spoke of the difficulties which today are disturbing or can disturb the faith of the People of God. They also mentioned that these difficulties arise in great part from the modern crisis of civilization and of human culture themselves.

The Second Vatican Council expressly treated of this crisis, especially in the Pastoral Constitution on the *Church in the Modern World,* which the Fathers often cited in detail. For example, some noted that in secular life there is an evolution of structures and of the very way of thinking, and doubt is being cast on the traditional image of man and of the world. This happens partly, at least, because of the remarkable progress of science and of secular civilization, by reason of which men are often completely caught up in the demands of their work; partly also because of "an ever increasing awareness of the evolution of the universe, and of man's own life and history." All this is reflected in a kind of anthropology, which is expressed also in philosophical systems, by which man so exalts himself and his earthly responsibilities, that the "vertical dimension," by which he is related to God and to supernatural salvation, becomes obscure and so man is easily led to atheism, either practical or theoretical. And so it happens that not a few men, imbued with this

---

[1] Regarding the principles and proposals given in the second and third parts, the Venerable Fathers will be invited to give their opinion in writing: the principles taken as a unit, and the proposals one by one.

mentality, reject the Church or religion itself, at least in practice, as an institution which impedes rather than promotes human progress.

Therefore, some Fathers, citing the words of John XXIII, stated that the Church cannot remain silent in these circumstances, and must express in new formulations the revealed truth which she has always handed down, formulations adapted to a new view of conditions, keeping, of course, the same meaning and the same thought.[2] This work is altogether necessary, although it is difficult and brings with it dangers which are not to be minimized. The Pastors of the Church, however, from the very beginning of the Council, under the leadership of the sovereign Pontiffs, earnestly entered upon this task.

That the work of the Council might bear its fruit, many theologians have already been working vigorously and successfully. They have carefully studied the great themes of the Council and illustrated their riches, especially in the fields of biblical, dogmatic, and moral theology, as well as in the fields of ecumenism and liturgy. All the Fathers agreed that this work is greatly to be commended. Also, a large number of priests dedicated to the care of souls have made great efforts to communicate a sound understanding of the Council to the faithful, and to foster the renewal of the liturgy and the whole life of the Church consistently with the Council. There is reason for joy, also as the Fathers remarked in the diligence manifested by many faithful laymen who earnestly seek to increase the knowledge of the Christian message as it is contained in the Sacred Scriptures and shines forth in the liturgy of the Church and her activity in the world.

It does not seem surprising, it may be noted, that the opportune and fruitful renewal which the Second Vatican Council brought to the Church, changing as it did many seemingly permanent customs and ways of thinking and giving a strong impulse to new thought and to the beginning of a new manner of Christian life and liturgy, has aroused difficulty and even uncertainty.

Nevertheless — and this is greatly to be deplored and was noted by a large number of the Fathers — in some places matters have reached a point such that it is no longer question of sound and fruitful investigation or legitimate efforts to adapt the expression of traditional doctrine to new needs and to the ways of modern human culture, but rather of unwarranted innovations, false opinions, and even errors in the faith. For truths of the faith are falsely understood or explained, and in the on-going process of understanding

---

[2] Cf. Address of Pope John XXIII at the opening of the Council; cf. also the First Vatican Council, Const. De Fid. Cath. c. 4.

doctrine, the essential continuity of doctrine is neglected. In a special way the Fathers deplored the fact that some actually call into doubt some truths of the faith, among others those concerning the knowledge we have of God, the person of Christ and His resurrection, the Eucharist, the mystery of the original sin, the enduring objectivity of the moral law, and the perpetual virginity of the Blessed Virgin Mary.

For this reason there is noted a state of unrest and anxiety in the Church, both among the faithful and among pastors, and therefore the spiritual life of the People of God suffers no little harm. This, indeed, is not felt in the same way everywhere, nor in equal measure among all groups of the People of God. It is more apparent, as may be easily understood, among men of more advanced education because of their special difficulties in reconciling faith with reason; but among the working classes there are some difficulties and problems about the faith and the Church, which are felt in a similar way in all parts of the world. In missionary lands and in certain other regions; where the first and greatest problem is the proclaiming of the faith and an adequate catechetical instruction of the people, the difficulties seem to be restricted to a few groups of priests and laymen. But the Fathers noted that it is to be feared that false opinions may soon spread and develop even in these parts of the world, with greater harm both to the apostolate of the Church and to the faithful themselves.

Of this unfortunate state of affairs the Fathers listed causes which must be carefully considered so that suitable remedies may be provided. Among the principal ones should be numbered: a certain decrease in the sense of supernatural faith among men conscious of their own natural powers; and, among many, a neglect of personal prayer to God; sometimes, according to the opinions of some, insufficient pastoral ministry in teaching the truth or preventing errors; an ignoring or a disrespect for the teaching and the authority of the teaching authority of the Church, whether of the Bishops or of the Roman Pontiff himself; a certain arbitrary and false interpretation of the spirit of the Council; and not always a well understood distinction between those matters which belong to Catholic doctrine and those which are left to the free and legitimate discussion of theologians.

A problem special to our time arises from the fact that publications and other means of communication immediately spread any news of religious nature to the whole world; and such news gives an easy occasion for scandal whether because of the deforming simplicity with which it is sometimes reported or because of different circumstances of religious life in different parts of the world, or finally, because the meaning of the traditional doctrine is not sufficiently taken into account. Sometimes these matters are imprudently spread about even by priests, religious, theologians, educators, and others, without sufficient regard for the way in which the faith is taught.

After faithfully noting the above, there is no reason why in this brief report we should dwell on particular deviations from the Faith, and the Fathers did not do this either; rather we shall immediately set forth, according to what they said and in an ordered way, the pastoral principles to be observed in these circumstances.

II. Principles.

1. *The necessity for the unceasing proclamation of the faith.*

By Catholic faith we embrace the good news of God who reveals Himself in His Son. This we do in keeping with the nature of this message which was entrusted to the Church for safekeeping and is proposed by her living teaching authority for our belief (cf. Dog. Const. *Dei Verbum,* par. 10). This faith of ours is a divine gift by which we who believe are drawn to God by a movement of reverence and commitment, a movement which is the beginning of salvation but which also depends on the preaching of men, according to the words of the Apostle: "faith comes from hearing" (Rom. 10:17).

It is necessary, therefore — especially in today's circumstances — that the faith with which man makes his response to God, Who speaks through Christ in the Church, be constantly cultivated and strengthened. This task of cultivating the faith belongs first of all to the Bishops along with their collaborators in the priesthood and among the religious who help the Bishops. But it also belongs to those laymen who are engaged in teaching the faith and catechizing; it belongs, in fact, to all the faithful and in a special way to parents with regard to their children. All the sons of the Church, therefore, each according to his charisms, must feel responsible for passing on the sacred gift of faith to the men of our time. This is something the Synod most gladly calls to mind during this "year of faith" which the Supreme Pontiff has decreed as he pursues his untiring, zealous dedication to the duty of preaching the faith.

2. *The individual and the collegial exercise of the authentic Magisterium.*

According to the teaching of the Church, the office of teaching on questions of faith and morals authentically, that is, with the authority of Christ, has been entrusted to all successors of the Apostles. It belongs to the Roman Pontiff personally and to the episcopal college gathered in Ecumenical Council to meet the needs of the Christian people by the conscientious exercise of the Magisterium. But it is not limited to them, since every Pastor of the Church, each in his own see or region, is by the reason of his office bound by the same heavy responsibility. Today this sacred work is done more fittingly when it is done collegiately through the Episcopal Conferences. In accomplishing its mission, each of the Conferences should be mindful of the communion in teaching that is to be maintained with the College of Bishops throughout the entire world but especially with the Apostolic See. This will result in support that comes from mutual help in the avoidance of turmoil, and in the strengthening of unity, while account is taken of the needs of all the Churches.

All the faithful, in any case, are to be taught clearly, and in ways adapted to the contemporary mentality, about the filial obedience and sincere adherence owed to the declarations of the teaching authority in the Church, all according to the different nature of different pronouncements, as is taught by the Second Vatican Council (cf. Cons. *Lumen Gentium,* II, par. 25).

3. *Pastoral approach in exercising the Magisterium.*

In fulfilling their office of teaching, the Bishops must be concerned both with faithfully preserving the deposit of faith and with protecting their flocks from the dangers that threaten them. But a positive way of setting forth the truth will usually be more fitting than a mere negative condemnation of error. Insistence should always be placed on those things which present revealed mystery as a true message of salvation meeting the problems and aspirations of modern man. Above all, Pastors should be aware of how legitimate and even necessary it is for preserving the deposit of faith that there be progress in the understanding that takes into account the progress of the sciences and culture and the ever new questions that face mankind. Therefore, before they teach the faithful concerning new and difficult matters, they should consult attentively theologians and other experts and seek the prudent advice of their priests and of the laity (cf. *Lumen Gentium,* IV, par. 37). Indeed, "since it is the mission of the Church to enter into dialogue with the human society in which she lives, Bishops especially are called upon to approach men, seeking and fostering dialogue with them" (Decr. *Christus Dominus,* II, par. 13).

This way of acting must not prevent the firm exercise of authority in directing the Church of God, according to the mind of the Second Vatican Council, to the exclusion of abuses and deviations either in doctrinal matters or in pastoral or liturgical questions. Those who are rash or imprudent should be warned in all charity; those who are pertinacious should be removed from office. The Apostle himself gives a warning about the firmness to be shown "with all patience and teaching" toward those who do not hold sound doctrine (cf. 2 Tim 4:2 f.).

4. *The activity and responsibility of theologians.*

Although the office of teaching authentically does not belong to theologians, nevertheless their office in the Church is an outstanding one and the service they render to the Church is indispensable. It is their expression of the divine mystery and in this way to do all they can to provide an answer to the new questions which continually arise. For them to be able to accomplish this task adequately, it is beyond doubt that they must be given the necessary freedom to investigate new questions and to further the study of old ones. However, they must put themselves humbly and faithfully at the service of the word of God, and they must never make use of it to favor their own opinions. True freedom must always be contained within the limitations set by the word of God as it has been constantly preserved and as it is taught and explained by the living magisterium of the Church and especially of the Vicar of Christ. Let theologians be aware of their responsibility, which is indeed great, in seeking the truth with scientific honesty and in communicating their conclusions in such a way as to imbue their brethren with a spirit of love and reverence toward the Word of God and the Teaching Church. The Bishops should encourage the cooperation of theologians among themselves and particularly they should favor the establishment of contacts between the theologians and the Magisterium, especially by means of Episcopal Commissions on Doctrine.

5. *The diffusion of doctrine*

All who in any way diffuse theological teachings should be persons of special pastoral prudence, above all because the instruments of social communications reach so many persons so rapidly. If this diffusion of theological teachings is to have positive and not negative results, sound pedagogical principles must be respected. First of all, let what is certain and fundamental be proposed as the unshaken basis of the faith and of Christian life; then what is new should be presented in such a way that a fitting explanation will manifest the continuity in the faith of the Church; finally hypotheses should be put forth with that grade of probability which they in fact enjoy and with attention to the ways in which it is foreseen they will be understood. Account must also be taken of the difficulty which arises from the fact that some persons incline to give an exaggerated interpretation to every word which at first sight seems to be different from the accepted way of conceiving or expressing the truth. As a result of this inclination, it happens that even theologians who are always careful to think with the Church sometimes can unjustly be considered, in the estimation of the faithful, to be imprudent revolutionaries!

Bishops should see to it that in a world which is every day becoming more united, the faithful are prepared to acquire more mature faith. But they must also see to it, with prudent and vigilant charity, that, especially in the matter of publications, the faith of the whole community does not suffer harm from lack of qualifications or lack of prudence on the part of a few.

Let all those, then who teach, write or preach be aware of the duty which obliges them to act in communion with the Magisterium and according to its directions.

6. *The witness of teaching joined to the witness of life.*

Bishops, with the collaboration of all the faithful and especially of priests and religious, must give witness to their faith not only with their words but also in their actions, most of all with authentic charity, in imitation of Christ who loved us. In this regard, it must be stated emphatically how necessary it is that the Church, thanks to the united efforts and activity of her pastors and her faithful alike, and especially of those who hold more responsible posts in civil society, be seen as effectively concerned with justice and charity not only in private matters but also on social and international levels. Indeed, this important witness to justice and charity, a witness adapted to the conditions of our times and in keeping with the teachings of the Second Vatican Council and the encyclicals *Mater et Magistra, Pacem in Terris,* and *Populorum Progressio,* is essential if the Church is to be truly recognized as the sign raised up among the nations (Is. 11:12) by the multitudes who throughout the world are victims of widespread poverty, social injustice, or various kinds of discrimination.

III. Proposals

In addition to these pastoral principles, the Synodal Commission has brought together statements from the Fathers to formulate two proposals to be offered to the Supreme Pontiff.

First proposal: *The setting up of a theological Commission.*

a) Does it meet with the approval of the Fathers that a commission be set up composed of theologians of diverse schools, to be appointed for a definite term, all men of intellectual ability, recognized as scholars, who reside in various parts of both the Western and the Eastern Church, whose duty it will be, acting with all lawful academic freedom, to assist the Holy See and especially the Sacred Congregation for the Doctrine of the Faith, principally in connection with questions of greater importance?

b) Does it meet with their approval that the names of these theologians be proposed to the Supreme Pontiff — leaving the final selection to his discretion — by the Episcopal Conferences themselves whose members, having duly consulted universities and theological faculties in their territories, believe that they are in a position to recommend the names of competent theologians?

Second proposal: *The drawing up of a declaration concerning questions of faith.*

Does it meet with the approval of the Fathers that, having heard the views of the Episcopal Conferences, the Holy See draw up a positive pastoral declaration concerning questions involved in the doctrinal crisis of today, so that the faith of the People of God may be given secure direction?

APPENDIX 7

Pope Paul's Address at End of Synod of Bishops, October 29, 1967

We now direct Our words especially to you, Venerable and beloved Brothers, who have taken part in the Synod of Bishops; and we are happy to note how timely and meaningful it is that the conclusion of your great meeting should occur on this festive day, on which the liturgy of the Roman Church prayerfully honors Christ the King.

We think it most fitting that, before you return to your sees, we should celebrate with concordant voices and intimately united minds this feast, which presents to our eyes so pleasing a vision of light, of grace, and of grandeur; this feast in which Christ is shown to us resplendent with the brilliancy of His Godhead, as Saint Paul describes Him: "The image of the invisible God, the first-born of all creation; for in him all things were created, in heaven and on earth, visible and invisible . . . He is the head of the body, the church; he is the beginning, the first-born from the dead, that in everything he might be pre-eminent" (Col 1:15–16, 18).

This feast, falling immediately before the commemoration of All Saints, proclaims the praises of Christ and illuminates His relationship with the Church which He has founded. From these two doctrinal points, inherent in today's feast, we would derive subjects to propose to you at this solemn moment, on the eve of your departure, for your encouragement and consolation.

First of all, we must raise our minds and hearts to the kingly rank of Christ, both to broaden and protect our sure belief in divine things, and also to be animated by an ever more ardent love in our daily lives. Christ is the Son of David, as foretold by Sacred Scripture, to Whose coming the Patriarchs and Prophets looked forward, to Whom His very persecutors bore unknowing witness by writing over His cross — then a symbol of shame, later a sign of glory — the title: "Jesus of Nazareth, the King of the Jews" (Jn 19:19).

As Peter, the Prince of the Apostles, proclaimed on the day of Pentecost: "God has made him both Lord and Christ, this Jesus" (Acts 2:36); for in Him human nature is hypostatically united with the divine nature, and what is more, being both true God and true man, He is the Son of God made flesh.* For we read that Saint Paul has written of Him: "(Him the Father) appointed the heir of all things, through whom also he created the world. He reflects the glory of God and bears the very stamp of his nature, upholding the universe by his word of power. When he had made purification for sins, He sat down at the right hand of the Majesty on high, having become as much superior to angels as the name he has obtained is more excellent than theirs" (Heb 1:2–4). To this universal primacy pertains the principle of unity of government, of love, and of salvation, which is exercised by Him alone, but is also in His merciful wisdom communicated to His Church. For "Great indeed, we confess, is the mystery of our religion: He was manifested in the flesh, vindicated in the Spirit, seen by angels, preached among the nations, believed on in the world, taken up in glory" (1 Tim 3:16).

Hence, as we have said, arise the relationships between Christ's kingly power and His Church. Jesus reigns indeed over the Church, but not yet over the world; although David's ancient prophecy, openly referred to by Christ Himself and in the first preaching of the apostolic age, promises Him sway over all peoples, it still has not come to pass (Acts 2:34–36; Mt. 22:44). For it is written: "Sit at my right hand, till I make your enemies your footstool" (Ps 109:1). In fact, the powers of darkness strive to retard the spreading of the kingdom of Christ. But this kingdom concerns naught else

* And, since by His passion and death He is the Redeemer of mankind, the authority and power which, as God, He wields over all created things, pertains also by both native and vested right to His human nature.

but the spirit of men, as Christ testified: "My kingship is not of this world" (Jn 28:36). This is the kingdom of truth and life; the kingdom of holiness and grace; the kingdom of justice, love and peace (Preface of the Feast).*

Now, however, the Catholic Church represents among men the royal, prophetic, and priestly power of Jesus Christ, since She has received "the mission to proclaim and to establish among all peoples the kingdom of Christ and of God. She becomes on earth the initial budding forth of that kingdom" (Decree "Lumen gentium," No. 5). Hence, although the Church is endowed with authority, and this is Her first relationship with Her divine Founder, and although She has Christ with Her, living in Her by grace and the word of salvation, and in Her continually renewing His sacrifice through the Sacrament of the Eucharist, wherein is located Her mystical relationship with Christ — yet She is not to be considered a Queen, when this title is given a temporal meaning. In fact, She continues among men the mystery of the humility of Christ, Who "came not to be served but to serve" (Mt 10:28). Moreover, the Church, like Christ, Her model and sanctifier, intends to serve men, and by pastoral means to lead them to salvation, sowing in their minds the seeds of life. This is clearly set forth in the Constitution "Gaudium et spes" of the Second Vatican Council.

Wherefore the grave responsibility falls upon us, the Shepherds of the Church, to perform the same duties and offices toward men as the Church Herself performs.

As you return to your sees, then, Venerable Brothers, remember that you have been sent forth to announce the kingdom of Christ; and that you have been sent forth by Him Who once sent forth others, saying: "Preach as you go, saying, 'The kingdom of heaven is at hand' " (Mt 10:7); that is to say the kingdom, which, although not fully realized now on earth, will one day become the perfect kingdom of God.

Meditate upon this, Venerable Brothers, that you are sent in the name of Christ, nay more, by Christ Himself, Who said: "Behold, I send you out" (Mt 10:16). Yet consider that you are also Shepherds of the Church, and hence that for Her we must expend our strength, our care, our solicitude, our labor, our sufferings and, if need be, our lives. Since the Synod which we have held aims only at the good of the Church, each one of us must promise, like Paul the Apostle, to

---

* This kingdom seeks souls for no other reason than that the word of God should be sown in them as in a fertile field; it seeks men wandering afar to bring them together into one family (Jn 11:52).

"spend and be spent" (2 Cor. 12:15) for the Spouse of Christ.

Finally, before you leave us, permit us to give each of you, as a pledge of love, a symbol of union, and a proof of brotherhood, the kiss of peace. We wish also to present to you the gift of a pectoral cross, confident that when you wear it you will remember the days you have spent here with us, and will consider it a bond perpetually uniting yourselves to us and to one another.

APPENDIX 8

Pope Paul's Address to the Members of the Congress for the Lay Apostolate, in St. Peter's, October 15, 1967

Beloved sons and daughters!

Before all else, greetings!

You have already received and exchanged very beautiful, very cordial and very significant greetings: they could not be lacking in a meeting such as this. Well then, receive also our greeting: it is not conventional, it is not rhetorical, it is not superfluous. Our greeting speaks of the heart with which you are here welcome, the heart of one who in Christ is to you a Shepherd, that is to say, bound to you by duties, by feelings, by hopes which pledge sentiment, thought, life. Yes, the heart of him who in Christ is to you a Father, a Brother, a Friend. This greeting, as those which, for the rest, have already been extended to you, tells you that none of you here is a stranger. You are here in your own home: the home of the common faith; the home of central charity; the home of Christian unity and universality. It is necessary that all of us should be conscious of this fundamental and living communion, which in vain we shall look for elsewhere. Let this greeting also speak to you of our joy to see you gathered around the tomb of St. Peter, on whom Christ has willed to found His Church, and to recognize in this gathering a sign and a hope of humanity which finds in Christ its vocation, its brotherhood, its peace, its destiny. There takes shape in our spirit the vision of the peoples from whom you come and whom you represent, and there lights up in our heart a great, supernatural affection for each of your nations: your presence increases in us the consciousness of our mission, of lover of mankind; and there increases in us the trust that its history will one day surrender to the divine plan which guides it to find in Christ its meaning and its end; the trust, we say, that this great unitive plan, still hidden in the heart of God, will be hastened, also with your collaboration, the efficacy of your commitment in the world, the ardor of your participation in the apostolate, of which the radiant Roman days of your Congress are for us the promise and the dawn.

There echo in our memory, almost prophetical, the words of St. Augustine: "there is in the field, that is, in the world, till the end of time, the growing wheat of Christ" (*sunt per agrum, id est per mundum, usque ad finem saeculi crescentia frumenta dominica." Contra litteras Petiliani,* II, 78; *P.L.* 43, 313). You are witnesses of this spiritual vegetation, you are for us a "sign of the times"; welcome, beloved sons and daughters, a blessing on you!

But we cannot forget that there participate in this praying assembly, in communion of prayer and of sentiment, also all the Fathers of the Synod of Bishops, and representatives of the universal episcopate, gathered here in Rome in their most solemn sessions of study in order to offer their collaboration in the universal government of the Church. It is therefore your Bishops who, in the persons of these, look on you with immense sympathy, and in them, encourage and greet you.

And now the humble Successor of Peter expresses His respectful fraternal greeting to all of you, venerable members of the Synod, here before the splendid and multicolored picture of the Catholic laity of the world; and he presumes to say to you, as a brother: Wish your laity well, *your* laity! May you be their faithful guide, far-seeing, open, and endowed with all their confidence, which will not be deceived! It is the Council that asks it of you, and the Pope who exhorts you, certain of finding in you men who know how to stimulate the generous energy of the laity.

We give a warm greeting from Our heart, filled with affection and esteem for the Observers of the various Christian denominations who honor this assembly by their presence. It gives Us great pleasure to note that you have come in such numbers; and it would please Us very much that you tasted in its fulness the beauty and the fascination of this meeting, according to the inspired words: "Behold how good and how joyous it is to dwell together as brothers!" (Ps 132:1.)

We thank you from Our hearts for your presence, which has such significance, as there rises in Our heart the hope and the prayer — which We know is shared by you and your brethren spread throughout the world — that we may all one day celebrate together the perfect communion in the unity willed by Christ, the last desire of His heart.

In the course of this brief conversation We think it necessary to sum up with a few fundamental statements the Church's thought about you, dear members of the Catholic Laity. As those who sail across immense seas take bearings on their journey to fix their position and set their course, so we think that your Third World Congress demands that prominence be given to the doctrinal acquisitions proclaimed by the Church in this more recent phase of her history, notably in the Second Vatican Ecumenical Council.

They are not new, but they are true and important; for you, hearing and pondering them now, they are fruitful and full of life. The first is this: the Church has given to the Layman, a member of the mysterious visible society of the Faithful, her solemn recognition. There we have, if we may use the expression, an age-old novelty; the Church has reflected on her nature, her origin, history, and functional aspect and has given the most fitting and richest definition of the layman belonging to her; she has recognized him as incorporated in Christ and as a sharer in the priestly, prophetic, royal function of Christ Himself. At the same time she notices his special character which is to be a secular member or citizen of the world, to engage in earthly pusuits, to follow a profession in the world, to have a family and devote himself in every field to temporal pursuits and interests.

The Church has proclaimed the dignity of the layman, not only in virtue of his membership of the human race, but also because he is a Christian. She has declared him worthy to be associated with the responsibilities of the Church's life in the way and degree appropriate to him. She has judged him capable of giving witness to the Faith. She has declared that she recognizes the fulness of the rights enjoyed by the Laity, both men and women: the right to equality in the hierarchy of grace; the right to liberty in the framework of moral and ecclesiastical law; the right to sanctity in conformity with each one's state.

It might be said that the Church has taken a certain satisfaction in declaring this doctrine on the Laity. There are so many expressions to be read on this subject in several of the Council documents, expressions repeated and intertwined with one another. If it can be said that this has always been substantially the Church's thought, it must also be agreed that she had never expressed it so fully or with such insistence.

There we have the recognition of the Layman's "citizenship" in God's Church. We mention it once again to you, happy to confirm what the Council has said; happy to see in it the completion of a theological, canonical, and sociological development which had long been desired and by many penetrating minds; we are happy to base on it our hope for a Church that is genuine, a Church made young again and better able to accomplish her mission for the Christian salvation of the world.

But, dear Sons and Daughters, after recognizing and proclaiming that you are in God's Church, there is still more to be said. We must also recognize and proclaim what you can, and should, do in the Church, what you are in fact doing as Catholics who have freely devoted yourselves to the apostolate. This brings us to the heart of the matter, to the definition of your ideals and your efforts, to what the whole world can read in the title of your Congress: the Apostolate of the Laity.

Here we feel no small embarrassment: for we can only repeat in another form what the Council has proclaimed with an incomparable authority and in carefully studied terms, remarkable for both their precision and their richness.

The principle is laid down — and this is already sufficient indication of its importance — in none other than the Dogmatic Constitution on the Church. There we read, "The laity are gathered together in the People of God and make up the Body of Christ under one Head. Whoever they are, they are called upon as living members to expend all their energy for the growth of the Church and her continuous sanctification. . . . Upon all the laity, therefore, rests the noble duty of working to extend the divine plan of salvation ever increasingly to all men of each epoch and in every land" (Const. *Lumen Gentium,* n. 33).

Thus, you notice, the Church sees the layman not merely as a member of the Faithful but as an apostle. And in opening before him a well-nigh limitless field she confidently addresses to him the invitation in the Gospel parable, "You go into the vineyard too" (Mt 20:4). This work will be both manifold and varied. The Council's Decree on the Apostolate of the Laity, in its turn, firmly lays down the principle that "by its very nature the Christian vocation is also a vocation to the apostolate" and then goes on to devote two whole chapters to a detailed account of the "various fields" and the "various methods" of this apostolate. You are of course familiar with these texts. Let this reference to them suffice to strengthen in your souls, dear Sons and Daughters, this unshakable conviction: that the appeal the Church addresses to you in the middle of the twentieth century is a real one; that the Church places confidence in you and invites you to accept great responsibilities in order to advance Christ's Kingdom among your brethren and be to the full what the theme of your Congress invites you to be, "the People of God in Man's Journey."

At this point, an objection arises. In fact, one may say, if the tasks entrusted to lay people in the apostolate are so vast, should it not be admitted that henceforth there are, in the Church, two parallel hierarchies, as it were — two organizations existing side by side, the better to ensure the great work of the sanctification and salvation of the world?

This, however, would be to forget the structure of the Church, as Christ wished it to be, by means of the diversity of ministries. Certainly the People of God, filled with graces and gifts, marching toward salvation, presents a magnificent spectacle. But does it follow that the People of God are their own interpreters of God's Word and ministers of His grace? That they can evolve religious teachings and directives, making abstraction of the Faith which the Church professes with authority? Or that they can boldly turn aside from tradition, and emancipate themselves from the Magisterium?

The absurdity of these suppositions suffices to show the lack of foundation of such an objection. The Decree on the Apostolate of the Laity was careful to recall that "Christ conferred on the apostles and their successors the duty of teaching, sanctifying and ruling in His name and power" (No. 2).

Indeed, no one can take it amiss that the normal instrumental cause of the divine designs is the Hierarchy, or that, in the Church, efficacity is proportional to one's adherence to those whom Christ "has made guardians, to feed the Church of the Lord" (cf. Acts 10:28). Anyone who attempts to act without the Hierarchy, or against it, in the field of the Father of the family, could be compared to the branch which atrophies because it is no longer connected with the stem which provides its sap. As history has shown, such a one would be only a trickle of water, cutting itself off from the great mainstream, and ending miserably by sinking into the sands.

Do not think, beloved sons and daughters, that for this reason the Church desires to bridle your generous inspirations. Quite simply, she is faithful to herself, and to the will of her divine Founder. For the greatest service she can do for you, is to define your exact place and role in that organism which is intended to bring to the world the good news of salvation. "In the Church, there is diversity of service but unity of purpose" (Decree on the Apostolate of the Laity, No. 2).

From a generous laity, faithful to its leaders and well organized, what is it the Church expects? First of all, substantial aid for the good functioning of her institutions. Thanks to that theological progress of which we often speak, it has become easier to define the sharing of responsibility between clergy and laity. It is necessary, especially in view of the insufficiency of number of the clergy, both priests and deacons, in many parts of the world, that the laity, whether in the ranks of Catholic Action or not, should take over more and more those duties which do not necessarily require the priestly character. And if such duties sometimes prove to be very humble ones, such as the teaching of Catechism to children, or the varied exercises of the works of charity, corporal or spiritual, let them remember that such tasks are fundamental, and take them up with all their hearts, thereby bearing witness to the spirit of service to which all, priests and lay people, are invited by the Council.

Another duty falls to your lot, one expressed by a phrase which has become of general use in recent years; namely, the *Consecration of the world.*

The world is your field of action. By vocation, you are immersed in it. But the natural movement of this world, influenced by a thousand factors which it would take too long to examine here, tends toward that phenomenon which several contemporary thinkers have competently analyzed, to their joy or to their anguish, under the various names of "secularization," "laicization," "desecration." We say it with sorrow: there have even been Catholic writers who claim it to be their desire, in opposition to the twice millennary tradition of the Church, that the sacred character of places, of times and of persons should progressively be diminished and disappear.

Your apostolate, beloved Sons and Daughters, must act in direct opposition to these currents. The Council has told you again and again: " It is the laity who consecrate the world to God"; they work for the "sanctification of the world," for the rehabilitation of the institutions and of conditions of life in the world — these are the very expressions used in the Council documents.

And what does all this mean, if not the re-consecration of the world, by infusing into it once again that powerful breath of Faith in God and in Christ, which alone can lead it to true happiness and to salvation? The late Cardinal Cardijn expressed this many times, in most moving terms. We said it recently: "The laity must assume as their own proper duty the renewal of the temporal order. It is up to them . . . to compenetrate with the Christian spirit the minds and customs of men, the laws and the structures of their community of life" (*Populorum progressio,* 81).

We now strongly assert it to you again: give the world of today the the energies which will enable it to advance on the paths of progress and freedom, and to solve its great problems: hunger, international justice, peace.

In conclusion, beloved sons and daughters, a few words concerning the spirituality which must characterize your activity. You are not hermits who have left the world, the better to dedicate yourselves to God. It is in the world, it is in action, that you must sanctify yourselves. The spirituality which must inspire you will therefore have its own characteristics, and these the Council did not omit to illustrate in a lengthy paragraph of the Decree on the Apostolate of the Laity (No. 4). Let it suffice to say it to you in one word: Only your own deep personal union with Christ can ensure the fruitfulness of your apostolate, whatever it may be. You will encounter Christ in Sacred Scripture, and in active participation in the liturgy of the Word and the liturgy of the Eucharist. You will meet Him in silent and personal prayer, for which there is no substitute to ensure the contact of the soul with the living God, the fount of every grace.

The compromise of the apostolate in the midst of the world does not destroy these fundamental prerequisites of all spirituality, indeed it supposes them and even demands them. Who was ever more "compromised" with the world than the great Saint Teresa, whose feast this year occurs today, the fifteenth of October? Who better than she found strength and fruitful results for her activity in prayer, in union with God at every instant? One day we propose to give her due recognition, as to Saint Catherine of Siena, with the title of Doctor of the Church.

Finally, We add this: May the grace of this Congress, the grace of this meeting with the Vicar of Christ, the grace of Rome, accompany you and sustain you! When asked to speak to your Second World Congress in 1957, under Our Predecessor Pius XII, We thought it well to say to you then: "Have confidence! Rome is going forward, and the Pope guides you!" Let Us repeat these same words today, in the humble knowledge of our limitations, but with the selfsame joyful certainty, strengthened still more by the splendid experiences which the Church has lived through during the last ten years.

May Our voice resound with all the fervor of Saint Peter's faith, all the ardor of Saint Paul's love! By their authority, we impart to you all, with all Our heart, Our Apostolic Blessing, and We extend it to your families, your nations, and to the Catholic laity of the entire world.

Index of Names